Cabin Comments

Cabin Comments

By The Bettys

Text by Betty Lemon
Sketches by Betty Anderson

Published by
Teton Bookshop
Box 1903, Jackson, Wyoming 83001

ISBN 0-933160-08-9
HARDBACK
ISBN 0-933160-09-7
PAPERBACK

Library of Congress Catalog Card Number: 80-53090

*Dedicated to the readers
of "Cabin Comments", who, over the years,
with their warm letters, friendly visits and
encouraging words, have brought great
happiness to the Bettys at Moose.*

The Bettys

BETTY LEMON, chief author of *Cabin Comments* and sole author of *Teton Christmas Tales,* as well as several English textbooks, graduated from the University of Chicago at the age of eighteen and received an M.A. degree from Northwestern University. She was the daughter of Jeptha Lemon, a distinguished educator. At the time of her retirement at the age of fifty, she was Principal of Milwaukee-Downer Seminary. Betty died of cancer at her home near Moose, Wyo., in September, 1977.

HÉLÈNE WITTMER was born in Héricourt, France and came to the United States at the age of eighteen. She is a graduate of the University of Lyon. After a distinguished career as a teacher of French and Head of the Language Department at Milwaukee-Downer Seminary, she retired to live near Moose, Wyo., with her friends, Betty Lemon and Betty Anderson.

BETTY ANDERSON was born in Buffalo, N.Y. She received an Ed. M. from Harvard University and an Ed. D. from Columbia University. After teaching in Massachusetts, Oklahoma, Oregon, and New York City, she retired as Headmistress of Milwaukee-Downer Seminary in 1961.

THE BETTYS have had an exciting life since they gave up city living and "took to the wilderness". Their pleasures have been in their log cabin on a bench overlooking the Snake River, in the flora and fauna of the Jackson Hole Valley, in their garden and greenhouse, in their tame animals and, above all, in the mountains surrounding them.

Introduction

DURING THE SUMMER of 1962, Betty Lemon and I wrote a column for *The Jackson Hole Guide,* entitled "Around the Valley". We were dubbed "The Bettys" by Floy Tonkin, then editor of the *Guide.*

Having tasted the joys of publication, and wanting to share the wonders of our wilderness living, we decided to purchase a mimeograph machine and publish our own paper. Thus *Cabin Comments* was born.

This paper was entirely homespun. Betty Lemon did most of the writing, but not all. I did most of the sketches, but not all. Hélène Wittmer did most of the editing, but not all. We all pitched in to help with the formidable task of mimeographing, addressing, folding and mailing. There was no charge for the paper, but contributions to help with mailing costs were welcomed.

During the years of publication, and particularly since the death of Betty Lemon in 1977, readers have requested that a collection of *Cabin Comments* be made available in book form.

The issues of *Cabin Comments* are arranged in chronological sequence, but you may notice that some issues are missing. This is because we sometimes took a vacation from publishing, sometimes because the typewriter was out of order and sometimes because an issue reflected our "teacher" attitudes and seemed inappropriate to the theme of our wilderness chronicle.

I would like to express our thanks to Gene Downer, Publisher, for his inestimable help in producing both *Cabin Comments,* and *Teton Christmas Tales,* the latter a collection of Betty Lemon's Christmas stories, taken from *Cabin Comments* and published in 1979. Without his help we could never have completed our task.

Betty Anderson.

Design by Freeman & Associates
Typography by Twin Typographers
Lithography by Paragon Press

1963

JUST TWO WEEKS AGO we left some 1500 miles to the east a world which was breaking into spring; crocuses were coming into bloom, daffodil shoots were showing buds, and tulips were pushing through the warm, moist earth. During the week ends people were raking lawns and removing storm windows to replace them with screens, and children, dressed in summer shorts, were romping around. Roller skates could be heard on the city sidewalks, the creak of swings in back yards, and the steady thump of jump ropes and children skipping through them.

Now at the cabin we find about us a different world, warm during the day, sunny and clear much of the time, but still covered with snow, deep snow, twelve inches on the level. This is the time of year, we have been told, when nature in our Valley is the least attractive. We had been warned about mud, variable temperatures—one day warm, the next day cold. Never having experienced a cabin April before, we think, so far at least, that April is one of the most beautiful months.

We see robins fly about the cabin. There are sudden flashes of blue across the snow, and we know that the blue birds are here. Flocks of rose sided juncos perch in the trees and fly timorously to investigate the bird feeder which we have placed near the wood pile. The moose ponds below are nothing but black streaks of water cutting through the ice and snow, but each day great pieces of snow break off, melt, and more of the pond comes into sight. It will not be long, we say, before each duck and goose family will lead forth its downy brood. A pair of trumpeter swans rose high into the sky yesterday as we were eating breakfast. The howls and barking of coyotes can be heard from the distant bench or from our ranch across the river. Owls hoot mournfully to each other as it begins to grow dark. A cow moose with her calf tried to cross the river one morning, but the baby found the waters too deep and too swift, so the pair turned

1

back. Four graceful does leapt over the sage a few feet from our windows, headed for the bench beyond. And closer home, Richard, our ground gopher, peeked out from hibernation in the wood pile, sat in the sun on one of the logs for a while, but apparently became discouraged by the deep snow and the icicles, and turned back to his warm bed for a little while longer. The willows in the pond below are brilliant yellow and green, and a wild rose branch just outside the window was caught in a ray of sun and flashed crimson. The snow has gone from the bench just below the windows, and the shoots of new grass are fresh and green.

And yet—and yet—yesterday we awoke to strong winds and sheets of fine snow blowing over the flats. We could barely distinguish the outlines of the saddle shed and corral only a few yards away. After breakfast when we went out with the puppies, the wind and the snow bit into our faces, and our feet broke through the top crust and the drifting snow and we floundered in knee-deep. This is a real blizzard, we thought, and we planned a day indoors knitting and reading before the fire. We ventured out again in mid-morning, however, this time dressed in sturdy parkas and snow pants with long heavy woolen socks under our knee-length rubber boots. We fitted on our snow shoes and found traveling thus much easier. An hour or so later, the sun was shining brightly, and there was little trace of the former threatening blizzard. Spring had come once again, but as we lifted our eyes to the mountains, there were still heavy clouds and snow showers there. We stood and watched for a few minutes and suddenly through the heavy mists shone out the highest and mightiest peak of them all, its lower slopes becoming visible by the second as the sunrays picked out first one crag and then the next. The sky shone blue as we gathered up the puppies, and dodged the steady drip of water from the roof, deciding that pancakes, hot syrup, and sausages would be an aesthetic lunch on a day like this.

April 27, 1963

THIS MORNING when we awoke none of the peaks were visible. It was a wintry world, a wet world, but through the mist and the fog came the cry of robins and geese and ducks from the pond below. As we ate our breakfast, multitudes of rose sided juncos came swooping through the trees to the ground just below our windows, and we caught our first glimpse this season of the white-crowned sparrow, the large one with the black and white striped head.

It was a world which was soft and gray and completely delightful, but no day, we thought, for the picnic we had promised the three children from the Circle H Ranch. As mid-morning came, there were no signs of sun or clouds' clearing, so we phoned and asked the children's mother if they would be disappointed if we postponed the picnic or, if so, would they be willing to have it indoors in our basement study before a big fire. She said that she feared they would be bitterly disappointed, so we decided to picnic indoors and set about to get things ready. About eleven o'clock three little figures appeared on the sage flats, dressed in warm, gay rain clothes and boots. As soon as they spied the cabin, long before they could see us waving to them, they rushed ahead, stumbling through the soft deep snow. We opened the back door as they approached, and they tumbled in breathlessly in a mass of cold fresh bodies and feet, slightly damp around the edges. They took off their rain outfits, we felt of their feet, and found most of them wet, so we hung socks up to dry by the fire and supplied heavy woolen ones of our own to take their place. Each child had brought a present he had found on the way, a gnarled piece of wood that looked, as its donor said, "like a dragon's face," a handful of brightly colored pebbles, a sprig of fresh, fragrant sage.

Steven took the hot dogs downstairs, Bill the bag of buns, and Ann, too little to carry more, walked carefully down with her spoon. Soon the fire was crackling, willow twigs were festooned with hot dogs, beans were simmering, and three pairs of children's eyes were watching intently a roasting feast. Our puppies, Fica and Tia, jumped about in delight at the crumbs which frequently fell, and soon the children learned to hold their food high or soft puppy mouths and sharp puppy teeth would snatch it away. Our guests ate all over the room and on the steps, too, on the window seat, on the floor, on the hearth, and occasionally sat sedately on the chairs provided. In this cozy atmosphere of lunch by the fire, delightful intimacies were revealed by the children. Bill showed a tooth which "might have to be pulled" as a new tooth was crowding it out. Ann told of the bright blue leotards she was wearing under her jeans, and Steven, the eldest, recited the multiplication table for us "way up to the sixes." Suddenly Steven spied a horse across the river, no it was a deer, and then Ann, in her frenzy to be first to identify it correctly, shouted, "An ephelant!" When the binoculars were called into use, the dark, shadowy figure munching tender willow twigs was proved to be a moose, and she was watched from the distance by ten eager eyes as she moved slowly from one bush to another. This incident recalled to Ann that she had seen "a lady spider" the day before in the snow. And then, comfortable on the inside with her favorite peanut-butter cookies, and warm on the outside, she burst into "Jingle Bells" and offered graciously to sing other "Chritmas" songs if we would like

3

to hear. Paper and crayons were called for, and as the boys drew pictures of the new ranch tractor, Ann showed us proudly how she could print her name forward or back with equal dexterity and abandon.

As a last treat the children were told we would drive them home in the Ski Doo, and shouts of delight greeted the announcement, followed soon by arguments of who was to sit where. Steven and Bill had sat on the back the last time, so Ann was allowed to sit there this time with the boys bumping along on the sled behind. Shouts of happiness and pleasure rose as they piled into the Ski Doo and were driven off, hands waving, kisses thrown, and a last call over Bill's shoulder, "You are some of my very best friends!" What more gallant thank you from a young gentleman could there ever be than that?

On our mantle are a few colored pebbles, a piece of dried wood, and a sprig of sage. The laughter of children has filled the cabin for a while, and we are happy and content in the generosity, the good will, and the sincere simplicity which three little neighbors from the near-by ranch have shared with us on this mountain April day.

May 13, 1963

NO MATTER if a brief snow shower comes, no matter if there are cold rains, no matter if a chill wind sweeps over the flats—now it is spring. Spring may come slowly and teasingly, may arrive one day in sunshine and warmth which invites us to take our noonday sandwiches out on to the porch. Spring may withdraw tantalizingly the next day, but she cannot fool us now. The Ski Doo has been drained of oil and gas, the battery has been removed, and it is now in the saddle shed for the summer. We have been able to drive our car down our little road to the cabin for over two weeks. On April 30 we found on the island across the ponds the first tiny yellow seedum, pressing close for warmth and nurture to the earth. The very next day we found the first minute salt and pepper flower which tosses off a shower of black dust when it is shaken, and the same evening when we took the puppies out before going to bed, we were startled to hear the first croaking of frogs in the pond. A robin is busy from morning till night looking for the best place to build a nest in the cottonwood just outside the kitchen window. And Harriet, our friendly little deer mouse, is devouring voraciously the crumbs we set out for her on the front window sill each evening.

We were eager to see if spring had arrived on top of the bench, so we went there a few days ago. We found great patches of snow still clinging to the trails and under the trees, and when we tried to cross

4

them, we sank in ankle deep and came back with our shoes wet and the legs of our jeans damp. But we exclaimed with delight when we found the first fritillarias, cold and fresh, at the very edge of the snow. Tiny upside down tulips they are, as delicate and dainty as an elf's golden cup. On the way to the post office we stopped to view a whole bed of them and in between saw the earliest spring beauties, still tight and pink, not daring to open their fragile petals to the brisk winds. Three elk were grazing on the new grass on the bench above us and four curious, soft-eyed does watched the car as it turned near the ponds.

Wanting to celebrate the spring ourselves, we had a buffet supper recently and tried our new electric ice-cream freezer. Tom, one of our guests, had indicated a particular preference for mocha ice-cream, so that was the flavor we chose. In between courses we put the freezer in the center of the room, poured the ice-cream mixture into the container, packed ice and salt on the outside, and set the motor churning. It hummed in a business-like fashion for a long time, every once in a while dropping a few notes which meant that the ice-cream was hardening. Finally it stopped, and all rushed with dishes and spoons for the first taste. Hot home made chocolate sauce was waiting on the stove, and we were happy to see how much ice-cream and sauce were consumed. It was a successful occasion and the puppies thought so, too, as they, in a very unsanitary but delightful manner, licked the dasher.

We were invited yesterday for cocktails by Albert and Fern, friends just across the river from the cabin. We went at four-thirty but did not return until nearly ten. They said they had bought a steak which was far too large for the two of them, so they decided they would "keep us for dinner." And what a dinner! Good drinks, good food, good conversation, and, as a special favor, they showed us the water colors they both had done at the art school they attend each winter in Arizona. The colors in each painting were delicate yet strong, and one could feel the sensitivity and power in all of them. We witnessed a show which would be hard to equal, and were pleased to hear about Albert's and Fern's aspirations for further study, saw their faces light as they spoke of advanced work they hoped to do, and when we left, felt that we had experienced a rare evening with thoughtful, highly talented people who have a true gift in art and are happy and generous enough to share their work with others.

We stepped out to our car from their warm, cheerful home into a blizzard, and great sheets of snow flew before the windshield as we drove home. Upon entering the cabin, we were greeted as usual by the puppies, crazy with delight to have us home again. To amuse themselves while we had been gone, they had taken, one by one, our riding boots from the closet and deposited them in helter skelter fashion on the living room rug. No damage had been done except to the top of one of our older boots which showed unmistakable signs of puppy licking and gentle chewing.

June 1, 1963

TWO WEEKS AGO we hitched our big trailer to the car and started for Twin Creek Ranch where our burros have been wintered. As we approached the meadow, we saw the three of them, Fidelity, AT&T, and Esso in the distance, grazing peacefully. Since they were far away from the gate where we parked, Stan saddled his horse and rode out to get them. We had brought carrots and oats for them, and they came up eagerly to take them from us and seemed to want us to pat their heads and rub their soft noses. They recognized us and we were happy.

They all looked very well cared for, and Fidelity and TNT had changed not at all in appearance except we thought Fidelity in her three year old maturity seemed more feminine and even more beautiful than she had been in the fall. We had left Esso at the winter pasture in October when she had been only eight weeks old. From the moment of her birth she had been a beautiful and graceful little animal—but now! We could hardly believe what we saw. She is well formed and handsome and carries her head proudly, tossing it back, just as her father does, when she is confronted with something she does not understand or of which she does not entirely approve. Now she is a very light dun color whereas she had been gray before, and her cross has turned from black to brown. Her eyes are still as soft and expressive as ever and her ears straight and long, but she still wears her winter coat of fur, inches and inches long. There is long hair on her cheeks, but fortunately a straight part runs up the center of her face and down her back. On either side of the part grow five or six inches of hair, and she resembles nothing so much as a thatched roof. Soon, we hope, she will lose her winter coat and will be as sleek and smooth as her parents. She is shy and timid with us. Before too long we hope we shall be able to approach her with a curry and brush off some of her long hair.

We let down the tail gate to the trailer and put Fidelity in first with little trouble. TNT seemed to understand what he was to do and sedately walked up the tail gate and allowed himself to be snubbed to the hitching ring next to Fidelity. Esso, who did not remember having ridden in a

6

trailer, thought it was a jolly game, and she romped around and around and skillfully eluded each attempt to catch her. Finally we cornered her behind some thick willows, Stan gently dropped a rope over her neck, and she was led up to the trailer, and with only a little pushing and persuasion joined her parents for the trip home.

Upon arrival at the cabin, the two older burros recognized at once where they were, but Esso was a little confused and stood still, looking over the flats, at the corral, up at the mountains, trying to remember and get things straight in her mind. The familiarity of home came to her at last, and she joined her parents in visiting their old haunts, the watering trough, their favorite rolling spots in the dust, the window ledges of the cabin, and at last the bird feeders where they stretched their necks and lifted their mouths, hoping to find bird seed which they could munch and enjoy. After circling the cabin several times to make certain everything was just as they had left it last fall, they raced down the slope in the back, and we saw the three of them set off contentedly down the road, headed for the pond.

This is the time of year when our Valley is busily preparing for summer guests. Dude ranchers are painting, shoeing horses, opening cabins, mending fences, and getting in shape generally for the summer season which is nearly upon them. We asked our friends at the Circle H what we could do for them and were told it would be of help if we would stain the window trims and doors of the cabins. Bob had already done a fine job of spraying stain on the cabins themselves, but our work had to be done with brushes so that stain would not splatter on the windows. For several mornings we went down and had great fun doing the staining, being helped occasionally by little Ann and by the boys when they were home from school on week ends. It was glorious to be out of doors all morning, working under no pressure and simply for the joy of it. There was a fine spirit of camaraderie on the ranch as everyone went about his particular job, stopping every now and then for visits or a coffee break in the ranch kitchen.

The element of surprise is great in our Valley, and one never knows what treasure lies in wait for him at the next step. On one of our mornings at the ranch, we found a fragile snake skin which had been left behind by some harmless snake, the only kind we have here, as he slithered to the ponds below the pool. We brought it home to examine through the microscope and discovered one example of nature's artistry in the myriads of colors revealed in an apparently insignificant dry and gray body of cells.

Coming back from the corral one late afternoon, we happened to glance up at the blue sky and were stopped instantly at the sight above. Seventy or eighty pelicans, large gray and white birds with a wing spread of nine feet, were riding the air currents above the river, gliding up, then down, as if by a pre-arranged signal, turning, showing first snowy white, then in the next second, gray against the sky. Up, up they would fly, then glide down with not a feather or a wing stirring, turning, turning, never knowing or caring what beauty they were creating or how their invisible earthbound audience below was held enraptured by their flight.

Two robins have built nests, one just above the other, in one of the cottonwoods in back of the cabin. The building of the nests was a miraculous thing to watch, each twig and piece of string carefully worked into the structure, the robin smoothing down the mud with her breast to round out the interior. And now each mother is sitting placidly on her eggs, and we are watching for the arrival of the first tiny, hungry bird. One of the robins flew against our window the other day, fell forward, and seemed lifeless when we rushed out to see. We picked her up gently, however, and although her eyes were nearly closed, her bill wide open, there was a slight movement and life still stirred in the little body. We carried her around the yard, stroking her back and head and discovered that her wings were uninjured and her legs still strong. Slowly her eyes opened farther, her bill began to close, her breathing became normal, and her heart stopped beating so furiously. We sat in the sage with her, finally dared to perch her on our knee where she remained perfectly content, with one black shiny eye cocked at us. She tried her wings, stretched on her legs, then settled back for more stroking and kind words. At last, she spread her wings and flew into the cottonwood.

One morning as we were driving to the post office, we heard in the distance a child's voice coming over the sage flats. We stopped the car, waited a minute, and again heard the call. Finally we distinguished four year old Ann running toward us; she had seen the car start and wanted to attract our attention. She bounced over the flats to meet us, the customary merry smile on her face. We knew that her parents hesitated to let her take the long walk alone up to our cabin and Ann knew this, too, but she had told us earlier in the spring that some day she was going to come up alone and not tell anyone. This she had done, and she was delighted by her success. She wanted to go with us to the post office, so we drove down to tell her mother where she was, and off we started. Sitting between us on the front seat, her sunburned little legs sticking straight out in front of her, Ann felt in the mood to unburden her childish miseries to us. She had fallen against the door that morning and bruised her forehead, her brother Bill had snipped off the end of the nose of her favorite doll, and both brothers, she said, had hit her and pushed her down. We wondered, after Ann's recital of her woes, if she could defend herself effectively against her brothers. We asked her what she in turn did to her brothers when they pushed her around. She looked up with set chin and determined eyes and said, "I sock 'em!"

Yesterday when we walked over our ranch, we looked in wonder at the beauty there. The johnny-jump-ups were opening in abundance, the fritillarias covered part of one meadow, and the Oregon grape was blooming bright and yellow. The streams were low enough for us to cross by stepping from one stone to the next, the trees were showing shining leaves, and the birds' singing was sweet and clear. The sky was cloudless, a deep blue, the mountains were sharp and brilliant, and the meadows, as we came from the grove of trees, stretched green and lush before us. A flash of orange in a nearby bush showed us the first Western tanager we have seen this year. The cottonwoods and sage after the recent rains were more fragrant than any perfume a human being could distil from the most precious flower. There is nothing in the world, we think, which can equal the scent of the sticky cottonwood buds except perhaps the tiny purple shooting stars which we found in profusion. We stopped to pick a few and as we smelled their spicy, clean perfume, we knew that not all the rare and expensive perfumes on this earth from Paris to Arabia could possibly compare with the scent given off by this little wild flower growing so freely on the sage flats.

Nor could any expensive city entertainment compare with our morning's experience, walking through the trees near the river, across the meadows beyond, hearing the spring call of myriads of birds, and lifting our eyes to the mountains above and beyond. No price could ever measure our freedom, our joy, the absence of pressure and strain, the unlimited beauty we had met.

July 1, 1963

THE ROBINS who built nests, making our cottonwood tree into a bird apartment, have hatched their babies. Apartment B was first with its young, but Apartment A was not far behind. All day long at the sound of the mothers' approach, the scrawny necks would be stretched, and delicacies poked into them. We watched and saw that the babies' eyes were open, and soon feathers began to grow fast. On cold and rainy days the mothers looked uncomfortable as they sat on the nests keeping the little ones warm. Frequently a long bill and neck would be thrust out

9

from under the mothers' wings, or a leg would be poked out from the other direction. One day as we peered down into the lower apartment, all occupants had gone.

One day while looking for Morel mushrooms, something made us stop among the trees, glance down, and there only inches from our feet was a gray sage hen huddled in the grass, one black shiny eye upon us. She had become frightened at our footsteps and as we came upon her, she flew a few feet away. As she rose, what looked like ten or a dozen black periods scattered in all directions. As we looked more closely, we saw that they were tiny chicks, alarmed by their mother's sudden flight. We were too startled to move for a second but then turned and moved away as slowly and quietly as possible. The mother, still close, made a soft clucking sound, and we hoped her babies would hear and scamper back safely to her. When we walk through the sage, we shall tread softly and watch carefully so that our footsteps will not cause such family havoc again.

Over ten years ago we traveled in France and visited a village called Le Puy. The women there were noted far and wide for their beautiful lace making. We bought a piece, delicate and perfectly wrought, and have cherished it ever since. We thought of Le Puy and the talented lace makers when we glanced over the bench from the back window not long ago. Even if we shall no longer visit Le Puy and see the magnificent laces there, at least we can see something equally magnificent and delicate from our very window. Down at the edge of the pond, were the first two water hemlocks in bloom, white, lacy, perfect in symmetry and shape and design. And there, we thought, is our Le Puy lace which will return in abundance for us year after year.

We looked up from lunch the other day, seeming to hear music in the distance. It came over the sage flats again and again, too far away to be distinct, too low to be clear. We thought no more of it, believing our ears had deceived us, but on the way to the post office a little later, we joined a line of cars which for some reason has been stopped on the road. We got out to investigate and found that the delay was caused by a herd of cows with their calves being driven to summer pastures. The bellowing and the bawling ahead as the cowboys drove the herd along made us realize suddenly what had been our mysterious "music." And indeed it did sound musical, not like a symphony or a concerto, but rather like the tuning up of a mighty orchestra. Calves were breaking loose and scampering into the brush by the side of the road, cowboys with ropes after them. One little fellow was determined to get away for good. We saw him in the distance, running fast down the center of the road, all alone, sending forth loud and terrifying cries of distress. As we passed later when the herd had stopped for the night to graze and the cowboys were pitching tents for their well-earned rest, all was well. Each calf was by its mother, and the entire herd was grazing peacefully or looking sleepily with drowsy long-lashed eyes blinking contentedly. The tuning of the orchestra continued, muted and subdued.

A mountain storm carries great excitement in its approach. The other evening just after dinner, we saw huge dark clouds sweeping in from the west. The mountains looked angry, and there was something ominous in the air that increased as the wind rose and swept all before it. The puppies raced in their pen and finally sat together on the roof of their little house, close to the window, watching, as we were, the clouds racing in and making the heavens black. Their fur stood up on end, and their ears were blown back by the gusts. We watched the horses on the flats moving in closer together until all were standing huddled in one spot. Harriet's crumbs which we had placed on the outside window sill, were blown in every direction. Distant thunder rumbled, and lightning flashed. The telephone gave one short, sharp ring which meant that lightning had struck the wires somewhere near. Then as if by a sudden command, the wind stopped, and a dead silence took its place. A second or two later the rain began, sharp, staccato beats on the windows. Then came the downpour which made the panes glisten. The fire crackled indoors, the puppies lay down before it and licked their wet paws, and we ourselves moved in closer, cheered by its warmth and comforted by its cheerful snapping.

At sundown to see the Alpine glow on the peaks to the north, to look west and east and south and see the sky aflame with apricot shading to mauve, turning by the second to soft gray, to see colors no artist could possibly reproduce and cloud formations beyond man's poor power to capture—this is nature's way perhaps to conclude the day and become tender and comforting in the reassurance that even though men may come and go, man's simple but earnest strivings for the good may yet be realized, that the sun will shine tomorrow and skies be blue.

July 15, 1963

THE FLAX is blooming now, and parts of the sage flats and mountain meadows are blue with it. We have seen, too, flying from flower to flower a tiny blue butterfly. Each year at the time the flax blooms, this winged creature appears, so similar in color to the flower. When we first

11

spy the little butterfly, we are deceived into thinking that a petal of the flax has blown away and has suddenly and by magic developed the ability to grow wings and fly free.

We have heard that a doe will first have one fawn, but after that usually will give birth to twins. We have seen on the bench, in the ponds below, and on the flats many does with their twins. The other day while we were riding on the bench, on the trail just ahead of us was a doe, and at her heels, were twin fawns, not more than a few hours old. Their mother quickly hurried them out of sight into the brush nearby, but we had time to see their tiny forms, their inquisitive soft eyes, their large ears, and their miniature hooves. They lingered a few seconds to view us as we approached them, then turned, and the last we saw were two tiny white tails, following the larger one into the trees.

Last Sunday evening we were sitting quietly in our living room when suddenly we were startled by a clatter and banging, growing louder by the moment. We stepped to the back door and peered into the darkness but could see nothing. The banging continued, and again we went out to investigate. This time, although we still could see nothing, we heard voices calling our names and as we stood on the back porch, a team of horses and a large hay wagon came into sight down our back road, driven by Bob and carrying some of the children, members of the crew, and guests from the Circle H. All cried to us to join them, so we got jackets and climbed aboard. All was smooth for a few feet over the level ground, but soon we hit dips, rocks, and ruts which threw us from side to side, tossed us into the air, and rattled our teeth. But the harder the bumps, the better all of us liked it, and we were delighted when Bob pulled up the team for a minute to warn us all to hang on doubly hard, just before we hit an especially deep rut and were almost thrown off the wagon. We drove for a couple of miles, stopped to catch our breath before starting back, and then retraced our steps with the same wonderful jolts and bumps. Talking was impossible, and as one of the Circle H guests wisely remarked later—it was no wonder the first people to cross the country on similar wagons were strong and silent since it would have been impossible to be anything else. Just as we were turning into the road near the cabin, the full moon shone out, lighting the last lap of the journey. We tumbled out, hay in our hair and on our clothing, happy to have been invited to join such wholesome fun.

One of our favorite local stories concerns Beaver Tooth Neal, a poacher who came into this country many years ago and lived by trapping beaver, all of it done illegally. The game wardens had been watching

12

Beaver Tooth for a long time, but he was far too skillful and canny to slip into their clutches. They could not catch him trapping his beaver, did not know where he hid his pelts, and they had never been able to discover how he got them out of the Valley to sell. One time they came upon Beaver Tooth's wife in town and were shocked by her battered appearance—two black eyes, bruised body—plus a tale of woe about how Beaver had beaten her up and of how she was leaving him for good and was now looking for a way to get out of the country. The game wardens, compassionate at her plight, offered to give her a ride to Victor, Idaho. This she accepted with alacrity and soon she and her trunks were in their car and all were on the way. A week later, however, she returned to her husband and their life together was resumed as peacefully and happily as ever. And the beaver pelts? They had been in the trunks. And the means of smuggling them out? None other than the unsuspecting game wardens who, needless to add, dared not show their faces in the Valley for quite some time.

We have seen our Valley's mighty river and its banks many times and from different places, but not until a week ago have we floated this river in a rubber raft. Del was our skilled guide, and he drove us early one morning to the mouth of the Buffalo where we put in. The day was clear, the wind brisk. We can imagine no more spectacular way to see this amazing river than from a raft, following the current down the flow and around the many bends. We appreciated the silence, the peace, the occasional rushing sound of the current. We laughed with delight as we got slightly damp while shooting the rapids and heard the waves slap and spank against the raft. We saw dense forests through which the river cut its way, we saw open meadows, steep banks, and always, always as we turned each bend, there were the mountains, remaining the same but looking different as approached from different angles. Often we found ourselves speaking in low tones or even whispers.

There is a feeling of mid-summer in the air in our Valley these days. Sitting by our living room windows, we can see the cotton from the cottonwood trees blowing aimlessly to the ground. The other day a real blizzard of cotton blew through the air and drifted past our windows down the bench. The summer winds have blown soft tufts of it into corners where it clings until the next breeze starts it on its way again. There is often a summer mist on the mountains, and the high snows are disappearing rapidly. The meadows and roadsides are ablaze with summer flowers. The lupin on the flats has almost gone as has the wild columbine, but the wild geraniums, the flea bane, and the arnica are now at

13

their height. Wild hollyhock and Indian paint brush make the roads and trails brilliant. The choke cherry blossoms which festooned our little road are brown on their branches. The "sarvis" berries are turning red. The days are warm, but jackets are needed in the early mornings and evenings.

August 15, 1963

Morning's hues:
Crimsons, blues.
And a humming bird flies to our cottonwood tree.
Noons hold
Sun's gold.
And a humming bird nests in our cottonwood tree.
Twilight rays:
Mauves and grays.
And a humming bird stirs in our cottonwood tree.
Purples claim
Evening's name.
Jewels afar:
Moon and star.
Hush of night,
Moths' delight.
And a humming bird sleeps in our cottonwood tree.

September 1, 1963

SOME OF THE happiest experiences we have had during the summer have been at the Circle H Ranch cook-outs by the river. In the evening about six o'clock we drive over to the ranch and then walk down the road over the bench, through the woods, and into the open space where the fire is burning, hungry people are gathered, and the aroma of frying hamburgers, potato salad, and hot coffee meets our nostrils. Guests at the Circle H sit around on logs or fish in the river till Bob calls, "Come and get it!" Sunday morning cook-outs are a special treat when the fare is scrambled eggs, ham, and hot cakes. Whether in the morning or evening, the air is always fresh and cool, the skies are clear, and the sound of the river makes a pleasant accompaniment to the friendly talk. Food out of doors tastes better, people's spirits seem lighter as they tell of the day's adventures, and meals indoors afterward seem dull in comparison.

14

We wouldn't trade the best champagne cocktail for the lemonade there in paper cups or the finest filet mignon for the hamburgers broiled over the open grate or the most delectable pastries at the Waldorf for one piece of Esther's home made cake.

During the night for several days past our puppies have been restless and have occasionally broken into sharp barking. The other evening while Tia was in her pen, she barked in a way we have not heard before, a loud bark ending with a long, mournful howl. We stopped what we were doing to listen, and her sister Fica, too, cocked her head in wonder. Tia repeated this call again and again. Suddenly we realized the reason for her prolonged, sad cry. From the bench above us came the clear call of a coyote and our little Tia was doing her best to answer it in similar fashion. Soon there were cries from other coyotes, from the bench, from the river bottom, from our ranch across the river. We wondered, with something of sadness in our hearts, if this were not the reaching out of a little domesticated animal for her friends and close relatives in the forests, a yearning sometimes in the lives of all of us to go back to the wilds from which we came.

Our Valley, we think, appeals unusually to a person's sense of smell, from the time the first sticky buds appear on the cottonwood trees until there is the unmistakable smell of snow in the air. It is this season in late August that we like to ride the mountain trails and come out of the shadows into a patch of hot sunlight. The smell of pine is strong, and occasionally when we bushwack away from the trails, we catch the sweet smell of a huckleberry patch. Then we get off our horses and search through the low green bushes for the dark berries which are so good on breakfast cereal, in muffins, or in pancakes.

Four of us were sitting in our living room one afternoon, watching a fierce storm sweep down the Valley from the peaks above. Suddenly a blinding flash seemed to burst in our very faces, and a deafening clap of thunder followed immediately. One of our guests facing the window pointed toward three cottonwood trees growing on top of the bench, only a few feet away from our front porch. The sparks were flying, but no flame or smoke appeared, and when the storm had abated sufficiently, we went out to inspect. In the flash of an eye, three trees had been split directly down the trunks. We hope and think they will live, but it brought home to us as little else could have done what destruction an electrical storm can cause and what damage can be created when nature shows her wilder, more ruthless aspects.

15

FOR SEVERAL DAYS at a time during the past few weeks storms have built up on the other side of the mountain ridges and have finally poured over into the Valley. Thunder rolled, lighting flashed, and the rains came, to be broken only occasionally by rays of the sun. The weather has grown colder, and we have gone on numerous wood gathering expeditions for twigs and branches to serve as kindling for the fires which are now so welcome. On the third or fourth day of the storm, at last the clouds lifted, and we saw them catch the sun, finally disappear into the ever widening patches of blue sky. All eyes were on the lifting clouds and soon, wild with excitement, we saw rising in grandeur above us the peaks themselves, dusted with the first snow of the fall season. Of course the first powdery snow will disappear fast in the bright Indian summer sun, but we know, too, that soon we shall awaken in the morning to see another cover of high snow and then another, and then we shall see the most glorious sight of all—white, shining snow reaching down from the mountains to meet the blazing reds, yellows, and greens of the forests below. Green, blue, and golden days these, with the cloudless blue of the sky above, the gold of the aspens and cotton woods, and the green of the pines. Each draw on Black Tail Butte is yellow with the changing leaves. The Western dogwood is already a rich crimson. Such sights, such silence, such freshness and cleanness in the air—as heady as a first sip of the rarest vintage of wine. We wish you could return now, all of you summer guests and friends who love this country during the summer months. Return to see and marvel at a Valley ablaze with the last wild, ecstatic burst of glory before all is enveloped in the silence of the winter's snows.

The recent rainy days, spent indoors except for an occasional walk with the puppies or a trip to the corral to let the burros out each morning and to put them back with an abundance of fragrant hay in the evening, were happy ones, and we accomplished things which we had been postponing until the storms would come. There were pantry shelves to clean, drawers to put in order, wood to stack in the basement, and mending and knitting to do. New books and magazines had been accumulating. And now there was time for all of this, enjoying the feeling of contentment and satisfaction when all was in order and we could sit by the fire and knit or read or play canasta or shanghai. We had time to try tempting new recipes, to set our ice cream freezer going again, and to indulge in a perfect orgy of bread baking. We are contemplating many later fall activities before the real winter sets in, getting our Ski-

Doo in shape for rides over the snow, bringing down heavy clothing for cold winter days, waxing our skis, and, more immediate, helping Bob at the Circle H peel logs for a fine new corral to be built there.

One of the nicest evenings we have spent all summer was at the Wilson rodeo grounds watching the barrel racing. It was cold, and we were grateful for the heavy blankets which we wrapped all around us, but we soon forgot chilly fingers and toes in the fun of watching the skill with which the women and girls took their horses around the barrels, the lightness with which they raced in and out of the poles, like deft and graceful skiers slaloming. And finally came the square dancing on horse-back with gay music and calling in the background. A good share of the enjoyment for us was watching Rosemary on her beautiful Tuffy, racing around the barrels and winding her way in and out among the poles. Everyone had tremendous fun, the riders even more than the spectators. We enjoyed the performance to the utmost and thought it an evening which we shall want to repeat next summer when the good sport begins all over again.

An amusing thing happened at the Circle H a few days ago. A fisherman had thoughtlessly left his creel filled with a fine catch of brook, native, and rainbow trout on the porch of his cabin. It was dusk, and the fish were to be taken to the ranch kitchen. But they never got there. A particularly audacious bear smelled them, thought they would be a delectable feast, so up he lumbered to the porch, in full sight of the people within the cabin, sniffed around the creel for a second, and then scooped up the fish in his massive paw, savored a few, and made off over the edge of the porch with the rest. His huge bulk disappeared over the bench, his body swaying with contentment, his ears and nose twitching slightly with the coup d'etat he had so successfully maneuvered.

A float trip by day is a marvelous thing, but even more so, we have discovered, by moonlight. At the last full of the moon, we were invited to join a group from Moose who was taking such a trip, and we accepted their invitation with alacrity. Someone had forgotten the oars, so while he went back to pick them up, we built a camp fire on the bank of the river. Perhaps this was the nicest part of the whole trip, and we were all rather pleased about the forgotten oars which gave us a chance to sit in the darkness, only the camp fire below and the moon above shedding light. There is something about a camp fire which induces silence or soft talk; people's thoughts seem to be more gentle and speech accordingly so. When the oars finally arrived and we put in, there was something of the same silence. The river flowed around us with an eerie light of the moon, the trees on the bank seemed taller, darker than usual, and dead branches assumed grotesque shapes. The water lapped against the float, the dip of the oars was almost inaudible, and all that could be heard distinctly was the plunge of a beaver into the water or the slap of his broad tail. When the wraith-like mist rose, the waters became black, the faces of the others indistinct, and we seemed to be floating alone, without company, without a boat beneath us, suspended between the waves and the air in a magic, mysterious kind of way. It was incredibly beautiful, unearthly, and when we put out at shore two or three hours later, we were almost startled to see around us familiar sights and well-known surroundings. We had been in a world which man had seemed never to enter, visited places which had never known a human voice or foot. The river, as we stepped from the float, was just the same as it had been when we had been drifting down it, the moon above was the same moon which had shone on the water, the trees, the rocks which we had passed were no different from usual, but it was the same and yet not the same. We were in the world of man again, having stepped so short a time before from the world of mystery and silvery spell.

These are the days for fall planting, and we have been taking advantage of every spare moment to do this before the weather turns and becomes too cold. Witty, who will join us permanently next June, sent us an enormous box of daffodil bulbs, at least a thousand. We got ourselves trowels and so far have planted over half, just behind the cabin along the bench. It is difficult to plant them on such a steep bank, but we hang on tightly to every twig or shrub with one hand and plant with the other. We have found it easier if we lie flat with our toes digging into the earth and pebbles beneath us for a good foot-hold. The fresh moist earth feels good in our fingers, and the fragrance of it and the leaf mould is delicious. Each bulb is put lovingly into its own small hole, covered carefully and firmly with earth for its winter bed, and given a happy thought for the time we shall see in the spring the miraculous evidence of the beauty which can come from a hard, brown, little bulb.

And we have been planting other things, too. Yesterday we went across the river to our ranch: We took shovels in hand and went in search of little trees which we were planning to transplant to the cabin. We found ten or a dozen and set to work. Tiny, eighteen inch spruces they are, each full and perfect. It was not difficult to dig them up as the earth was moist, and soon we had our trees, carefully laid into our canvas log carriers. We moistened the roots well and hurried home with them where we had holes already prepared. We set them out and watered them well.

We invited Ann, our four-year-old neighbor to go on a picnic to our ranch with us. We started off with a knapsack full of lunch, Ann clutching a clean paper bag into which she wanted to put "treasures" she hoped to find on the way. We walked through the meadows and found a lovely sunny place, just on the other side of the buck fence and near a wide stream, to spread out our sandwiches. It was a happy, free occasion for all of us, the food tasted unusually good, and the water from the stream was clear and cold. We sat and rested there for a while, looking at the peaks rising above the trees, seeing a fish jump suddenly from the water, and hearing the gentle moo-ing of the cattle in the meadows beyond. Ann took a nap when we returned home, and from the next room we could hear her singing softly and telling herself a little story before she went to sleep. Her "treasure" bag was filled, and contained, as she showed us later, a butterfly wing, two delicate mushrooms, a scarlet leaf, a pretty pebble, some thistle down, an orange lichen, and a few bright berries. What finer treasures, we thought, could anyone, child or grown-up, choose than these.

October 15, 1963

THIS IS A COUNTRY of music. We are charmed daily by cries of wild geese flying overhead in a perfect V formation, hundreds of them, honking and calling as they fly southward. At sundown the elk on the bench begin to bugle, and their flute-like cry can be heard far into the night. The whirr of ducks' wings is a common sound these fall days as is the nervous chatter of the chipmunk gathering his last cheeks' full of food before the winter. The dry rustle of falling leaves is in the air all day long. Our burros are musical, too, braying raucously to be given hay at the corral in the morning. These are all sounds with which we are now familiar and which we have grown to love. But one evening we had the opportunity to hear more sophisticated music when we were invited to the Circle H to listen to recordings on the magnificent new Magnavox stereo there. We were given our choice of music and chose first "The Mysterious Mountain" of Hovhaness. This was an experience in musical listening indeed, and we readily understood how this composition has recalled to many listeners this very Valley and its surrounding mountains. It made us hope that we can hear soon on recording "Teton Mural for Orchestra" by George Hufsmith, composer-in-residence for this Valley, which we have recently heard in concert. Our next choice was Mahler's First Symphony. We were held under the spell from the first note. Knitting and conversation were forgotten as we listened to the orchestra's interpretation of one of our favorites. The power and tremendous force of the music in addition to the purely melodic parts, the humorous parts, the sad and wistful and compassionate parts was enough for one evening, and we could absorb no more. We wanted nothing else to intrude upon the effects just produced, so we quietly picked up our things and drove home down the little back road through the sage, a full moon shining high above. We wondered what other setting could be so perfect for music.

The other night Tia, one of our puppies, whimpered to go out, so we put her into her pen. It was black and windy, and we could see or hear nothing, but no sooner had Tia run around her pen, sniffing the ground, than she began a ferocious and fearful barking. We sensed that something must be wrong, so went out to investigate and found a large, bristling porcupine at one end of the enclosure. We tried to grab Tia and ward her away from the danger but her curiosity got the better of her, and before we could seize her, she had gone up to the porcupine and given an inquisitive sniff. A yelp of pain immediately rose, and she tore around the pen, trying her best to extract the cruel quills. We got her into the house, slammed the door of the pen shut so the enemy could not escape, and held the wriggling, whining little animal until we had pulled out all quills from her soft nose and face. There were not many, and fortunately they had not worked in, but it was an agonizing process nonetheless. We phoned the Circle H, as we always do when in trouble, and Harry, Senior, came over promptly, armed with a gun. We did not want to run the risk of other mishaps with the puppies, the burros, or the horses, so with one clean shot, the bristly animal rolled over and was gone.

We have made many kinds of jams and jellies before this fall, but rarely have we ourselves picked the fruit we have used. That, we have discovered, is the most fun of all. First came the choke cherries. We tied buckets to our belts so that we could pick with both hands. At first there was a rattle when the cherries dropped into our containers, but as we picked more, the bottom of the pails soon became covered, and there was no longer any sound as we continued. Some branches were so heavy with fruit that we could pull a whole handful off at a time. It seemed minutes only until we had as many as we could carry. We removed all leaves from our pails, washed the cherries, added sugar and a little water, and set them to boil. As soon as the mixture tested right, we took the juice from the stove, bottled it, and now we have sweet, purple syrup.

And then came the rose hip jelly and syrup. The hips were growing in profusion along our road, so again we strung our buckets to our belts and started off. Again we heard the rattle of fruit in our pails and again they filled in a miraculously short time. We sat on the front porch in the sun and pulled the blossoms off each hip, a laborious process, but finally we finished. During this part of the task, all three burros came up to the porch, and we gave them each a rose hip, not dreaming where our folly would end. So delicious were the hips, the burros thought, that nothing would do but they must have more, many more. We shooed them away, but persistently they would return, and before we knew it, a burro nose was in each of our kettles of precious fruit. Finally in desperation we finished our job indoors, being watched by three pairs of burro eyes at the windows, each pair of jaws chewing blissfully on a mouthful of hips. The jelly and the hot cake syrup turned out beautifully, both a golden orange color, fragrant as a day in fall. When wintry gusts blow about the cabin and when sheets of snow swirl across the sage flats, we shall have a hot cake or waffle breakfast and relive all the joy of these autumn days, enjoying the taste of autumn and the aroma of autumn from our bright colored jars and bottles on the basement shelf.

November 1, 1963

THIS MORNING, October 30, there was snow on the porches and just enough snow to dust with white powder the sage flats and the bench beyond. The pine trees there emerged from the mists covered with white. The mountains were completely hidden by snow and clouds. A few wet flakes were falling to the ground, melting almost as soon as they fell. The cabin was warm, but we lit a small fire for cheer as we ate our breakfast and then leisurely put on slickers and boots and headed toward the corral to give the burros their morning hay. It was misty, and the corral and saddle shed were difficult to distinguish. But slowly from the mists the figures of the burros became distinct. We were startled and delighted to see, close to Fidelity, a tiny figure with unmistakably long ears. The baby had arrived at long last! We quickened our pace, and as soon as the family saw us coming, each member started toward us. Fidelity with her wobbly baby bringing up the rear. We put the mother and the baby into the corral, exclaimed with joy at the perfect little figure, the curly hair, the soft gray eyes, the tiny hooves, the beautiful cross down the back. It is a little girl, and we named her Loli for Long Island Lighting stock, so that she would feel as if she really belonged to our stock-named animal family. Her mother is called Fidelity, short for Fidelity Fund, her father TNT, short for AT&T, and her little sister Esso for Standard Oil.

21

We rigged a tarp at one side of the corral and spread burlap bags on the ground underneath so the newborn child could keep dry, and then piled in good green hay for the mother. All members of the family are happy with the new addition, and TNT and Esso spend most of their time peering in through the corral logs or talking with Fidelity over the top log. Later in the day we put the mother and baby out for a while. Little Loli romped and played through the sage, even bucked several times, nuzzled her mother frequently, and finally lay down to take a quick nap before going into the saddle shed for the night. She thinks life is completely lovely and the world created just for her pleasure. The puppies are wild with delight and have welcomed the new baby with barks of joy. All of us wonder and marvel at the tiny, long-eared Hallowe'en sprite which has come and now belongs so dearly to all of us.

We received word that our horses would be picked up and taken out of the Valley to their warmer pastures. We saddled them for the last time and rode them across the river to our ranch where they would feed on the lush meadow grasses till later in the week when they would be trucked off. We stood at the top of the bench, saddles and bridles in the car, and watched the twenty-five Circle H horses and ours in the meadows below. Frost was on their backs, their winter coats were thick, and, feeling gay and strong in the cool air, they galloped down the meadows, racing and jumping the ditches, hooves resounding, tails and heads high, in the finest of spirits. They finally stopped and began to graze and from where we were watching above, we called, "Good-bye, Royalty. Goodbye, Dividend—till next spring. Winter well and keep strong and happy!" Our two horses, recognizing our voices, raised their heads at once, pricked their ears, and stood still as statues watching us. Then with a toss of their heads in one last farewell they were off and away, free, young, joyous.

Anne, now almost five, loves her dolls, loves all young things, and finds great satisfaction in caressing and cuddling Jet's new puppy. But she is already beginning to think of her own home and the children she would like to have. We asked her the other evening how many children she was going to have, and she promptly answered, "Three—all boys."

"And what will their names be?" we asked.

"The oldest will be Steven," she said, looking at her brother Steve. "The next Billy," and this time a glance went to her brother Bill.

"And what about the third?" we inquired.

"He will be called Grandad," she said, casting an affectionate look at Harry, Senior. "And when I call, 'Come here, Grandad,' it will be Big Grandad who comes. Then I will say, 'No, it is Little Grandad I want so I can give him his dinner.' So I shall call again, 'Come, Grandad,' and this time Little Grandad will come running for his dinner. That is the way it will be."

The skies looked ominous as we left the cabin early one afternoon two weeks ago to go to hunting camp. The barometer had dropped during the morning, not very low, but low enough for us to tuck into our duffle bags at the last moment an extra wool shirt and heavy socks and gloves, just in case. Riding along the highway, snug in the cab of the Circle H pick-up, we could see that many of the aspens back of Shadow Mountain had shed their leaves in the winds of the morning. The clouds behind the mountains were dark and were slowly enveloping the peaks. But the sun was still shining across the sage flats, and we were warm, almost hot, in our blue denim clothing.

Arriving at our designated campsite, it was clearly evident that Bob had been there before us. Four tents were neatly in place, one large one for the cook tent and living room, and at one side in a tidy line a small white tent for us, an extra sleeping tent for Bob and other male visitors, and a large tent for the storage of saddles, feed bags, saddle blankets, the chain saw, axes, pack saddles, bridles, halters, tarps, and other assorted gear.

We unloaded the pick-up, panier boxes to the cook tent, saddles to the barn tent, folding chairs to the "courtyard" in front of the other tents, our sleeping bags and duffles to their proper places. By late afternoon the stove was ready in our tent, the kitchen was in order, wood cut, and a dinner of hamburgers, salad, potatoes, apricots, and cookies was on the table. At this point the threatening clouds opened and the rain descended upon us. Although we hoped for snow, the temperature stayed too high. We all stayed dry and warm under the tents, but outside the ground was soon soaked and muddy.

Bob had the little stove roaring with flame and warmth when we turned in for the night. Our sleeping bags were comfortable, but before morning we realized that we had not yet worked out the right formula for blankets, sleeping bags, and tarps. With a resolve to plug the drafts and re-arrange blankets in a different order the next day, we crept deeper into our respective bags, shivered, and went to sleep.

We could see a heavy frost over everything when Bob came into the tent early in the morning to start a fire in our stove. Within minutes our tent was warm, and we were ready to crawl out and dress. The cook tent was as comfortable as any city living room, and a breakfast of eggs, fried potatoes, hot cakes, and coffee tasted better than room service fare at the Waldorf. The first rays of sunlight shone into the tent as we were eating, and we could see that the skies were cloudless. By the time the breakfast dishes were washed, it was warm, and we shed heavy jackets and hoods. Looking down the green Valley, we could see in the clear atmosphere fresh snow glisten on the distant peaks.

In the afternoon Bob said, "Let's go up that ridge and see what's up there," so we saddled Bent Arrow and Cimmaron and were off on game trails, up steep ridges, across small creeks, winding through forests until an hour or so later we arrived at the high meadows of Whetstone Mountain. Through the meadows the everlasting blossoms gave the illusion of summer even as the dried leaves and grasses crackled under the horses' hooves.

There were many spots in the meadow grass where the elk had bedded down for the night, but no fresh tracks did we see. The rains had washed the land clean. A big doe bounded ahead of us, her white rump startling among the browns of the grasses, the gold of the aspens, and the blue green of the giant spruces. The view of our beloved Valley was a glorious panorama, the mountain range blue and white in the distance, the flats brownish green, Mount Leidy looming up nearby, serrated with streaks of fresh snow. As the sun sank and the sky became pink behind the mountains on the horizon and deep rose on the rocky ridges just above us, we put on our heaviest jackets and were glad that we had thought to bring warm gloves. We felt the cold of our saddles if we shifted position, and our toes began to tingle before we reached camp at dusk. Warm tents, a hearty dinner, and early to bed. Tired, perhaps, but peaceful, happy, and free.

To us who have not had the opportunity to camp in the hills for some years, being in a snug, warm tent, sponge bathing in the cold creek when the sun quickly warms us, watching the sun rise and the sun set, living so intimately with the weather, the Steller Jays, and the Camp Robbers, helping to keep camp tidy, admiring the ingenious Bob as he arranged the griddle on a peg so it would swing freely on and off the top of the stove, playing gin rummy in the tent when it rained, watching the hills close by and the mountains in the distance—all of this is satisfying and good. As a visiting hunter from Detroit said to us, "I don't much care whether or not I get my elk. I like to ride the hills, see the country, hear the streams, enjoy the woods. These are the things that make hunting worth while." He had expressed our feelings precisely.

THE APPROACH of winter here in our Valley has a vastly different meaning from the coming of winter in most other places. There is excitement in the air, a sense of looking forward to some great event, an anticipation of high spirits and happiness. Everyone looks to his wood pile and silently measures its size against the length of the months to come. The garages in town are busy putting snow tires on cars, and engine heaters are stacked within easy reach of buyers. Our own snowmobile, the little SkiDoo, has been put in fine shape and is even now facing forward in the saddle shed, completely prepared to be driven out when the snow becomes so deep that our road is impassable and we have to park the car at the Circle H gate. Our freshly varnished snow shoes are already stuck into a bank of snow within reach of the back door. Our pacs have thick warm socks in them, and our peg board in the hall closet is gay with bright-colored hoods and mittens. The snow shovel is on the front porch and another in the car as a precaution against trouble on the road. The tow started to operate on the Pass a week ago, and every week end skiers of all ages are skimming and twisting and sometimes tumbling down the slopes.

We walked outdoors a few minutes ago and went along the edge of the bench above the river. The air was fresh, cold, clean. We found branches of dead sage protruding through the snow and picked up several to add to the fire crackling in the fireplace, not that we expected any real warmth from the wood but simply because it is delightfully fragrant and fills the cabin with a pungent aroma. One of our great joys is to gather wood in the forests, pack it into the back of the big station wagon, and bring it to our wood pile just outside the back door of the cabin. For many days now we have been concentrating on wood gathering because we know that soon the snow will be so deep that all the good chunks and sticks which we use for kindling will be hidden.

The wild animals are coming down from the high country to more plentiful feed below. As we were eating lunch the other day, a young buck deer came up the back road, paused, looked fearlessly at the cabin, and then bounded toward the river. Fifteen deer raced over the sage flats recently, and a beautiful big buck deer with a mighty spread of antlers was standing near the road as we drove to the post office yesterday. A cow moose with her calf comes out each afternoon from the trees on the bench above, and the cry of ducks and geese can be heard all day long over the river. Our tamer friends, Fica and Tia, love to spend hours in their pen, playing and romping in the snow, running their noses through it, eating it, tossing their old shoe and sticks high into the air, and chasing after them to see which can get them first. At night under the

25

nearly full moon, the coyotes' call can be heard all around the cabin, and the puppies answer it in long, mournful howls. The cry is taken up by Jet and Bullet down at the Circle H, and the call of the tame and the call of the wild mingle in prolonged and weird sounds.

The sun sets early these days, and by five in the afternoon our lights are turned on and the fire is lit. There are long evenings to enjoy with friends, to play shanghai, to knit, to read. The new magazines are stacked high, and, currently, Joseph Wood Krutch's autobiography, *More Lives Than One,* and Franz Kafka's strange, powerful, but unearthly novel, *The Trial,* are within close reach. One evening we had a sumptuous duck dinner at the Circle H and listened to a recording of Beethoven's Ninth Symphony afterward, being caught as always when we hear it in the tremendous grandeur of the music, the infinite compassion of the third movement, the free and magnificent and joyous music of the great choral movement.

We wanted to do something special on this our first Thanksgiving in the Valley. We could think of nothing finer than to have a hearty breakfast and soon after drive over to our ranch across the river to see how it looked in the snow. When the sun had risen high enough to warm the atmosphere—the thermometer had dropped to eight above zero the night before—we got into the frosty car and started off, down the little road, across the bridge, and finally into the road which leads to the ranch. We parked momentarily at the top of the bench to look over the wide expanse of land with the woods beyond, and then drove down, parked the car, and set off over the snowy meadow to the old buck fence near the first fishing stream, our favorite spot to sit and look around at the land which is ours. There were innumerable wild animal tracks, ranging in size from the big ones which elk and deer had left to the smaller snow shoe rabbit tracks, the tiny deer mice tracks, and the delicate tracks which small birds had left. There was a perfect network of these, and although we saw no game, we sensed it near and heard from the river beyond the call of wild geese and ducks. The little twigs of sage and fragile weeds still reaching through the snow were covered with slim, delicate ice crystals which glittered in the bright sun. The sage was aglow with tiny lights, twinkling gaily as if each bush were sending secret messages over the flats to nearby bushes. The sky was never so blue, the peaks never so majestic, the snow never so clean and sparkling and white. We walked back to the car after an hour or two in the fresh air, feeling content and peaceful, wanting nothing more, needing nothing more, but filled with unprecedented thankfulness that we are here and can think, hopefully, of years upon years to spend doing the things we love in the place we now so joyfully call home.

1964

THE VALLEY WINTER has now arrived in earnest, and if there has been any question about our driving the car to the cabin or being able to travel over the snow on foot without snow shoes, such a question is now decided.

But this idea of being snowed in is a pleasant one to all of us. Our neighbors and we have parked near our front doors our fine motor toboggans which will take us anywhere in all manner of snow conditions and weather, and, much as we like to think we are snowed in, we all know that with our SkiDoo we can reach the main plowed road just as quickly as we do with our car in the summer. After fresh snows which in one night can build up to several feet or after the occasional winds have drifted the snow over our toboggan track, we go out and make new tracks which become as hard and as firm as a cement walk and over which we can walk with no fear of sinking in.

Wild animals can be seen in great numbers now. The other morning as we were eating breakfast and looking over the island to the river beyond, sixteen deer passed below us, entirely unconscious of the humans and the puppies watching them. A few days later we saw on the island two immense bull moose, black against the white snow. They faced each other, and for a long time, either in seriousness or in jest, seemed to be arguing with each other by putting their heads down and clashing their antlers together. This morning a cow moose and her twin calves passed within a few feet of the cabin and then sauntered off towards the bench above, their long, thin legs carrying them without effort through the deep snow.

A trip into town in the summer time is often something to be done quickly and put behind one. But in the winter time, a trip to town carries gaiety and a feeling of conquest. Harry, Senior, used to tell us about bringing in mail and groceries by dog sled, helped by his fine, massive malemute, Kim. We also remember Mae's account of how she traveled to town by covered sleigh which was heated only by a small stove, and how many long days the journey took. Our travel these days is much easier, but there still is the same feeling of adventure when we put on heavy socks, pacs, hoods, jackets, and mittens. We always are sure the snow shoes are in the SkiDoo before we start, just in case we should need them to cross the snowy sage flats. We press the little chrome button on the dash board of the SkiDoo and hear the comforting sound of the motor. We cast a look to see if the long fiber glass sled in back is well attached, turn the motor to full force, and away we go, past the corral, down the little dip in the road, over the cattle guard, and onto the main road for about half a mile till we reach our car parked off the road at the Circle H gate. We turn the SkiDoo so it will be faced in the right direction for the return trip, wipe off the snow from the car, and we are on our way, down the snowy road, trees on either side white and stately, buck fences attired in queer shaped hats and bonnets, some standing straight, some lopping over in a ludicrous fashion. We pass the moose ponds, now only black streaks through the deep snow, we cut down and through the dugway, and in a moment pull up in front of the post office where we always meet and exchange gay greetings with friends, some of whom are hardly recognizable in their fur caps, heavy parkas, and stout snow pants. There is the friendliest of atmospheres at the post office, work is done quietly and efficiently with no sense of pressure or impatience or hurry. Often we can tell what the stacked packages in the back room contain by the very aromas which emerge. Not long ago we knew someone in the Valley had received a box of strong cheeses, and a large burlap bag, filled to bursting and emitting a strong odor, told us that Harry's fertilizer for his new bulbs had finally arrived. The roads to town are kept well plowed and free from snow, so we can drive on the highway at a reasonable speed, past the entrance to our ranch, past the airport, and on down the big hill, passing cars, most of them pick-up trucks whose drivers all wave in a happy fashion as they pass. All of the eating places, and many of the motels which border the town are closed now, but as we drive farther, we begin to see more people, busy shoppers, school children, store owners who are cheerfully helping customers with their purchases. The big sign on top of the REA building tells us what activities are imminent—bake sales, ski movies, rummage sales. Friends call to us as we pass, others wave from passing cars, and sooner or later we find our way to the bakery for a cup of hot coffee and a fresh doughnut. Here we always meet friends and interrupt our shopping briefly for a visit with them. Often we drive to Twin Creek Ranch to see our burros, each time amazed at how much the baby Loli has grown. The little family always recognizes us and comes over to nuzzle against us, eagerly eating the carrots we have for them in our pockets. When the back of the car has been well loaded and we have checked our lists to make certain we have forgotten nothing, we drive back down our little road to the waiting SkiDoo. We unload provisions from the car and pile them on the sled, start the motor, and back we go.

Although the holiday season is drawing to a close, we shall never forget this last Christmas morning. It was indeed a memorable occasion. After our own leisurely breakfast and the excited opening of our own gifts, we put our presents for the Circle H into our sled, got into the SkiDoo, and started over the snow, through the tall pine forest, heavy with its holiday garb of white, over the two new bridges by the corral, and around to the front door. Adults and children rushed to shout "Merry Christmas!" and we tumbled out and in, handing out their gifts and receiving ours. It was the first Christmas in their beautiful new home, and, although the move had been accomplished only days before, all was complete. Verna, Margaret's mother, handed us each a delicious egg nog, and we sat down before the big fire in the magnificent fire place to enjoy the morning. A little later Harry showed us his garden room, the many bulbs he had already planted and even one he had gently moved to see if it was really growing. Soon the children pulled us down stairs to their play room where there was an array of toys. Ann proudly showed us the tiny creche she had helped construct, the baby Jesus, Mary, and "Jophes." Everyone's face was happy and excited at the big rooms, the lovely furnishings, the kitchen compact and complete to the last detail. Jet and Bullet, the two black Labradors, raced about in the snow outside, and Rocket, the new puppy, who, now that he is older, we find of dubious heritage, slipped into the opened door whenever he could to join the gaiety and festivities within. At last we got back into the snowmobile and turned toward home, glancing back as we rode over the snowy meadow at the fine new house, the Christmas tree twinkling in the living room, a curl of smoke rising from the chimney, and knew that all was good, all was right. We greatly rejoiced that the house we had watched being built with such interest ever since mid-summer was finally complete, occupied, and now is home to our dear friends.

We had known that winters in the Valley would be spectacular so far as scenery was concerned and that the days and evenings would be filled with gay times with friends, but, we must admit, we had been somewhat concerned about bitter weather, biting winds, and day after day of sub-zero temperatures. Our friends from the East and Mid-West apparently had shared our apprehensions as many of their holiday greetings carried hopes that we "could get out once in a while" and that we were "not freezing to death." We realize full well that a good two months of winter still lie ahead and that much can happen, but so far our fears certainly have been allayed and our concern has been proved unreasonable. We think it only fair to tell our worried friends and all the summer residents who have not experienced a winter here that to this point we have been far warmer and temperatures have been far higher than if we had been in our city home in the Mid-West. The snow is deep, but it is dry and light, and one can walk through it and find boots and ski pants still dry as the snow does not cling. The temperature dropped to 27 below zero one night, but we did not realize it until we were told several days later by neighbors who had watched their thermometer more closely than we had done. Not a single day has passed when the sun has not melted some of the snow on the roof, and long icicles have been formed from the dripping water. Because the humidity count is extremely low, one does not feel the cold. Clear, dry nights, warm, bright days, with skies incredibly blue and sun unbelievably warm. We are as sunburned as in the summer time and have suffered not one moment's discomfort. And so, all you people who have feared a mountain winter, come to this Valley and try the skiing, the ice skating, the ice fishing, the snow shoeing, the traveling over the trails on a motor toboggan, the sitting in a snug, warm cabin by a fragrant fire of pine and aspen logs and twigs of sage, and you will know that we speak the truth and you, no more than we, will ever want to leave again.

January 15, 1964

WE WERE TALKING the other day about the various adventures which this life holds for us, and we began to ennumerate a few which we have come to accept now as usual and commonplace.

For instance, in the morning we can hardly wait to go to the kitchen to prepare breakfast, because we are eager to see what new birds are flying about and pecking at the suet which we nailed to a post on the back porch. When we took our Christmas tree down, we stuck it into the snow, just outside the windows, and tied more pieces of suet to the branches. As decorations when the tree was in the living room, we had gay little artificial birds perched on the branches, the prize one being a tiny, lifelike snow owl who gazed unblinkingly at us from his perch. But now since the tree is out of doors, the artificial birds packed away till next Christmas, we have real birds flying to and from our Christmas tree, mountain chickadees, black-capped chickadees, downy woodpeckers, hairy woodpeckers, and we are hoping to lure soon a pair of Steller's jays and nuthatches.

As we go to our woodpile to bring in armsful of kindling or split logs for the fireplace, we always stop for a moment to glance up at the snowy peaks or down the river which these days frequently steams in great white clouds. Often we see as many as fifty or sixty ducks riding the currents.

Last night we played shanghai at the Circle H, but it wasn't the usual card game and we did not go to it or return from it in the usual way. The thermometer read close to zero when we left, so for the first time this winter we wore our air force suits, light but warm pants and jackets against which no cold on earth can penetrate. We pulled up the comfortable hoods, edged with wolverine fur which cannot frost, put on our fur shoes, and for the two miles, riding in an open sled through the frosty night, we felt no chill, nothing but comfort and warmth. We parked the SkiDoo at the front door of the lovely new house, we saw a face appear at each window, and when we went in, a crackling fire greeted us, and one of our Shostakovich favorites was on the stereo. After good talk, a good game of cards, good music—everything which makes an evening a happy, satisfying one, we got into our air force suits again, turned the SkiDoo homeward, and back we rode over the snow, glancing up often to marvel at the closeness and the brilliance of the stars above.

We have missed our little deer mouse Harriet recently and knew that she and her mouse family probably were in their nest in our third and only unused flue. We liked to think of her there, warm and peaceful, and, judging from the vast amount of food she had carried away from our front window sill last summer and fall, we knew, too, that she and her brood were bountifully fed. But we missed her nightly visits and still put out food once in a while in case she should rouse herself and return. But the food remained untouched, and there was no trace of Harriet. This morning, however, we were delighted and excited to see that Harriet had returned and had come over the drifts straight to her dining area at the window sill. There unmistakably in the snow were her dainty footprints and the mark which her long tail had left. We are very glad that she has paid us this visit, and tonight after dark, we shall toss out some tasty, crunchy bread crumbs, which should delight her little mouse heart.

31

A group of us is starting skiing lessons soon. Not that we care about perfecting skiing techniques or doing any serious skiing, but just that we want to get out of doors, have sound and healthful exercise, and, most important of all, have hilarious, gay times, laughing at our mistakes, our awkwardness, and incidentally hoping that we learn how to handle ourselves with a modicum of skill.

And so it goes—a simple life, a good life, a peaceful life, but never a dull life or an ordinary one.

February 1, 1964

WE HAVE HAD many adventures in the past ten days. While the bath water was running merrily and abundantly for one of us, suddenly our pump groaned briefly and stopped entirely. A full flow of water one second, not even a drop the next. We looked at each other first in amazement, then in consternation, then in frenzy. We rushed to the other faucets and turned them on, and our fears were confirmed. Our first horrible thought was that the well had gone dry. That would be real trouble. Fortunately our dinner was nearly ready, a full pot of coffee was waiting to be heated, and there was no immediate cause for concern. We found all the big containers in the cabin, filled them with snow, packed it down firmly, and set them on the stove. Then, as always when in distress, we phoned the Circle H. It was dark and windy and snowy. Bob offered to come up immediately; we refused to let him, and he promised to come the next morning. We stored what melted snow we had in kettles and proceeded to melt more and more and more, each huge bucketful yielding about two inches in the bottom when it was melted. We got through dinner all right, did the dishes with clean water we scooped from the tub, and even laughed at our predicament. But the dreadful thought kept recurring—What if the well is dry? What do we do then? Move in with the neighbors? Rent a motel room in town? Go back to the city? But others have melted snow for water, and so can we. We'll get the whole process down to a fine science. Scoop snow, fill kettles, melt snow, store water. Scoop snow, fill kettles, melt snow, store water.

The next morning Bob appeared and, armed with a wrench, went to the pump in the basement. He examined it carefully, finally pulled up the plastic pipe, and found a little dirt in the foot valve. Nothing more. It was that simple. Down went the pipe into the well, but it had lost its prime. Losing the prime was a new expression to us. We could think only of a cow who loses her cud. Both of these disasters were equally vague in our minds except we knew they must spell trouble. When a pump loses its prime, one must pour water, water, more water into it in

32

order that it may begin to function again, so bucket after bucket, kettle after kettle of our precious melted snow went into the pump, and finally when the switch was turned on, the most beautiful sound resulted, the churn of the pump, protesting at first but soon swinging into its full tone. Then we tried the faucets and never have we heard such wonderful and miraculous music as when the water with a few first spurts and splutters gushed forth in all its power. We washed in slightly rusty water for a while, our ice cubes had a peculiar yellowish tinge to them, and we even drank water with a rusty cast to it, but it was water, good, fine well water, and soon it became as clear as crystal. This was adventure. We never had appreciated water so much before. We never had realized its tremendous importance or how we depended upon its flow. How careless and thoughtless in its wasteful use we had been! Even yet each time we turn on a faucet, we smile with pleasure and satisfaction and count our blessings.

And then there was the adventure with the electric power last Sunday morning. We had had breakfast and were heating water on the stove for more coffee. After an unduly long time of waiting for it to boil, we went to the kitchen to see what the trouble was, thinking perhaps we had failed to turn on the electricity. But the little indicator was marked High and still nothing was happening. We turned on the switch for a light in the kitchen, and nothing happened there either. We hoped that nothing was wrong with our wiring so decided to call the Circle H to see if they had power. Margaret answered the phone, sensed who was calling and what was wanted, so she didn't even say "Good Morning" as she picked up the receiver, but instead said gaily, "Yes, it is!" We were surprised at this greeting, hesitated a minute, and, sensing our confusion, she added, "I knew who was calling and what for. Yes, our power *is* off." We laughed with her and then phoned the emergency number for the Lower Valley Power and Light Company. A pleasant voice thanked us for calling and said the men were already on their way to locate the trouble. We built a huge fire in the fireplace and kept warm and comfortable. We began to plan lunch and found we could get together a very good meal over the wood coals. Just as we were finding ways to manage for a while without power and were testing our ingenuity to see what we could contrive, we saw the electric company truck going down the main road, and in minutes thereafter our lights went on, the electric heat clicked, and the pump began to churn normally. Two, at the most three, hours of inconvenience. But really not inconvenience at all since we managed beautifully, and, again, began to appreciate a little more something which before we had always accepted and taken for granted.

And then there was the SkiDoo. All we ever had to do was step out to our snowmobile and ride off. This day was different. Something had apparently gone wrong with the wiring for the starter, and the trusty little machine, for the first time, refused to start. We put the tarp back on it, went into the house, and decided to go for the mail some other day. And then the snows began. Not just a half-hearted, lazy kind of snow, but snow in earnest, inches accumulating within a very short time. We watched the hitch rack in front of the cabin grow shorter and shorter and finally disappear. We watched the masses of snow heap up on the wood pile. We saw the puppies' pen fill and the fencing around it grow less and less visible and finally disappear entirely. Such light fluff we never had seen; a shovel full was featherweight, and the whiteness of it! Now we really were snowed in, and there was no chance at all of getting out except on snow shoes. But there was no emergency, we had plenty of good food laid in just in case something like this might happen, we were marvelously comfortable and warm. And what we accomplished! Cleaning until the cabin shone, mending, ironing, knitting, reading, writing, cooking, keeping in touch with Witty in the city by phone, talking with friends at the Circle H and in town several times a day. When we wanted our mail or when our supply of milk and eggs ran low, Harry, who went out every day to take Steven and Bill to school, would bring them up and leave our little box of dairy products and mail at the main road. One late afternoon just as it began to grow dark, we snow shoed out the mile or so to the road, knapsacks on our backs, and brought in the mail and the milk and the eggs. How still and beautiful the world looked! The trees dusted with snow, those with heavy branches, loaded with it. The unbroken fields of snow all around us, the trees on the bench rising black and tall. And just as we returned with our provisions, we saw the great silver moon rising over the butte. And never was mail so appreciated, never did milk taste so sweet and good, never did eggs sputter and sizzle so gaily in the hot skillet.

And then one morning we awoke to clear, bright sunshine, the peaks rising in the distance, snowy against a blue, blue sky. The storm had broken, the air glistened, the thermometer having been in the twenties and thirties, dropped sharply. Bob got the SkiDoo going, took it to the Circle H shop, and put it in fine order so that now it runs better than ever. And yesterday, the first time in nearly two weeks, we drove to town, our car having been cleared of its mounds of snow by kind friends at the Circle H. We were greeted everywhere by "So you finally got dug out!" or "We began to think we wouldn't see you till spring," or "Had a little snow up country, I hear."

And all this within ten short days! Such magnificence of scenery we have never witnessed, such kindness and thoughtfulness and concern on the part of neighbors and friends who realize that this is our first January here and feared that we might not be inured to the rigors of a wilderness winter. And such comfort! Food never tasted so delicious, hot water never felt so good, our faces never were so sunburned, our bodies never felt so strong and healthy. It is good for a few short hours, to be deprived of those things which we have always casually taken for granted.

March 1, 1964

SINCE WE have never before this year spent the month of February in our Valley, we were interested to know what kind of weather to expect. Some of the local people have told us that this time of year is likely to be "hard cold" and that temperatures may drop to incredibly low points. Others have said that some days can be mild and that we may even have thaws and occasional rains. From what we have heard, we imagined that if we wanted to leave our Valley for a short trip, this would be the month to do so. Perhaps to New Mexico, Arizona, Hawaii, the South Seas, or Japan. But now that February is spent, we think that certainly not during this month would we want to leave for fear of missing too much here. There has been snow in February, there have been high winds of short duration, there has been cold. We think we would never tire of snow; high winds when one is sitting comfortably around a blazing fire can bring only the feeling of excitement and adventure and gratitude that he can be warm and snug within; the cold has not once been unbearably bitter or even objectionable to us. As we ride over the snow on our SkiDoo, we can only rejoice at the freshness, the crispness which we feel on our faces, the dryness and crunchiness of the snow underfoot, and the increasing sunburn on our faces. No, we think, February is not the month we shall want to leave the Valley. Some other month perhaps, but certainly not this one, and each of us wonders which month it will be and knows secretly that such a month really does not exist.

The animal and bird life seems to be increasingly interesting. Besides our usual chickadees, woodpeckers, and Clark nutcrackers, we see the black and white of magpies flash through the bare trees, the harsh call of ravens is frequently heard, and yesterday in town we saw a pair of Bohemian waxwings, glorious with their rosy-gray crests and bright yellow stripes on their tails. Cedar waxwings have been seen along the road to town, and not long ago we caught a glimpse of the great bald eagle. Yesterday afternoon we looked from one of our back windows and were startled to see lying in the sun a brown furry body with a small head and pricked ears. He scampered toward the porch, then back again, watching us every minute with his sharp little eyes. He came closer to the window and daringly peeked in. He looked like the kind of animal one wants to pick up and cuddle in his arms, feeling the little face pressed close. We discovered he was a young marten and marveled at the beauty of his sleek, shining fur, known as American sable. We think he has made his home under our front porch. This morning we saw his footprints in the snow, leading from the cabin toward the river, and this afternoon we saw the footprints headed back. We hope he has come to stay and will be peering into our windows again. We call him Jeremiah.

We had our first real encounter with three moose on the road. We had heard for a long time about how a moose will sometimes be trapped on the road, reluctant to plunge through the deep banks of snow which the plows have left. We had heard how terrifyingly angry they may become and how, if pressed too far, they may even charge a car. One morning we were on our way to the road on the SkiDoo, our sled behind. We stopped at the Circle H to pick up Ann and Margaret who were going skiing with us. Bob and Rosemary decided they'd like a ride to the road with us, and before we started, out of the house came Harry, mail knapsack under his arm, rushing to jump on and get a ride, too. We attached their sled in back of ours, and the merry, laughing procession started, everyone shouting and happy. We wound past the open spot which is used in summer for barrel racing, the barrels now resembling enormous marshmallows in the snow, and suddenly one of us looked back and saw that the last sled of our caravan had snapped loose, and Bob and Harry were left behind, looking bewildered and surprised at their sudden plight. We stopped the SkiDoo, they grabbed their sled and ran to catch up with us, attached it again, and the long procession began once more, continuing this time safely and with no mishaps. We took three cars from the parking area, Harry going first, we following, and Bob bringing up the rear with the pick-up truck. Along the way we noticed that Harry was going slowly and more slowly. Finally he stopped entirely, and we could not imagine what was wrong until one of us caught a glimpse of a huge bull moose trotting along ahead. We all laughed at the spectacle we made, a moose leading three cars down the road. We stopped our cars, Harry got out of his, Margaret rolled down the window of our car and called jokingly, "Honey, can I help you?" At one point the moose looked back, put his ears down flat, and for a moment we feared smashed headlights and fenders. Harry asked Bob with the stronger pick-up to

36

drive ahead, so we all pulled off the road till he had passed. Down the road Bob went, the moose leading, we following the pick-up. After a mile or so of this, the moose found a place to jump over the snow bank, and as we passed, he looked at us haughtily, not at all disturbed that he had been in our way, but only humiliated by his injured dignity. A few nights later we were returning late at night from a delicious lobster dinner at Fran and JB's home. We wanted to make good time as they had asked us to phone when we arrived home, and we wanted no delay in our arrival to cause worry and concern. Again, as we rounded a bend in the road, there were two moose, a cow and her calf. The lights of the car blinded and infuriated them, and although they trotted ahead of us most of the way, they turned back often and stood still in the middle of the road, looking at us as if daring us to proceed. Their ears were flat, their eyes gleamed bronze red in the lights of the car, and once or twice they even started slowly toward us which caused us without hesitation to back the car out of their way. We inched our way along, backing occasionally, and finally the pair disappeared down the road beyond the Circle H main gate and our parked SkiDoo. We waited a minute to make sure they would not return and then got out of the car, cast the flashlight gleams on our little motor toboggan, got on, started the motor, and we, too, disappeared into the night, although we must admit we cast glances behind us once in a while just to be certain the red eyes were not still fixed upon us.

Another reason we cannot leave the Valley in February is because of the excellent skiing. Five of us, all beginners, began early this month to take lessons from Bill. We all met at the bottom of the hill for the first lesson, boots and skis on, poles in hand. Bill said first, "All right, girls, now line up in front of me." All, awkwardly watching our feet with concern as to where our skis might take us, obeyed. First walking on our skis gingerly, learning to slide a little, then trying the kick turn which most of us executed the first few times with amazing results, one ski generally pointing due north, the other due south, poles in between somewhere, legs we knew not where. Finally we got the first fundamentals learned well enough so we could, step by fearful step, begin to climb the smallest hill. Skis were crossed, righted again, legs were twisted, turned around and on up we all went, Bill patiently in the lead. Other skiers whizzed down around us, mostly children, but we were too intent on what we were doing, concentrating too fiercely, ever to give much notice. Then came the snow plow, practicing skiing down our short incline, falling, learning how to get up with the least amount of trouble and effort, and near the end of the lesson we were taken to the bunny

37

tow for our first trip. We were taught how to grab the rope easily at first, then tighter so that our ascent up the hill would be slow, how to get off, how to snow plow carefully down. Most of us in our first fear and anxiety gripped the rope at first for dear life, hard and fast, and found ourselves carried to the top with alarming speed, suddenly, breathtakingly fast, so dismayed by our whirlwind trip that by the time we reached the top we were only too glad to release the rope and fall off in any way we could. We practiced and practiced between lessons, finding the most disconcerting thing of all perhaps the pre-school age children flashing past us, no poles, speeding up on the tow ahead of us. We were all waiting at the bottom of the tow one day, each apparently reviewing in her own mind the fundamentals we had been taught, when red-clad five year old Shane bounced ahead of all of us, grabbed the rope with one small mittened hand, started up, looking back and calling as he zoomed off, "See yuh!" Another mite, hardly old enough to walk steadily, let alone ski, wearing ski boots not more than four inches long, said to one of us as he got on the bunny tow, "I usually ride the chair lift but Barry, my teacher, told me to meet him here." We looked up to the heights of the hill one morning and were highly amused, not to say envious, to see a tall instructor with seven dots behind him, seven three or four year olds, learning to come down the steep incline. They looked like heavily bundled periods in the distance, each working hard on his lesson, each succeeding nobly. We never feel conspicuous or stupid as there are all ages of people, learning at all stages, and at the foot of the tow we exchange funny experiences or bits of advice we have learned. We feel quite proud to be known on the hill as the Ladies Auxiliary. One business man from town takes time during his lunch hour to take lessons or practice on the bunny tow. His face is determined but happy, and he is taking great satisfaction in his very obvious improvement. "I'm doing what they told me to do," he said as he put his hands on the rope and let it slide through his fingers for a minute. "I don't always understand why, but I'm doing it, and it's working fine." And then as he tightened his grip on the rope and began to move up the hill, he cast over his shoulder with a grin, "If my eight year old kid can do it, so can I." With much more practice, many more lessons, learning more each day, gaining increased confidence at each turn on the hill, we took our first trip up the chair lift to the first station, got off and saw the terrifying sight below, the hill so steep and long we dared look at it only out of the corner of one eye, the little town below, set out in neat squares, with doll-like houses and buildings, the ants we knew were people at the bottom of the hill. Our hands, moist with cold sweat, our legs suddenly weak and unsteady, we began with Bill the easy descent, trembling every minute, falling where we should have handled our skis well, stopping often for instructions or to wait for a fallen comrade behind. Finally, finally we got within sight of the bunny tow and breathed easily as we knew we were near home territory. And when Bill said to each as we passed him, "All right, ski all the way down, turning as you go," we knew we had made it and could have burst with pride. More practice, more lessons, and now we go up the chair lift like veterans, skiing back in a fraction of the time it used to take us, feeling confident and relaxed. We are beginning to feel the rhythm of skiing, the joy of manipulating our ankles, our knees, our hips, our shoulders properly. We know that there is much for us to learn, that we have made only the faintest beginning, but we all know enough to realize that we love it, consider skiing the greatest of sports, and, as Bill said, are learning much more than mere strengthening of muscles and controlling body and legs. Now we can hardly wait to get to the hill, we experience a delicious chill run through us as we get on the chair lift, we feel exhilaration as we begin the downward slopes. We are more relaxed, easy, comfortable, and love the swinging, the turning, the gliding down, daring to shoosh at the bottom where we still look with comfort and affection at the bunny tow.

Day after day this month the skies have been brilliant blue; the peaks rise in all their snowy dignity and power. The river steams morning and night, and the trees glisten in the early morning sun with sparkling frost feathers. The roar of the river below reaches our ears each time we step out of doors. On some days the air is as soft as spring, and the songs of the birds carry the music of April. One can almost smell the fragrance of the sticky cottonwood buds. Everything and everyone seems to be waiting, waiting expectantly for something to happen, and we know by the warmth of the sun, by the longer and longer daylight hours, that it will happen soon. May told us she saw four robbins eating tallow in her yard yesterday, and that perhaps was the first sure sign of all. But it is still winter, the snows are deep, the early mornings and evenings are cold, and we are happy that there are days and days of skiing ahead. No—February is too exciting, too expectant, too promising for us to leave the Valley. We cannot miss one golden day or one mountain sunset which touches the snow, the bench, the peaks, the clouds and snow plumes above them with colors glorious beyond belief. We shall remain here always during this month, we know now. The Southwest, Hawaii, the South Seas, and Japan will have to wait for us till we find in our Valley a month less attractive, less fascinating than February.

PERHAPS IT WAS the absolute silence out of doors when we awoke. Perhaps it was the unaccustomed darkness at the windows. Perhaps it was the unusual unwillingness of the puppies to leave their warm beds and venture out. At any rate, when we looked out and when we tried to open the doors leading to the porches, we knew it had come in the night, the heaviest blizzard of the winter. We rejoiced that we had no appointments that had to be met, no duties in town to discharge. We could spend the whole glorious day at the cabin, going out only long enough to shovel the porches so the doors would open, making a path through the snow to the wood pile and SkiDoo. This we did soon after breakfast, and we knew then that we could get plenty of kindling and plenty of logs to keep a fine fire going all day if need be. The cabin was warm, we had a good supply of food to last for days if this should continue, and we settled down, knowing we need have no worries.

There is so much to do when one is snowed in! We don't care how often it happens and welcome each snowed-in experience as much as the last. We take joy in leisurely cleaning the cabin, in polishing silver, in knitting, in writing, in reading, hearing the wind howl around the corners and the snow peck at the windows.

Not the least enjoyment we get from the snow is the certainty that the ski hill will be in fine shape and that there will be lots of good powder. We like best to ski during the week as we have almost the whole hill and chair lift to ourselves and need have no fear of bumping into anyone or having to get out of anyone's way in a hurry. Lately the days have been warm, unusually sunny, and the snow conditions just right. We were proud at our last lesson when Bill said, "Today we go to the second station" which meant two-thirds of the way to the top. It was not half so fearsome as going the first time to the first station, and we felt like old hands on the chair lift. The distance down looked longer, the hill a little steeper, but we had had more practice and instruction in making turns and in side slipping, so we felt more confidence. Then there is the coming down over the broad, sweeping slope that runs between two groves of trees. We had often looked up from the bunny tow or first station runs to this particular spot and thought how much fun it would be to take this way down. And now we find ourselves at this very spot, coming down the same way, maybe not so easily, not so smoothly, not so effortlessly, but anyway we are there and have made our own faint beginning on the faster slopes. We tumble, fall, roll, are covered with snow, but as we progress further, our confidence seems to strengthen, and we make the bottom proudly, if somewhat breathlessly, eager only to get on the lift and try it again.

April 1, 1964

WE ARE PROUD to live in the United States and know that no other country in the world could hold the advantages and charms for us which this country does. There is no one in the world with whom we would change places. We realize full well that there are many in down-trodden, Communist-ridden, starving countries who would only too gladly change places with us. It takes money to support a country, and if it is our tax money and the tax money of others which helps to make this nation good and great and strong, we think that no money anywhere could be spent more wisely. We would willingly give even more than is required of us if by so doing we could be assured that the United States would continue on the path which has made it the most civilized, the most humane, the most honest, the wisest of all nations.

But many doubts have been nagging us lately, and we are beginning to wonder if our tax money and the tax money of others really is contributing to this country's good. Could all the millions and millions of dollars which pour into the United States treasury each year from the American public, we wonder, be contributing instead to the detriment of this country.

We have done no research on taxes and how tax money is spent. We are writing here only of things which we have witnessed with our own eyes, have read in reliable papers and magazines, or have heard. We realize that anything we may say in protest to the ways our tax money is being spent will make no effect whatsoever. Sometimes, however, making such a protest clears one's own conscience. Paying taxes, we know, is inevitable; wasteful use of much of tax payers' money apparently is inevitable, too. But before April 15 we want to state that we are becoming alarmed and at times saddened by what we know. We are not resigned. We know we must bow before the inevitable, but we shall not do so submissively.

A person would be considered not only wildly extravagant but childishly simple if he bought a car worth several thousand dollars unless he first examined that car carefully and compared it with others as to appearance, durability, performance. Who would dream of buying a fur coat or a piece of jewelry worth the same amount without first inspecting that coat or that jewelry? But millions of Americans turn over comparable amounts of money or more each year to their government and never

41

question its use or its expenditure. They do not demand to see honest, good results come from their money. They simply hand the money over, forget it, and if they are prudent start saving for next year's hand-out. In the hands of scrupulously honest, conscientious government officials this complete trust might be understandable, but in the hands of anything less, such trust is preposterous and unthinkable. And yet, all of us do it every year.

As long ago as November, 1962, we were staggered to read the cost of maintaining the President in the White House. Over two million dollars to protect the President and his house, 250 police force members, an office staff of nearly 300, and transporting the President with Boeing 707 jets, propeller driven executive transports, helicopters, a fleet of White House limousines, elaborate and expensive water craft—at a cost in all to tax payers of ten million dollars annually.

Last summer the President and his staff of over 100 people flew into this Valley, on, what was called, a mission of conservation of natural resources here. For days before the President arrived, planes of all kinds flew in and out. It was reported that before the arrival of the executive plane, the President's fire engine was flown in at terrific expense so that in case his plane should catch fire, the flames could be quickly extinguished. A large hotel here was kept open beyond the season's closing date to accommodate the Presidential party. Someone even telephoned from Washington to see what time it was here in the Valley as it was apparently too difficult for him to figure out the time differences across the country. We saw the great silver Presidential plane arrive at six o'clock one evening. Shortly after we saw three helicopters taking part of the Presidential party to the hotel. The next morning at nine, exactly on pre-announced schedule, the helicopters flew back, and shortly thereafter the great plane rose into the air and left the Valley. What could have been accomplished in that short time in regard to conservation, people in the Valley wondered. But a few suspicions were confirmed when later papers and news magazines frankly stated that the trip, although called one for conservation purposes, actually was entirely "political." We wondered what the cost of this elaborate but short trip had been and who had paid for it. It was without question the American tax payers. If a tour is political in nature and intended primarily to win votes in coming elections, perhaps the party which would benefit by such a tour should pay for it. Perhaps it would be more honest if the President himself called such a trip political instead of having news magazines and papers make the announcement for him. But such evasion, even such subtleties in hand-

42

ling the truth, have grown common, and, what is discouraging, are accepted by the American public as natural and defensible.

We were disturbed to read recently of the incredible waste of the Air Force. Hundreds of thousands of dollars of furniture was bought when the furniture already in use was perfectly adequate. And this simply because there were some unspent funds in the Air Force treasury. Computer systems leased when new ones could have been bought and maintained for about half the cost of the leasing. Fifty million dollars, plus the interest cost, wasted annually in maintaining in stock such things as nuts and bolts when such things could be purchased almost anywhere when and as needed. Would Air Force officials who order such items or who are responsible for such expenditures of money be so ready to do so if the money came from their own pockets? Is not one doubly careful when handling the money of others? Does one not guard the interests of others with even greater caution than his own? And these are the things which sadden us—members of the United States government and Armed Services who have become so willing to waste and fling about extravagantly money which the American public has worked hard to earn.

Everyone is familiar with offers to Republican Senators and their wives of as many as five trips abroad, all expenses paid, if when the Senators return they cast their influence in passing White House programs which are being met with opposition in Congress. This is not only a misuse of tax payers' money but a deliberate attempt to bribe Congressmen to vote the way the White House wants them to vote. Not only do we dislike seeing our money being spent to send Congressmen on expensive and needless trips, but we dislike even more seeing our money spent for dishonest, corrupt purposes.

At the beginning of last month came the news of two employees of the Interior Department who said that they had been given no work to do since August. Their combined salaries totaled nearly $20,000 a year. One is gratified somewhat to know that there are two members of the government who do not wish to see tax payers' money misspent, even on their own salaries, but one wonders also why they waited nearly seven months to make their state of idleness and waste known.

And then there were the radio and published news reports of how the President, in order to cut expenses, went around turning off lights in the White House. Psychologically this was a master stroke. There probably are few families in the country, the members of which have not been cautioned at one time or another by the head of the family or the breadwinner of the family "to turn off lights; save expense." Naturally

43

when these millions of families read the report of how the President of the United States himself was trying to be careful about electrical expenses, they smiled with satisfaction that he, too, was in their class and wanted to help save their money. Later reports came through, however, that just as soon as the President left some of the White House rooms in darkness, one of his staff went around quietly and turned all the lights back on again. The expense of keeping a 100-watt bulb burning for ten hours in Washington is less than 2 cents. Also tax payers read not long ago that certain government officials were being denied use of their tax financed limousines and chauffeurs. These officials are permitted to have cars, but hereafter they must drive themselves. All of this may sound impressive at first, but compared to the billions being spent, the turning off of a few electric lights, the denial to a few of limousines and chauffeurs, important as any conserving of expense may be, is not too important and cannot make much difference in the public's tax returns next year. We wonder sometimes if these announcements of petty savings are not intended only as a sop to the tax payers to try to prove to them that much is being done to save them money.

We cannot take too much stock in these intended sops, however, when we read in the March issue of one of the country's most respected magazines of the incredible waste in defense spending. Since 1954, for instance, five billion dollars was spent on weapons which were proved either impractical or unnecessary. Work done in Navy Yards has been proved by a Navy survey, the survey ordered for the purpose of trying to disprove what another accounting firm had discovered, that construction costs in Navy Yards were 15 to 31 per cent higher than construction done by private firms, repairs 10 per cent higher, modernization 8 per cent more.

We are not impressed by the President's turning off lights in the White House when we read of elaborate entertaining by the Pentagon of Congressmen who are in positions to grant favors. Elegant breakfasts, gourmet dinners, fancy cocktail parties, transportation by liveried chauffeurs in limousines. Everyone in government seems to want to cash in on the lavish spending, the posh living, the wild extravagances at the tax payers' expense. It recalls in a terrifying way another era in another country when the people were taxed beyond endurance to satisfy the extravagances and licentiousness of another government, and the cry flung to the oppressed citizens was "Let 'em eat cake!" It brings sorrow and disillusion to think that there are high officials in this government who not only will tolerate but themselves are willing to snatch all they can get to spend upon their selfish desires and wishes. The money is not theirs to spend in such fashion and was never intended to be spent in that way by anyone.

Nor are we impressed with the recent tax cut. We cannot rejoice about tax cuts of any kind until there is concrete evidence on the part of the government that expenses and big expenses at that are being cut back first. If an individual finds that his expenses exceed his income, the only sensible answer to the problem is not in increasing expenses and cutting down income but in cutting expenses and increasing income. As Eisenhower said—never in the history of the world has an individual, an institution, or a nation spent itself into prosperity.

A year or so ago we were summoned by the Department of Internal Revenue to appear at a stated time, a stated place, in regard to our income tax returns of the year before. We entered a room filled with countless desks at each of which sat a man whose job it was to interrogate persons about their taxes. There were dozens of others like us who were called up one at a time, asked to be seated, and then the questioning began. We do not know what the attitude of the other interrogators was, but the man we drew had the attitude that we were naturally dishonest of course, hoped to cheat the government, and were doing all we could to circumvent the law. He was insulting in his questions, even more insulting in the manner in which he asked them. For example, he questioned our expenditure of money for books necessary to our work. He said, "Why is it any more important for you to have these books than for the man on the street?" It so happened that we were teachers, needed books for which the school could not pay, had bought the books at our own expense in order that our classes could profit by them. We thought that at least we could deduct the cost of such books from our income tax, as indeed we could. But to be questioned in such a derisive, patronizing manner about this deduction as well as all others was insupportable. Finally we said in high resentment, "We are honest people. We have no idea of trying to cheat the government. We have made deductions which it is stated in your own form we are entitled to make. If we have made a mistake, we shall be most happy to correct it. But we object strenuously to being treated in this manner." A shabbily dressed little lady who happened to be passing our desk at this moment, overheard what we had said, stopped a moment, and said in indignation. "That's how I feel, too. I'm a hard working office clerk. I want the government to have all from me it is supposed to have. But they've treated me here like a criminal who is trying to get by with some- ·thing. I don't like it either."

45

The following year we decided to consult the government's free service in making out our tax returns. We appeared at their offices at seven-thirty or eight in the morning, and already the line of people reached far down the long corridor. There were three desks at which were seated three youthful public servants who were there to help us with our problems and questions. Standing the entire time, we waited a full two hours until our turn came. When we approached the desk, no chair was offered. We continued to stand. We asked several questions and to each were given the answer with a casual shrug, "I don't know. I'd have to look that up." Finally we became discouraged and realized that the people put there to answer our questions knew even less about them than we did. We left, having received no help whatsoever, merely a brush-off, apparently for having been a nuisance and for not having known the answers to our questions in the first place.

Again—it was the attitude more than anything else which saddened and even frightened us. Is the government of this tremendous, powerful country so eager to squeeze every penny from its people that it will permit its agents to humiliate, to frustrate, to accuse? Will it, when sincere people go for honest help so they will be certain to make no errors on their tax returns, permit them to be met with indifference, ignorance, and a patronizing attitude from those hired to help them? It made us regret we had ever sought such help.

We were very pleased, on the other hand, to read another recent article which was entitled, "Where Money from Washington Is Being Turned Down." Where, we wondered, in a country where everyone seems to be snatching the most he can get of the tax payers' money where is such money being refused. On reading further, we learned that it is in the West where people are rising against the acceptance of federal funds. For example, Westerners are voting down tax payers' money for a dam in Montana. Private funds will build a dam in Idaho; federal funds were rejected. The West is giving such strong evidence of wishing to preserve the right to develop its own natural resources that the Secretary of the Interior recently referred to "the rising tide of antifederalism" in the West. Governor Babcock of Montana refused to sanction government aid in a recently proposed dam because, as he said, it was impractical. The dam would inundate 9,000 acres now irrigated and would irrigate no new land. Other Western legislators are saying with increasing force that too many projects have been proposed by the government which are not feasible, are economically unsound. These same legislators are willing to accept federal funds for projects of proved worth, but in so doing they want to make very certain that Washington will not control Western resources.

We heard another heartening story, again from the West. A friend of ours in this Valley, who is incidentally a government official, built a fishing stream on his ranch during this past summer. According to law, he was entitled to partial payment of the stream by the government on the grounds that it was fish and wild life development. He refused to apply for this aid, however, thinking that since he and he alone would benefit by the stream, it would be less than honest to expect tax payers to help pay for something from which they could reap no possible benefit. This same family of Westerners was notified by the school which their children attend that they were entitled to a certain sum per month during the entire school year. They live in an isolation area, they were told, and had to provide transportation each day for their children to and from the school bus. But, said the family, it was their choice to live there, they could afford to transport their children to the school bus each day. Therefore, why should tax payers underwrite the expense? Why should the family be subsidized in this way by the government? Needless to say, the offer of the tax payers' money was not accepted.

We do not intend this to be an outcry against the present party in power in Washington. It might be the same story under either party. Whatever the party, our protest would be raised just as loudly and just as vehemently. Is it possible, we wonder, that men in government, Democrats or Republicans, are so eager for election or re-election, are so determined to have their party in power, are so concerned about having prestige and influence and fame that they no longer care by.what means they achieve their ends? If this is so, we need not look with terror at any power which Krushchev can wield, or at any threat of which Castro is capable, or to any thermo-nuclear weapons which man has ever invented to find what is the most dire threat to the American people and to the American way of life. The most serious threat lies in the immorality which is being permitted to grow and flourish within our very boundaries and among the very men whose sacred duty it should be to uphold the honor and the trust of their offices instead of so flagrantly abusing them.

The above article, in its entirety, was printed in the Congressional Record Appendix at the request of the Honorable Milward Simpson of Wyoming on Wednesday, April 22, 1964. (Ed.).

LAST NIGHT it snowed. Not much, but enough to dust the porches and cover the unsightly ashes which were left from the bonfire we built yesterday to burn the boxes and other trash which had been accumulating in the basement all winter. This morning the thermometer dropped, and a cold wind, now blowing over the sage flats, whips up the tarp covering the SkiDoo, ruffles the puppies' fur and makes their ears stand up. A fire is burning in the fire-place, the first morning fire we have had in days.

In spite of last night's snow and in spite of the wintry wind, there is a change in the Valley. One senses and feels it in the very atmosphere. There is softness in the air, the song of the woodpecker from the cotton-wood tree is tuned a little higher, the call of the ducks and geese over the river indicates adventure. Skiers are speaking regretfully of the imminent close of the lift. There is a swish of tires as cars run through water on almost bare roads. The snow does not crunch icily underfoot. Woolen mittens make one's hands perspire. The snow in the canyons, on the flats, and along the sides of the road glistens with the moisture which melts during the day and freezes again when the sun dips out of sight. When we shoveled the snow away from the basement door, we saw strong, green shoots of grass on the unfrozen ground. The snows may still come and the cold winds still blow, but something is about to happen, and we, caught in the suspense, watch nature around us with more alert eyes and listen with sharpened ears, fearful lest we may miss one subtle sign or one whispered note.

We have seen more and more wild life coming out from sheltered places. Moose are swimming the river and trotting into the trees on the other side. The herds of deer we see near the road look sleek and as if they had wintered well. A carefree otter sped through the willows in the sun toward the moose ponds below, and we know it will not be long before the regal ermine loses his snowy coat in Cinderella-fashion and again becomes a brown and ordinary weasel.

Great heaps of snow had collected on our roof, but the steady drip, drip, drip of winter during the middle of the day in the sun made us realize that soon it would slide, leaving the black tar paper underneath clean and bare. We put on one shutter at the window most likely to be injured if the avalanche struck, feeling then more comfortable as we knew no damage could be done. One mild sunny day we looked up and predicted that the slide would come at three that afternoon. Shortly after lunch, about two-thirty, just half an hour before our prediction, we heard first a rumble, then a roar, and finally a crash. The slide had come. We could not open the front door until we had shoveled, and when we went around to look from the outside, enormous boulders of snow were piled twelve feet high on the front porch.

Each day we see more chunks of snow broken from the banks of the river, and the springs below the cabin are running freer and broader, their waters black and cold. Before long we shall go down the bench to investigate more closely and try to find the water cress we planted there last summer. The fishing season opened a few days ago, and already we have seen floats going down the river and fishermen standing with their rods along the banks. The tackle shop is humming with activity, licenses being sold and discussions running to the most effective kind of equipment.

The chickadees, woodpeckers, and Clark's nutcrackers seem no longer famished for the suet we put out, coming only occasionally for a peck in a half-hearted, disinterested way. On March 30 we were fairly lifted from our seats in the car when a robin flew across the road as we were driving to the post office. At lunch the other day as we were looking across the island below the cabin, we saw the great blue heron perched motionless on the topmost branch of a giant pine.

For so long our eyes have been used to the white of the snow, the blue of the skies, and the black of the pine trees that we are startled and delighted by other colors in nature which are beginning to become visible. Below the cabin in the ponds there is the rosy red and yellow of the willows, the sunsets are becoming softer in color, and we noticed how orange the lichens are which are now showing against the stark, gray rocks. Two trumpeter swans, snowy against the brilliant blue sky, flew down the river the other day, and the colors in reverse came when a flash of blue against the whiteness of the snow let us know for certain that the bluebirds are back.

Our first mountain winter is nearly spent, the most glorious winter we have ever had anywhere. Never has the approach of spring brought to us such a feeling of eagerness, tip-toe anticipation. Never has its coming brought so much joy in all that we shall see and hear and do. So let the winds roar and the snows blow. This is their last long farewell for another year. The gentle touch and voice of spring can afford to be patient. Their hour is at hand.

The Valley is now waiting.

THERE IS STILL at least a foot of soft, hollow snow and we still depend upon our SkiDoo to get us to and from the car at the road. It is becoming difficult to steer the little motor toboggan around the sage bushes and keep to our old winter trails. Occasionally as we ride along, we come suddenly to the weak snow around the sage and sink in and get unexpected jerks and bumps. Yesterday after one such bump, our clean laundry which we were bringing from town jogged off the sled behind, and we nearly lost a pair of jeans in the creek. But each day there are increasing signs of spring, and our eyes and ears are alert to catch each one.

This morning the great blue heron flew straight over the tips of the trees, several pairs of mallard ducks are nesting just over the bench, and their quacking and the honking of the wild geese can be heard day and night. The pink-sided juncos are back, the white-crowned sparrows, the minute pine siskins, and they come boldly to the back porch to peck at the seeds we have scattered there for them. Juncos fly along the road, too, stopping on either side to eat the seeds which the receding snows uncovered. Often we have to stop the car for fear of hitting one as they swoop and skim in clouds, first to one side of the road, then to the other. The bluebirds are searching for nesting places under the protecting eaves, the robins are looking over the possibilities in the cottonwood trees for their spring homes, the swallows fly low and are starting nests under the roof. The other day we heard a thump against the big windows in the downstairs study, rushed out, and found a young Cooper's hawk, stunned by his blow. We picked him up gently to be certain he was all right, and he turned his head and peered at us coldly with his yellow eyes. His strong talons clung to our fingers for a minute, he stretched his wings finally, and flew off to the trees near the pond. The hooooot-hoot-hoot of the Great Northern Horned Owl breaks the silence of the nights with its low, mournful note, and the puppies, in mock terror cower and growl softly when they hear it.

Recently in the wood pile we saw a familiar flick of a tail and knew that Benjamin, our chipmunk, had returned. He and the other members of his family dash over the bare ground and old logs on the bench, tails held high, and engage in thrilling games of hide-and-seek in the wood pile. The puppies are fascinated by them and sit near or on top of the wood pile by the hour, watching and waiting for the nervous little animals to appear. This morning Benjamin decided to investigate them and tip-toed to the very end of one long piece of wood, sat down, and watched the still little bodies of Tia and Fica sitting below, their eyes fixed just as intently on him.

Our wood pile is now completely uncovered, and piles of small branches, split logs, and mammoth whole logs have appeared to assure us there is plenty of fire place fuel for the rest of the season. For a while we had wondered, but we had forgotten the good supply we had laid in which had been snow-covered for so many weeks. It is hard to realize even this early in the spring that a few brief days ago we were walking on snow four or five feet above ground level and that we had to go down several steps to reach the doors to the cabin or the logs in the wood pile.

Last week end Cookie phoned us from the tackle shop and invited us to go on an early spring float trip. We met him in mid-morning, warm clothes in hand, a lunch packed in our knapsack. After pumping the float with air, we pushed off into the black water, snow banks on either side, to spend the whole day drifting and floating down the river. We let our fingers dip into the river and found them soon growing numb from the icy waters. In places the water was so clear we could see the brown and gray and red and rosy stones at the bottom. We rounded bend after bend, saw the brilliance of the spring coloring around us, the red and yellow of the bushes, the green of the first shoots on the banks. As we stopped for lunch in the warm sun on a pebbly shore, the only sound was the tiny splash of the rising white-fish. The sandpipers walked stiffly over the rocks on their long legs, the ouzels skimmed and dipped close to the water. Hundreds of ducks and geese swam around us, some coming in to land on the surface of the river, some rising with a whir and a whistle into the air. Beautiful in flight they were, graceful and easy and completely unconcerned by the human eyes watching them below. None of us talked much, satisfied with the soft sound of the dip of the oars, the creak of the raft, the wild sound of the water fowl around us. We returned tired and sun-burned to a deep copper color, but happy and content.

May 15, 1964

WE ARE NOW in the process of moving our furniture from our Mid-West city homes to the cabin here in the mountains. One of the problems which confronted us was the moving of hundreds and hundreds of books, but Witty, who will join us permanently in June, offered to pack and mail them during her spring vacation. Bob fashioned some excellent book shelves in our downstairs study in preparation. Into the cabin on our SkiDoo we brought carton by carton as each arrived, and now most of them are arranged on the book shelves. We feel that a very precious part of our belongings is here, making the study look more "lived-in" and furnished. With our books which provide enjoyment, inspiration, information, and beauty, we know that our crowded shelves are in reality windows open to the riches of the world.

Cries of delight arose as we were unpacking, finding an old friend here, another there, and frequently reading a few pages to refresh our memories about something we had nearly forgotten.

There were the Beatrix Potter books, worn and torn, some without covers, some scribbled in with a childish scrawl. We looked over the charming illustrations for *The Tailor of Gloucester, Jeremy Fisher*, all the tales of *Benjamin Bunny, Jemima Puddleduck, The Tale of Tom Kitten*, and we read parts aloud—"One morning a little rabbit sat on a bank. He pricked his ears and listened to the trit-trot, trit-trot of a pony." Or "It is said that the effect of eating too much lettuce is 'soporific.' *I* have never felt sleepy after eating lettuces; but then *I* am not a rabbit." Or a story which used to delight our hearts as children—"Then these mice set to work to do all the mischief they could—especially Tom Thumb! He took Jane's clothes out of the chest of drawers in her bedroom, and he threw them out of the top-floor window."

There were other childhood books, many of them illustrated by N. C. Wyeth—*Treasure Island, The Black Arrow, The Story of King Arthur*. Another carton brought *The Madness of Philip*—what a quaint old-fashioned story! The first line—"His mother, being a woman of perception, realized that something was wrong," and from that point on, the book continues with Philip's escapades and "madness."

We had forgotten the beauty of *How Green Was My Valley*, the descriptions of the Welsh people, the Welsh countryside, the love of a man for his homeland, and we leafed through it and were glad to read of true love between a man and a woman.

Then there is *Cry, the Beloved Country*, and again we read a page here, a page there, marveling at the beauty of its prose, almost Biblical in its simplicity and strength.

The *Collected Poems of Walter de la Mare*—we remembered we first had been introduced to de la Mare's writing by his charming story, *Memoirs of a Midget*. We ran our eyes down the table of contents in his book of poetry, and the very titles suggested his delicacy and sensitivity in writing—"Sea-Magic," "Silver," "Miss Loo," "The Keys of Morning," "Winter Dusk," "April Moon," "English Downs," "The Cherry Tree," "A Pot of Musk." The slender volume, *A Shropshire Lad* came next, and we read over and over that favorite of A. E. Housman beginning "O loveliest of trees, The cherry now…"

The Romances of Herman Melville appeared in the next carton, and we paged through what is to us the greatest of all American novels, *Moby Dick*—beginning with the famous opening line, "Call me Ishmael" on through the pure poetry found in the chapter, "The Whiteness of the Whale," to the concluding lines, "Now small fowls flew screaming over the yet yawning gulf; a sullen white surf beat against its steep sides then all collapsed, and the great shroud of the sea rolled on as it rolled five thousand years ago." The end of the dauntless Ahab and his ship, the Pequod, the end of one of the greatest tales in all literature.

There was the limited, definitive edition of Charles Dickens. Those books we put onto the shelves quickly, not bothering to do any more than glance at two or three of the Cruikshank etchings. But the limited edition of George Eliot was a different matter, and we spent quite a time looking over *The Mill on the Floss,* the descriptions of Maggie and Philip in the Red Deeps, the flood which carried Maggie and Tom into its turbulent, icy waters. Then on to *Daniel Deronda, Middlemarch, Adam Bede,* and the tale of Eppie and her step-father, the old weaver of Raveloe, *Silas Marner.*

One of our favorites, Conrad's *Lord Jim,* came next, and we remember having suffered Jim's agonies with him, his struggles to rise above his past deeds, his last fatal mistake, his noble death. We remember how Conrad saw something great and good in Jim and always spoke of him, in spite of his mistakes and weaknesses, as one of Conrad's own great company. "He was one of us." And he *was* one of them in his sensitivity, his courage, his deep feelings about places and people, his very gentility. "He was one of us." No greater compliment could Conrad give to describe this greatest of all his characters.

Over and over we have picked up the *Pensées* of Pascal and read a bit here, a bit there, not always agreeing, but always being stirred to thought.

Two English writers whom we love came next, Mary Webb with her lovely stories, *Precious Bane, Gone to Earth, The Golden Arrow*—all of which are beautifully written, but it is to *Precious Bane* that we turn most often, the story of Prue Sarn and her "dear acquaintance," Kester. The second of these writers is Constance Holme, and as we looked through her small books, *The Lonely Plough, The Wisdom of the Simple, Trumpet in the Dust,* we remembered her characters, the Westmoreland country where many lived, and all the wonderful tales she used in weaving the two together. Our eye caught one passage from *The Lonely*

53

Plough—"We all stand alone, if it comes to that. We drive our furrow single-handed, out of the dark into the dark, though we've got to reckon with the soil that others have left, just as others must reckon with our leavings after us. But it's our job while we're on to it, all the same. It's our job, while the light lasts, to make the best of it we can. It's always one man's hand on the lonely plough."

The Forsyte Saga is given a prominent place on our book shelves, a place easy to reach as we know we shall be getting it down often to re-read. How much we enjoyed the story of this famous British family! But perhaps even more than the story itself, the gentle, almost unearthly beautiful interludes between the various books, "Indian Summer of a Forsyte" and "Awakening." We certainly must read this one again as well as its sequel, *A Modern Comedy*.

More books came tumbling out of cartons, our beloved *Walden* and next to *Walden* we put Thoreau's *Cape Cod,* an edition we love especially with its quaint sketches on the margins of a windmill, a sandy shore, a sail boat, a wild flower.

Nearly a whole carton was given to Willa Cather, *Shadows on the Rock*—we remember how good the food always sounded in this book, the hot soup, the gooseberry and plum conserves—*Death Comes to the Archbishop, O Pioneers!, A Lost Lady, My Mortal Enemy*—we sadly recalled the tragedy and sorrow of that one. And finally our favorite of all of Cather's, *My Antonia*.

All of Robert Frost's were there, some first editions, and all inscribed in his own handwriting with an unpublished poem which he had written for us when we had met him in Vermont. "When I see birches bend to left and right across the line of straighter, darker trees, I like to think some boy's been swinging them, but swinging doesn't bend them down to stay..." Or "Something there is that doesn't love a wall, that wants it down"—"Men work together, I told him from the heart, whether they work together or apart." All, all were there, many of which we found we could quote from memory, so often have we read them.

And the other great American poet, she, too, was there, every line she had ever written for publication, Edna St. Vincent Millay, that glorious singer of youth and beauty and love. "Son, said my mother when I was knee-high, you've need of clothes to cover you, and not a rag have I" and "God had called us and we came, our loved earth to ashes left. Heaven was a neighbor's house, open-flung to us, bereft." Or "All I could see from where I stood was three tall mountains and a wood. I turned and looked the other way, and saw three islands in a bay." These, too, we quoted from memory as we put them on the shelves.

And Millay's great predecessor, Emily Dickinson, was added to our collection on the shelves, her little fragments of poems, scribbled by the hundred on the backs of envelopes, on scraps of paper, none ever published during her lifetime. The concluding lines of our favorite we spoke as we put the book down, "O some scholar! O some sailor! O some wise man from the skies! Please to tell a little pilgrim where the place called morning lies."

Kristin Lavransdätter was there and Sigrid Undset's own favorite of her writings, *The Master of Hestviken,* strong stories, powerful stories, full of Scandinavian lore and legend and interesting characters. We also found James Stephen's *Crock of Gold* with its unearthly, charming, strange stories of leprechauns and queer folk, told in gaiety, wisdom, laughter, tears. There was Samuel Butler's *Way of All Flesh, Barchester Towers, The Old Wives' Tales,* all British, all substantial, all good reading, and we promised ourselves to return to these soon. Another Britisher's writings came next—*Mrs. Dalloway* and *To the Lighthouse* by Virginia Woolf, delicately written novels, sensitive, elusive.

We came to the great writers of other countries, beginning with Count Leo Tolstoi and his *Anna Karenina* and *War and Peace.* Our favorite of all novelists, Dostoevsky and his *Crime and Punishment, The Idiot, The Possessed, The Brothers Karamazov.* Moliere was there whose humor we did not appreciate at first but now place him as the greatest of all writers of comedy. Stendahl's *The Red and the Black* we found, and Barrie—Barrie who makes us want to laugh and cry at the same time as we remember his plays, *What Every Woman Knows, A Kiss for Cinderella, Quality Street,* and our favorite novel of his, *Sentinental Tommy,* which begins by telling of Tommy as a child on a dirty London stair, hungry, but having been warned by his mother never to ask the neighbors for food. He would smell something tantalizing on the stoves in adjoining flats poke his head into the room, and shout, "I don't want none of your fish," or "I ain't hungry" or "My mother says I ain't hungry."

There are the works of Albert Camus which we read so avidly, only wishing we could read them in the original French rather than in translation. *The Fall, The Stranger, The Plague,* the plays, and the one we like best of all, the three or four page "Myth of Sisyphus" in which Camus gives his definition of the "absurd" life. We read again his last ringing lines about the man who was condemned through all eternity to

55

push the rock up the hillside only to see it slip down again for him to push back, those last lines which make any hard and dreary and interminable task bearable, "One must imagine Sisyphus happy."

But we have not finished our unpacking. There are hundreds more which we shall finger and leaf through lovingly, remembering the joy we had when we first read them, anticipating the joy we shall have when we re-read them.

June 1, 1964

NO LONGER can it be said that spring is merely on the way. Spring has come and has been in the Valley for at least two weeks. The sage flats are now completely green. The first week in May our road was bulldozed open, and our SkiDoo was regretfully put into the saddle shed until next winter. Now we can drive the car straight to the cabin door which is convenient, but we know we shall miss the adventure of starting off on various errands by motor toboggan.

A pair of otters has been romping joyfully over the island near the river, and a mother marten and her young one, probably Jeremiah, have found a happy home in a large knot-hole in one of the cottonwood trees. We see them going in and out and sometimes sunning themselves at the entrance to their tree house, watching what goes on below, yawning lazily, and investigating the ground below or the branches of neighboring trees above. A robin is unconcernedly building a nest in the corner of the eaves just above our kitchen window, and the meadow larks bring music to the sage flats all day long. Early in the morning and in the evening the ponds below the cabin are filled with bird symphonies, and the notes are free and joyous and clear. We saw twenty or thirty pelicans in the sky, turning and gliding through the air, and we caught a glimpse of another ten or twelve sunning themselves on an island in the river. Coming along our little road the other day, we were fascinated to see two Wilson's snipes doing their queer, ungainly mating dance on one of the last snow drifts. Their legs moved awkwardly in a hypnotic fashion, their necks and heads were thrust forward and back as if the birds were in a trance. We saw in the distance on the flats hundreds of small birds which swooped first this way, then that, rising in the air, then dropping to the ground. We later discovered they were the Rufous-crowned sparrows returning to the Valley for the warm months.

No sooner had the snows left, than the wild flowers began to appear on the flats in a brilliant dash of color. First came the bright yellow cinquefoil, daring to send forth blossoms right next to the vanishing snows. Soon the minute salt and pepper blossoms came,

56

huddle close to the earth as if for warmth and nourishment. Then under the sage bushes appeared the white and pink spring beauties with their long red stems. The perfectly formed fritillarias were next, tiny golden things like exquisite elf tulips turned upside down. And last came the fragile shooting stars, making sections of the ground purple with their bright color, and the air around them fragrant with their faint, sweet perfume.

The flowers we planted are in full bloom, too, bright daffodils and tulips over the bench in back, sky blue squills and grape hyacinths in front of the cabin. Six or seven sturdy hollyhock plants are growing lustily.

The cottonwood buds are full to bursting, and in the sun the air is heavy with their fragrance. When one touches a sticky bud, his fingers are scented for a long time afterward with a perfume of which Dior or Corday or Chanel has never dreamed.

This week we attached the trailer to the car and went to get our burro family. Now all four, the mother, father, and the two little girls are happily settled once again on their familiar sage flats, coming often to the cabin for carrots and loving pats. Any day we expect to see big trucks coming down the road with horses' heads peering over the top slats. We shall look excitedly to find our Dividend and Royalty among the rest.

The cabin itself is a center of activity these days. Hy and his men moved in as soon as the road was open, bringing their materials and tools, and we know that the additional rooms, planned and worked over for this winter, are really under way. The cement footings have been poured, the logs are in, carefully peeled, and are now being laid. We can begin to see the new rooms taking shape and form, two more bedrooms and bath on one side, a dining room opening into a greenhouse on the other.

Yesterday Harry, Margaret, and the children, Steve, Bill, and Ann, and we packed lunches and drove to our ranch across the river for a picnic. We walked over the meadow land, green and flower-covered, through the forest of mighty pine and cottonwood trees, to a spot near the swift flowing fishing stream. We all sat on the bank for a few minutes, watched the water rushing past, looked at the trees and budding shrubs around us, up at the snowy peaks beyond, and were filled with the beauty, the peace, and the silence. We walked along the old road next to the stream and under the mammoth trees, still catching glimpses of the mighty peaks, picked up a few of the cones which squirrels had tossed from the trees, stopped to look at the little pine trees growing straight and tall by the road, at a wild rose bush, shining red in the sunlight, or at one of the first golden dandelions. Soon we wandered back, gathered rocks to place in a circle, and the children happily ran about picking up sticks for the fire. We cut and sharpened small branches on which to roast our hot dogs, got out the potato salad, relishes, and lemonade, and finally sat down to a feast, delicious in taste, and in a setting unsurpassed. It was difficult for us to realize that this land was ours, the earth on which we stepped, the trees and streams which we admired—all belonged to us. And then the words of a famous American returned to us and made us understand their truth and wisdom as we never had understood before, "Enjoy the land but own it not." And that is what we shall always do, enjoy our ranch to the full, be happy that we have made parts of it available to others who love it as we do, but never shall we permit a feeling of ownership, of proprietorship, of avaricious possession to enter our thoughts and emotions about it. We consider ourselves as caretakers of the land, privileged to hold this responsibility for a while, and that is how we shall always consider it.

CABIN ANIMALS   *June 15, 1964*

WE BELIEVE that if a person likes animals, he should have them. The fear that a puppy may chew up a favorite pair of bedroom slippers or that a kitten may scratch the furniture are preposterous reasons, it seems to us, for surrendering the pleasure which these animals can bring. We are among the fortunate ones who live in the wide open spaces of the West where the possession of animals is encouraged and even considered necessary. So—animals it is for us, and it has become only a question of how many and what kinds.

Our animal kingdom began with two fine Western horses, with strong, sturdy legs, close-coupled bodies, fine heads, pricked ears, and alert eyes. These were a necessity for carrying us over the mountain trails, through the rocky streams, and for enabling us to reach places no car could possibly carry us. Our Dividend and Royalty are fine animals. As we lead them into the corral they nuzzle us or gently push us along with their soft noses. When they are in the meadow and see us approaching, they lift their heads, prick their ears, and start toward us, trotting the last few yards of the way. They know we have a handful of oats for them and a pat on the neck. Dividend was a skittish animal when he first came to us, a little temperamental, and very head shy. With kindness and care, however, he soon calmed down, allowing one to stroke his head at any time. Royalty is a young horse and needs much sleep as all young things do. Frequently he is sound asleep on his side when we go into the corral with his bridle and he patiently lets us slip the bit into his mouth, not stirring a muscle. As we gently put the bridle over his ears, he sometimes puts his head on our knee and continues his snoring, his upper lip ruffling up slightly with each contented breath. Finally he rouses himself to the extent that he will lift his head, a gentle tug on the reins brings him to his feet, and after stretching luxuriously, arching his neck with head down, he is ready to be off.

But horses are not enough. Our second choice came when we saw in town a pair of perfectly matched little burros, harnessed to a tiny carriage, their soft eyes looking at us curiously and their long ears pointed forward. We admired them, and felt they would contribute much to a person's animal kingdom. The owner said, "If you think these are snappy, you ought to see little Pete down at the barn." We went to the barn and through the door came first a tiny black nose followed by two big black eyes, and then two enormous ears. That was little Pete and he was coming out to his mother to nurse. Phyllis, his mother, happened to be sound asleep on the ground, so up to her little Pete went, sniffed around for a minute, and then, becoming impatient, took her by one long ear and tugged with all his might. Phyllis got up and little Pete had solved his problem. We put in our order for two babies for the following summer and were assured that they would be waiting for us. Sex didn't matter, color didn't matter, just so long as the babies were in healthy condition.

The next summer the six and eight week old babies with their mothers were delivered in a battered old horse trailer. There was a little girl burro, and a little boy burro, and they had never seen each other before. The little girl immediately developed a maternal instinct toward the little boy and took him under her wing for love and protection. And so it is to this day; if one is out of sight of the other, there are loud, raucous calls, scampers, frantic searching, until they are together. The little girl we named Fidelity, short for Fidelity Fund stock; the little boy, AT&T, TNT for short. Never have stock dividends brought more joy. Each of our new pets developed into handsome animals and before the summer was over, the mothers were returned to their owner, and the babies were on their own, frisking through the sage, bucking with glee, and kicking playfully at each other.

Now, three years later, they continue to be pampered and petted, and often we see their big eyes looking at us through the windows and see them taking delicious bites of the cabin window sill when they think we are not looking. Wood is a favorite delicacy with them, and the logs on their corral are chewed on the entire inside. The window frames of the saddle shed are also nibbled, and marks of their teeth are left on some of our neighbors' cabins where these animals have gone and affectionately left an imprint. It was suggested to us that their fondness for wood might indicate a vitamin deficiency and that different salt licks would perhaps help. We tried all kinds of salt licks, white, blue, red, but still the nibbling continues, so we have come to the conclusion that wood is just a peculiar burro food. The sound of tinkling glass is wonderful to them, so we have had to screen the windows of the saddle shed as all four panes were playfully knocked out several times.

But the most wonderful thing of all about the burros happened one day when we went to the corral as usual and as we approached, saw three sets of big pointed ears instead of only two. Fidelity and TNT had had their first baby! We hadn't expected it nearly so soon, but there she stood on her wobbly legs, stiff and stilt-like. Her knees were wobbly, her coat a mass of curly down, still wet from her mother's licking. She inherited her parents' handsome appearance and was a soft gray thing with a coal black mane and a perfect cross down her shoulders and back. Her eyes have an incredibly soft, gentle expression. News of her arrival traveled fast, and soon boxes of candy for the owners arrived, dozens of congratulatory cards, corsages of carrots, little bottles of licorice candy pills labeled "Pills for Parents," poems, and a photograph of Sally, the neighboring black mule who was sending her best wishes to her long-eared relatives over the fence. Pink and blue ribbons flew gaily from the corral gate. TNT left the corral for a few minutes and galloped to tell Sally and his horse friends the details of the good news.

Little Esso, named for Standard Oil, learned to romp and play and buck and kick playfully just as her parents used to do. They all looked happy and pleased as they came up to the cabin for carrots. Fidelity took the lead, then came Esso scampering along, looking like a huge black butterfly because all we could see of her through the sage were two big ears, and then came TNT, nodding his head approvingly.

Toward dusk one day when Esso was less than a week old, we were amazed to see standing only a few feet from the cabin a gigantic, magnificent bull moose, sleek and beautiful and powerful, with a mighty spread of antlers. He looked around unconcernedly for a while and then headed for the timber above the cabin. He unwittingly approached the corral where the burros were settled for the night, stepped on a twig, and startled them. We saw eight burro legs flying in terror over the five-foot corral, and the huge animal that had startled them high-tailing it for the woods, he as alarmed as the burros by the unexpected encounter. We rushed to the corral, fearing broken legs, shattered bodies, but there was Fidelity on the outside of the corral, inches from her baby, and TNT was standing guard a few yards away, both snorting and blowing their disapproval. The moose did not appear again; we think he has gone for good, and the little burro family has once more settled into its contented and peaceful routine.

And then, the following fall, on Hallowe'en to be exact, another wonderful thing happened to us and to our burro family. On the morning of October 31 we went to the corral and there, there before our eyes was a second burro baby, another little girl, the image of Esso. We named her Lilco for Long Island Lighting stock, Loli for short, and we and her parents and little sister welcomed her into the fold. She is a gay sprite, joyous and full of mischief, loving to tease us and her family with sly little tricks and sidelong glances. And now the family is complete and happy, Fidelity and TNT always grazing and walking together, little Esso and Loli romping around them.

A lover of animals likes to cuddle and pet small creatures who respond joyfully to such affection. One likes to run his fingers through soft animal fur as he sits by the fire or to feel the comforting snuggle of a furry body next to his foot. One can't hold a horse or a burro on his lap. So, when we read in our weekly local paper, that someone had border collie puppies who needed good homes, we immediately went to look over the litter and choose the ones we would adopt.

We were taken back to the big, airy barn, and one at a time, five tiny wiggling puppies were brought out for exhibit. We decided upon two, one a cream-colored little animal with a curly tail tipped in black, four white paws, black tipped ears and muzzle, and a stylish black necklace at her throat. She can innocently blink both her eyes in a charming fashion, but she can also wink with only one. When she looks up at us and gives us this sly message with one big black eye, we are completely undone. She sleeps with both eyes very tightly shut and thus is produced a look of strange intensity on her tiny face.

The other puppy is brindled and white with four white paws, a white tipped curly tail that bends over her back like a tea-cup handle, and a perfect white hour glass around her nose and down her chin. This one gave signs of developing dramatic tendencies so we playfully called her the Great Sarah. If she injured one of her paws ever so slightly, she would wail piteously, put her head over our shoulder when we ran to pick her up and soothe her. Then she would limp pathetically over the

61

floor until something more interesting attracted her attention. The limp would then be forgotten until life became dull again, when the limp and whimpering would be resumed. When her sister chewed her ear a little too vigorously, she would raise a howl, deafening in its intensity. The next second, however, revenge would take the place of acting, and she would tear into her sister with determination and vigor. She is doing better about this, however; perhaps it has made a difference that we have found her out and have gently but decisively called her bluff.

We chose the musical and exotic names of Fica and Tia for the puppies, one for F.I.C.A. and Social Security, the other for T.I.A.A. and Teachers' Insurance Annuity Association.

Their moods are varied and unpredictable, ranging from a gay, light, feminine mood when they play happily and quietly with each other or with an old shoe, to a mood of ferocity, when they growl and roar at each other, chase each other over the floor, rugs flying in all directions. At times theirs is a mood of petulance, also quite feminine, when they have been denied something they want, or a mood of just plain puppy hunger when they cry and beg and plead for their dishes of food. The most delicious fragrance lingers about them such as only puppies have, and they make little soft puppy sounds, usually when they first wake up, little blowing sounds with their noses, which tell better than anything else that they are happy and loved.

And this is our animal kingdom, not too large and not particularly unusual. Many people have horses and burros.

Even as we sit at the typewriter, composing these last few lines about our pets, we look up and can see the members of our family. The horses are tethered at the hitch rack after a long morning ride over the mountain trails. The four burros have taken a stance, each at a different window, and are peering curiously at us. The puppies are sitting close together on their red cushions just inside the window, looking outside at the rest of the family there.

July 1, 1964

FROM EIGHT in the morning until late afternoon there was the industrious sound of pounding of logs and nails, the whine of the electric saws, the singing and gay whistling of the men at work. We had become quite accustomed to it all and were taking things in our stride when a long distance phone call announced that the carpet layers would come in two days to spend the next three laying new carpets throughout the original cabin and in the two new bedrooms and bath just being completed. We looked at each other in dismay, dreaded to break the

62

news to the men who were working so hard to finish. But tell them we did, and their only reaction was to laugh and say they would speed things up a little and clear out in time. Bless you, we thought.

And then on the rainiest, muddiest day of all, the two carpet layers arrived, unloaded their massive rolls from the truck, we scurrying just ahead of them to carry out furniture, the builders rushing to drive the last nail and move their tools, equipment, and materials to another part of the house. We swept and vacuum cleaned the shavings from the floors, and close upon our heels began the measuring and fitting of carpets, the cutting, the sewing, the laying of the pad underneath, and at last tacking the carpets in place. For three days we stepped over men at work on their hands and knees, tried to avoid bumping into sharp knives, saws, cans of glue, boxes of sharp tacks. Not the smallest of jobs was attempting to keep the dogs from under foot. How we prepared our meals we shall never know, where we slept we can't remember, but three stout sleeping bags were most convenient, and somehow, someway, we lived through it. It helped to see the clouds lift and the sun's rays begin to shine through the Valley. Everyone's spirits rose as the mud dried and the air became sparkling and clear.

The furniture van was due to arrive momentarily, and each time we drove down the road to the post office, we watched fearfully from the corners of our eyes, expecting to see the enormous truck rounding a bend, days before we were ready for it. The builders told us that each time a car drove in, creating a little dust on the road, they looked up with apprehension for fear it was the van, but luck was with us, and the carpet layers had finished, the workmen had transferred themselves to the other side of the cabin to complete work there just before the great van appeared. From that moment until nearly dark the movers unloaded things and placed them properly. All we could do was sit around the edge of the living room and direct where things should be put, the basement, the attic, the bedrooms, the living room. We knew that we ourselves had packed box after box, and we had seen the movers pack dozens of them, but we had mercifully forgotten just how many there were. Scores of them plus furniture, much of which had to be uncrated and assembled, appeared from the van. We all silently agreed that from this point on we wanted our lives cluttered with no more things. The tyranny of them, we have learned, is incredible.

We had, however, two full days over the week end to begin the unpacking and settling. Each box had been carefully labeled, and the combination and assortment of contents were amazing. There was one box marked Dog Food and Blankets, another Yarn and Iron Skillets, and a third simply but frantically Odds and Ends. We think we shall keep that one until Christmas morning. Anything it has to offer will be by then a complete surprise. We can hardly wait.

We smile wanly at each other whenever we meet in the hall or various rooms, one armed with a paint brush, another with a screw driver, the third with a hammer. We say, "Well, anyway the worst is over," or in an attempt to be cheerful, "We really are progressing." The constant questions are "Has anyone seen my red moccasin?" or "I wonder where the juice squeezer is" or "I haven't yet located the shade to my bedroom lamp." As we were preparing supper the other evening, one of us was pacing about with a dazed, vacant expression. She had in her hand an apparently delicate object which was being carried most gently. No table or chair seemed the correct place for it. Another one of us went to see what the rare and valued object was and discovered it was an egg. She quietly led the bewildered one to the refrigerator.

July 15, 1964

WE HAVE NOT permitted the building and moving and unpacking to interfere too seriously with our usual activities out of doors, and we hope we have not had our eyes fixed so steadily upon new doors and windows and walls to forget to see also the sage flats beyond the cabin. In all directions the scarlet gilia makes the land crimson, and the tall, slender flowers rise above all others. The golden glow and the butter-weed send their brilliant coloring as far as one can see. The wild buck-wheat at this early season is creamy white. The wild flax with its perfectly formed blue flower is growing in great patches on the flats. The wild geranium is still bright pink along the road, and only yesterday the wild roses burst into bloom, making the air sweet with their delicate fragrance. On the mountain trails we saw the first red Indian paint brush among the blue of the lupin. The water hemlock is full and white, growing shoulder high near the ponds and mountain streams. The tops of the cottonwood trees are fluffy white and small bunches of the snowy cotton drift through the air all day long.

One evening as we were sitting in the living room after dinner, we heard a mysterious thump just outside the window, and we and the dogs rushed to investigate. There, walking carefully over the new porch boards, was a brown bear, tiptoeing his way into the dark as soon as he had realized he had roused us. We saw him disappear over the bench below, lumbering through the underbrush, down to the ponds.

THE BUILDERS finished their work on the new additions to our cabin last week; they moved out with their tools, their heavy saws, their materials. We miss their cheerful talking and whistling, and it seems strangely quiet with no more pounding of nails and humming of saws, but at last we are settled, a condition which two months ago we thought we never would attain. We have cleaned up the yard, swept up pieces of wood and scatterings of sawdust, and daily we have had huge bonfires to burn the paper and packing boxes. The attic is in order and the basement is cleaned, and our last job was to finish the wood on the dining room cabinets and on the louvered doors of the dining room and kitchen shelves. Now, at last, all is complete. We put down on the dining room floor our Navajo rugs and moved the dishes and glassware to the dining room cabinets. We have enjoyed breakfasts at the new counter and dinners elegantly in the new dining room. All is now unpacked and the living room free from packing boxes except for one small one which holds our records, waiting for the arrival of our new stereo. We have even had time to pick wild flowers to fill vases around the house, and at this moment some of our own purple pansies and gay orange nasturtiums are in a little vase on the coffee table. Our favorite pictures have been hung. We have brought in good rich earth for the greenhouse benches and already straight little tomato plants are standing there. Some seeds we ordered have arrived, and soon we shall plant sweet peas, nasturtiums, stock, and carnations. We have had time, too, to give more thought to cooking, and this afternoon the cabin is filled with the fragrance of a wild blueberry coffee cake. So—finally things are where they belong, we have the leisure to sit down and enjoy and admire it all. Miraculously all the confusion and turmoil of the past weeks have quickly faded away, soon will be forgotten, and if, in frantic moments, we ever wondered if it all would be worth it, we know now as a certainty that it is.

We now have time to ride and can take entire mornings to go over the mountain trails, through the forests on the bench above the cabin. We ride quietly, slowly, stopping by a mountain stream occasionally or on the sunny bench where we can look over the entire Valley below. Occasionally we leave the trails briefly to search for huckleberries or to examine more closely the tiny pink wintergreen or Pirola blossoms which are growing in profusion close to the ground in the forests. The other day we concentrated on the tracks which we could find in the soft dust on the trails and found fresh coyote tracks, moose, deer, and elk. We sense these animals near and can feel their sharp, wary eyes upon us from the safe cover of the trees.

We have been frightened lately by loud, raucous, human-like cries from the island below the cabin and more than once have rushed to the windows to see what could be making these strange, fearful sounds. We feared that some child was lost or had strayed too close to the rushing river and was in danger. At last we discovered that the cries came from a family of baby ravens who were being taught by their parents to leave their home and venture out alone. Each day during the lessons the cries rose in terrifying shrieks, but after a few days they grew less and less alarming. Now they have disappeared completely, and we know that the young birds are finally grown and independent.

As soon as it becomes dark in the evenings, we hear from the sage flats nearby, from the bench above, or from the island below the long, loud howls of the coyotes and the softer yap-yap-yapping of the puppies in the pack. First one coyote will begin, and then he will be answered by another until their calls rise in unison from many directions. Bitters, our city-bred dog who is fast becoming accustomed to the ways of Western living, raises his head, cocks his ears, but makes no attempt to join in the wild howling. Tia, however, is alert at once and puts back her head and gives a very acceptable imitation of her wilder brothers out of doors. We hear long, mournful howls coming from the bedroom, the dining room, or anywhere where Tia happens to be. Her sister, Fica, too, joins in the wild calling and does her best to make her little dog howl resemble that of the coyotes. Tia succeeds very well, Fica thinks she does, and we shall never tell her that her sounds resemble those of a barnyard Chanticleer at break of day.

Occasionally the evenings are mild and warm, and those are the times when the big windows are covered with myriads of tiny bugs and moths. This summer we have noticed an especially beautiful white moth, small, with delicately formed wings and body, and suggestions of fragile etchings on the wings. When quiet, this little moth resembles a minute Japanese fan, perfectly and exquisitely formed.

The Valley is humming with activity these days. Riders are planning trips to Surprise and Amphitheater Lakes or to the flower meadows beyond the canyons. Fishermen are bringing in fine catches and spending day after day on the river, the lakes, or mountain streams. Climbers are scaling the peaks, hikers are finding new trails, campers are enjoying the thrill of out-of-door living. Wild flower lovers and bird watchers are finding dreams come true. We are reminded of the opening lines of Edna Ferber's fine new book, *A Kind of Magic,* in which she says, "To be alive is a fine thing. It is the finest thing in the world, though hazardous. It is a unique thing. It happens only once in a lifetime. To be alive, to know consciously that you are alive, and to relish that knowledge—this is a kind of magic. Or it may be a kind of madness, exhilarating but harmless." We at the cabin, too, are feeling this same exhilaration, this same madness, complete peace and happiness. We, too, have been brushed by this "kind of magic" and can only feel gratitude that, looking back, we know at last that all paths for all our lives have been, without our conscious knowledge, leading us here.

September 1, 1964

EVER SINCE the burros were babies, they have wanted very much to come into the house with us and have stood at the edge of the porch, asking with their big eyes to be permitted to follow us up the steps and into the rooms beyond. Now we *do* have burros indoors. They behave wondrously well, are completely mannerly and polite and never dream of taking advantage of their position to do anything but with the greatest decorum. We can see their long fuzzy ears, almost hear the swish of their short tails, and can easily imagine the devilment they are planning as they put their heads together.

About a month ago a famous portrait painter of animals, Emilie Touraine, came into the Valley, and we were privileged to see some of her fine work. We sat before it, amazed and incredulous that anyone had been able to capture not only the image of animals but, more important, their souls and temperaments. A glorious palamino horse came to life before our eyes, a handsome apaloosa turned and looked at us. A miniature French poodle looked down at us with a pert, saucy glance from under his white curly forehead, his eyes sparkling with intelligence. Then came her portraits of classic horses, powerful, beautiful animals of true royalty. There was Bucephalus, Pegasus, the steeds of Paris. We gasped in admiration as we saw these mighty animals portrayed with sensitivity, strength, imagination.

67

After we had spent some time talking with her and seeing her work, we noticed a twinkle in her eye and she laughingly said, "Now there is something else to show you." This was the final surprise of the evening. Her manager Jack, brought out several large paintings which were portraits of the dearest, furriest little burros that anyone could imagine. Some of the paintings were of only one burro, some of two or three, and one of four. They were slightly caricatured, but not so much so that they looked grotesque, rather just like real burros with their happy, funny traits slightly exaggerated. Their long ears were pricked at something they saw in the distance, their little bodies were alert, their tails almost twitching with excitement and interest, and each little animal had his own distinct personality. Each painting had a clever name, High Society, Up to Something, Mischief-Makers. We exclaimed with delight as we saw them, and when the painting of the four burros appeared before our eyes, we said with one voice, "That one we must have." How we admire them! How we love them! We found the ideal spot in the living room and before we knew it, our little burro family, all four of them, was looking down upon us with all the mischief and gaiety which we see in the corral and on the sage flats and at our windows. We spent the rest of the evening before the fire, our eyes wandering frequently to our wonderful new painting, all of us getting up now and then to view it from different angles.

Emilie had heard about our Cabin Comments and asked in the course of the evening if we had any stencils which we used for mimeographing. We gave her several, and as she talked, she took the stylus and sketched other burros for us, a replica of the large painting we had bought, a Christmas burro, and many others which we will use for a long time to come so that our readers may share with us Emilie's great gift for capturing on paper with a few strokes of a pencil their spirit and character. The sketch on this issue is of the burros looking into our window, probably admiring our painting and recognizing in it surely their own little forms and faces. Such generosity, we thought, as she left, and such kindness!

A few days later, Emilie saw our live burro family, and, dropping what she was sketching at the moment, she took her canvas, brush, and oils in hand, and quickly, deftly, surely, sketched each one of our real burros. There was Fidelity, stately and dignified, AT&T looking out at the others with a benign, fatherly expression, Esso craning her neck curiously to see something just ahead of her, and the baby Loli, looking out at the world with gentle, inquisitive eyes, ready, however, to scamper off at any moment and get into mischief. These sketches, of course, we

68

decided we must have, too, and now they are each carefully mounted and adorn the most important wall of our dining room.

Last night when we took our dog family for its last walk before bed, the air was so clear that our voices echoed back to us. We shouted in turn just one word, and it came back to us from the river, from the flats, from the cold, clear distance. "Happy!" "Happy!" "Happy!" loud and strong at first, then diminishing into the distance and perhaps bounding at last along mountain streams and trails in soft continuance "Happy!" "Happy!" "Happy!"

September 15, 1964

WITTY, WHO NEVER in her life has ridden horseback, decided the other morning to borrow a horse from the Circle H corral and accompany us on a ride to the trails above. She enjoyed this first experience so much that when Rosemary offered to sell her Bent Arrow, a fine eight-year-old, Witty promptly accepted, and now she, too, has her own horse, and many have been the rides we all have taken over the trails along the bench and through the forests. The trails are nearly deserted now, we can ride all morning without meeting other riders, and the silence is deep and unbroken. The underbrush is turning color, most of it a rosy red with splashes of yellow. Yesterday on the trail we saw two doe who turned and watched us pass; and a little farther we came upon another doe and her fawn who looked at us quietly with no alarm. Occasionally as we ride, we break out of the woods into the open from where we can see the entire Valley, the highway nearly deserted of cars now, the autumn haze softening the buttes and river bottoms, and we noticed on the nearest butte the first suggestion of the brilliant gold of the aspen.

There has been only one thing we have missed greatly at the cabin, and that has been music. A telephone call one afternoon last week announced the arrival of the stereo, and we were transported with happiness and anticipation. We could not wait the day or two for the truck to deliver it, so we ourselves went into town in our Jeep Wagoneer to pick it up. The box which contained it was so large that it protruded far beyond the back door of the Jeep, but that daunted us not at all, and down the road and through the sage we bumped along with it. Our nervous and eager fingers tore off quickly the crate and heavy packing box, and then inch by inch we carried the enormous instrument into the place reserved for it in the living room. We read the book of instructions carefully, did precisely as we were told, but when we put the first record on, nothing happened—no sound came forth, and we stood in despair before the machine. We called Harry at the Circle H who has had long practice with his own fine stereo, and almost before we had left the phone, one of the guests at the ranch appeared to help us. Bill knows a tremendous amount about such instruments, and after working with ours for a while, calling for a screw driver here, a hand mirror there, he put on a record and the room was filled with mighty music. We were deeply grateful, and from that moment on, we have been playing almost constantly our old favorites and our new discoveries. Last night we felt in the mood for stirring marches, the morning before we heard Dohnányi's delicate Variations on a Nursery Song. When Margaret and Harry came to hear our new instrument, we felt in the mood for Sibelius and concluded the evening with the glory of Beethoven's Ninth. The next night we all were stirred by Verdi's great Requiem Mass. This morning we heard Milstein's recording of the Bruch Concerto for Violin. So it goes. Old friends in music, new friends, too, and now we agree that everything is perfection. Out of doors the stir of the wind in the trees, the rush of the river, the call of birds, the cry of coyotes, the bugling of elk. Indoors the sound of music. And always above it all, augmenting every human delight, enhancing the mightiest to the most infinitesimal in nature, lending enchantment and magic, power and might, the peaks rise snow-capped, strong, silent.

October 1, 1964

OUR OWN ANIMALS are in the highest of spirits on these clear, cold autumn mornings and evenings. On the trails the horses are alert with pricked ears and watchful eyes, eager to see everything in the Valley before they are taken to their winter pastures two hundred miles east. They step lively, occasionally think they see ferocious beasts behind each

70

shrub, like to break into a trot, and raise their heads high in the wind to let their manes feel the cool air and be tossed about. The burros graze quietly, and then suddenly for no apparent reason race through the sage, all four running at top speed as if pursued by some unknown danger. Since feed on the sage flats and meadows is becoming sparse now, we put out hay for them not only in the evenings when they go into their corral, but also in the mornings when they are led out. This, we find, sends them off happy and well fed for their day of wandering. We have noticed that they will eat their morning hay just outside the saddle shed for a few minutes, and then something seems to startle them and off they go, heels kicking, backs humped in bucking. We have wondered what scared them away from their morning meal, but today we discovered their cause for alarm. AT&T, the only male in the group, frequently is nudged away from the hay by his more greedy wife and daughters and is forced to the edge. But he is a wise one and has his own tricks. As the others were feeding, we discovered, he quickly gives a start, tosses his head, brays the word of danger, and his more timid and extremely gullible women folk raise their heads, accept his word of warning, and prance off to avoid whatever he says is threatening. AT&T follows them at a more deliberate pace, and when Fidelity, Esso, and Loli are sufficiently far away and nibbling the grasses, he returns alone to the hay and feasts to his burro heart's content.

Green and golden days. Blue and golden days. Splashes of red and rose and orange. In this entire Valley there is no direction one's eyes may wander that does not hold color and light and glory. We have taken several drives to places where the color has been exceptionally vivid, drives down the canyon, over the Pass, toward the other Pass on the far side of the Valley, and up the narrow, stony road to see the glow of the golden aspen against the red cliffs. There were low places where the willows grow, now a russet yellow in the sun. There were high places where the mountain ash, sumac, and maple shone scarlet and orange and where clusters of their berries gleamed like jewels in the sun. The dark green of the pines lent an artist's background to the brilliance of the other trees, and with each bend in the road, we gasped anew at the splendor which was incredible in its various shadings and startling colors. In this Valley, we all agreed, nature is lavish, holds nothing back, and paints with bold strokes. Here there are whole mountain sides of flaming foliage, great blond fields of wheat and oats and wild grasses stretching into the distance and out of sight. There are great stands of golden trees; one can drive through whole forests of aspen, the atmosphere yellow with their reflection and glow, the ground a massive

71

carpet of golden leaves which have drifted down. There is nothing brown or drab about autumn here. The Valley, having given abundantly all summer in more delicate colors of mauves, pinks, blues, yellows, now in one gloriously abandoned climax, gives a last burst of riotous color before the silent white snows come to cover all.

November 1, 1964

IT IS NOT OFTEN that one is awakened at four o'clock in the morning by flashing headlights of a car outside his window. It is not often that one slips into a robe to go to the door and finds a delighted man outside who, upon entering, grins happily and says, "It's a girl!" But such happened to us early one morning recently. It was Harry on his way home from the hospital in town where he had taken Margaret a little earlier. He came to tell us óf the arrival of Kathryn Sue. We had a joyful celebration on that morning of October 18th, saw the early light appear in the sky, saw the first rays of the sun glow upon the peaks as we talked about the new baby. A few days later we saw her, sweet, alert, and perfect in all ways. She strongly resembles her mother, but in an expression or two we saw also a likeness to her five-year-old sister Ann. As we held her and looked down into her small face, we thought of the many days ahead when she would bring fun and joy to all of us and of what a privilege it is to live so near a tiny baby and be able to watch her growth and development.

THANKSGIVING, 1964   ## November 15, 1964

One cannot pause for long. The domed sky above, the fragrant earth
    below
Hold promises too sweet and beauty ever-changing. But for one fleeting
    moment
To look and think and thankfully remember. To lift one's eyes, to
    stretch one's arms
Briefly in spirit with senses quick and sharp to encompass with
    adoration,
Final and immutable,
All the great, life-giving earth.
To feel all, to permit not one leaf or petal or shining star
To pass unnoticed. To recall in happy gratitude,
In peace and beauty and cleanness and joy.
To think midst snows
Of the first flowers pushing through cold, moist earth,

Their fragile beauty—pink and white and yellow.
The miracle of tender green upon the trees, golden in the rising sun.
The strong feel of damp earth, new forming, sticky buds,
Filling the air with assurances of even more abundant life to come.
The rushing creeks and streams, freed
At last from the grip of ice and snow,
Foaming and roaring in white waters over red-brown pebbles,
As if to compensate for time spent in imprisonment.
The meadows—a-flame with multi-colored blossoms.
The paths and trails winding higher and higher toward the peaks,
Promising excitement, expectations as they lift, lift upward.
Dust, gray and soft as goose feathers, beneath the horses' hooves.
The sun more hot, the skies more blue and cloudless.
And then the gentle rains and gleaming, glistening leaves,
The sage odors, shrubs and grasses fresh-washed and clean.
The young creatures of stream and field and wood, playing, pausing to
    look
Upon new life with soft and questioning eyes—eager, strong, vigorous.
The days bursting with such richness
That ear cannot listen to all, nor eye perceive.
One's senses growing giddy in attempts to grasp it in entirety.
Grasses then slowly fading, leaves beginning
To rustle and whisper in soothing murmurs, drifting to earth.
Hesitantly changing from summer greens
To crimsons, tawny yellows, golden russets.
A blue haze on the sky-line and over the peaks.
Air frosty, clear, and cold.
The moon and stars shining with a sharper silvery light.
The rains more cold, the winds more keen.
The tang of wood smoke in the air.
Graying skies and massing clouds, thick and black.
The quiet arrival of the snows, transforming each twig and branch
To elf and goblin shapes.
And traced upon the snow's soft surfaces
The delicate etching of tiny bird and mice feet.
A hush, a silence falls upon the earth,
All growing things sleep still and deep beneath the snows.
And for a moment one takes pause
To think, to feel, and gratefully to remember.

73

1965

IF AN OLD YEAR'S closing and a new year's beginning are any indications of the nature of days to come, all of us are prepared for jolly, exciting, and fun-filled months ahead. Our excitement and adventures began on Thanksgiving morning when we awoke to a mountain blizzard with snow piling to incredible heights in minutes. We looked out the window and saw our red Jeep Wagoneer standing there, completely covered with snow, our SkiDoo under its tarp cover equally obliterated, snow piled high on the porches, and great sweeps of snow blowing over the sage flats. We knew we should have to work fast in order to get the Jeep to the Circle H parking lot by the main gate, so after breakfast one of us drove the SkiDoo through the swirling snow to the road and back, making two firm tracks; the other two dug the Jeep out and followed in the tracks, already filling and becoming indistinct in the snow and winds. We were successful. The Jeep was parked at the road where it will be until May. By then it was nearly noon, and we were soon due at Fran and JB's home for Thanksgiving dinner. Watching the blizzard become worse, we decided not to press our luck too far, so we phoned to say regretfully that we feared we could not make it. We hated to miss the fun and delicious turkey, but our decision to remain at home proved wise when later we heard that Eileen, another dinner guest, had been marooned there and could not get home for two days. Shortly after we had phoned, the electric power went off, and we busied ourselves in piling up more logs for the fire and in getting out the clever contraption Bob and Rosemary had given us for cooking over the fire in the fireplace. We found candles in case the power did not come on until after dark and filled the hibachi in the greenhouse with charcoal to keep the temperature there as high as possible. And then we waited. The power came on briefly in the early afternoon, long enough for us to wash the lunch dishes, but then the lights flickered once or twice and went out again. We cooked a dinner of hamburgers on our fireplace grill, warmed

74

coffee on the hot coals, and managed beautifully. After dinner the lights came on again, but again flickered once or twice and went out. We were just ready to go to bed several hours later, when the lights came on and this time remained steady, so we knew the trouble had been located and remedied.

We had had an adventure-filled day. From reports of neighbors and friends, the same had been true with them. We heard of several families who had resorted to wood stoves for the preparation of their Thanksgiving dinner. One family prepared the turkey, planning to take it to relatives twenty miles away who had prepared the rest of the meal. This family was left with turkey only for dinner, the other with potatoes, relishes, vegetables and pumpin pie only. One friend of ours was caught for a forced overnight stay with relatives and, being a diabetic without her insulin, caused considerable concern. Her hostess saddled her horse in the raging blizzard and rode to the main highway where she hailed the snow plows which turned in, plowed out the road, and made the insulin available.

From Thanksgiving on, with a few gloriously sunny, blue-skied days in between, there have been snows in the Valley, quiet, steady snows, filling up the SkiDoo tracks, filling up the puppies' pen, filling the five-foot corral up to and finally above the top log. We have found our way out almost daily, loving the rides in the SkiDoo to the car, finding our little road more beautiful than ever with trees and bushes along the way heavy with a soft white covering. We staggered from the SkiDoo to the parked car, sometimes stepping off the hard-packed trail purposely to see how far we would sink in and not being surprised to find ourselves thigh or waist deep. We have loved walking out on snowshoes or skis, breaking a trail in the soft, pure snow, leaving behind us a beautiful, symmetrical design. The dogs have loved it, too, rolling happily in the snow, swimming through it, leaping over drifts. We have enjoyed our trips to the post office, returning with tote bags bursting with packages and Christmas mail. We have loved our trips into town, seeing the gay Christmas decorations, visiting with friends, buying Christmas gifts and finding such shopping a pleasure with no rush, no crowds, and no frantic clerks. We cut our tree from the woods at the Circle H this year as our ranch across the river was snowed in, and we decorated it as usual with brilliantly colored birds, most of which we had to put on the higher branches as one of our puppies found them on the lower ones and could not resist slyly pulling them off. She thought they were lovely playthings, put there solely for her joy and amusement.

As we were stepping from the SkiDoo to the car one day, someone shouted, "Moose on the road!" so we climbed quickly into the car and waited for her to pass. The cars were parked close together without more than two or three feet between each, and to our surprise and momentary horror, the big cow moose stopped a minute right in front of the Jeep and then turned in, passing between our car and Harry's, so close she brushed the side of the cars as she passed. Another morning when we awoke, we saw just outside our bedroom windows, almost to their bellies in the deep snow, an enormous cow moose, followed by her yearling calf. We remained silent and motionless, and not once were they aware of the fascinated eyes watching their every step. They made a deep track through the snow along the fence and finally stepped easily over the top strand of wire, the only one visible, and made their way across the flats to the willows beyond.

Finally the snows stopped, the faithful drivers of the snow plows had the roads entirely cleared, and again we were invited to Fran and JB's for our long anticipated turkey dinner. We were met at the door by faces with long, pained expressions. "We have a sad tale to tell," they moaned as we came in and were taking off our fur boots and heavy parkas. "A sad tale?" we queried. "But maybe," we added, "it has a happy ending." "Well, the ending is yet to come," they said. "You are the victims. There is no turkey!" They had gone to the freezer that morning to take out the half turkey to be defrosted, and although they took everything out several times to make sure, they had had to come to the dreadful conclusion that the bird had flown. We were aghast at first, then realizing the humor of the situation, all of us burst into hilarious shrieks. No one knew where it was, how it had disappeared, or whose table it might be gracing at that very moment. We were served delicious chicken instead.

And finally the mystery of the Thanksgiving turkey has been solved. Cookie, seeing the object carefully wrapped in foil in Fran's freezer, thought it was one of his prize fish, took it out, and presented it grandly and magnificently to his friends, Jim and Ginny. They were surprised the "fish" had been transformed into a fowl when they opened the package, but thought Cookie had had Thanksgiving dinner with friends who had presented him with the uneaten half turkey when he departed. They thawed it out, ate it, and thus the mystery is concluded.

Some friends had dinner with us one evening and spoke enthusiastically of a recent trip they had taken to Scandinavia. We have always wanted to see the fjords of Norway, the clean, magnificent cities of Sweden and Denmark, the rich farmlands there, and have hoped some day to visit and luxuriously buy some of the handsome silver work at Georg Jensen's. Another friend is going to Japan soon, and that is another land we have always wanted to see. A friend writes from New York of the many Broadway plays, the opera, the concerts. We saw pictures of the impressive Los Angeles Pavilion and thought it would be interesting to fly there and hear a concert or two. Momentarily perhaps we plan a trip to one of these distant places and think of all we shall see and do, but our enthusiasm is short-lived. All we have to do is look up to the snow-covered peaks, take a walk over the white, unbroken snow on our snowshoes, or sit before the fire listening to music at its grandest, visit with dear friends who share our enthusiasm, to relinquish gladly our plans for a trip out of the Valley. "Sometime," we say. "Sometime we shall do this, but not yet. Not yet can we bear to leave any part of this Valley. All things in good time, but for the present this is what we want and what makes us content." And, although no one of us says so, we each secretly know it will be thus for a long, long time to come.

January 15, 1965

IF WE REMEMBER correctly, we said in our January 1st issue that after one storm followed by another since Thanksgiving, the snows finally had stopped. We were mistaken. New Year's Day was bright and sunny and cold, but the clouds gathered the very next day, and with only an occasional bright day thereafter, the snows have continued and only now do the skies look completely clear and cloudless. Talk of the heavy snows has dominated all conversations, and even old-timers in the Valley find it difficult to remember a winter when the snows fell so steadily and became so deep this early in the season.

We have loved it. We have welcomed the excitement of each new storm, watching delightedly the wind blowing over the sage flats, carrying the snow before it and piling it in unbelievably high drifts around the saddle shed and neighboring buildings. We snowshoed to the saddle shed the other day, and although there was an area immediately around it which the wind had swept entirely clear, a few feet from the door the snow lay six feet deep. The corral has completely disappeared except for the two high posts on which the gate is hung. Little white mushrooms indicate the tops of the steel posts on the wire fence, and on the roof snow reached a depth of seven feet or more. When we rode the SkiDoo to the parking lot, we found our Jeep like a tremendous white marshmallow, doors, windows, front, and rear completely indistinguishable. But the snow was soft, and the car assumed its normal appearance after a short period of brushing and shoveling. The cabin seems much lower than before and apparently has nestled comfortably into the deep snows for the winter. Long icicles hang from the roof and now are glistening brilliantly like jeweled pendants in the sun.

The mountains appeared rarely in the last few days, but when the sun managed to emerge briefly, they rose out of the mists in an awesome, almost eerie fashion, and we could see, before the next cloud enveloped them, that the peaks were entirely snow covered with no rocks visible at all.

We have spent much of our time lately by the windows, watching the snow fall and accumulate. Sometimes the soft flakes were almost the size of silver dollars, sometimes they were fine and felt sharp against our faces when we ventured out. And venture out we did—many times. There was the woodpile to locate in the snow and to dig out before we could bring in plenty of logs. There was the kindling pile to clear, too, and small boards and tree branches, completely dry under the heavy snows, to carry in and put into our huge copper kettle on the hearth. We set a ladder against the roof and climbed up, standing waist deep in snow as we shoveled the top white layer of fluff to the ground. We kept the doorways clear, but aside from that, there was no shoveling at all, and we were free to snowshoe over the great white expanse or simply sit by the window and look out. No appointments which had to be kept, no necessity to do anything but enjoy all the wonders out of doors.

Our binoculars were in constant use. Seven moose we spotted one morning on our ranch across the river, and we heard that there were many more, so many that our friends who live near had to walk out of doors with considerable caution for fear of bumping into one of these unpredictably tempered animals. One day, perched on the very top of an enormous pine tree on the island below, we saw a massive bald-headed eagle who stayed there quietly for us to have a long look at him. Then with no warning he swooped down on his mighty wings and easily and silently flew to his nest in another large tree on the other side of the river. We have kept our bird-feeder cleared of snow and have refilled it often with fresh suet and seeds. The chickadees come by the dozen as do the woodpeckers, and occasionally a magpie will fly in for a meal. Their sweet songs are heard all day long in the big cottonwoods in back of the cabin.

Today we can truly say, however, that the snows have ceased. We felt it toward sunset last night when we saw the western sky aglow with crimson banners and clouds. The sky looked like a vast mirror for an enormous, raging fire below—streamers of flame reached higher and higher. The highest mountain on the other side of the Valley stood out in the dusk with an unearthly glow. "Red at night, sailors' delight," we chanted.

This morning the peaks rise stately and sharp against a blue, blue sky. Their summits are pure and shining in the sun, the trees at the base powdered heavily with snow. In the clear, still air one sees occasionally a great puff of white sifting from their branches to the ground. The river flows slowly, glistening deep blue in the sun, and the air itself is filled with myriads of brilliant sparkles. Never was snow so clean and pure, never was air so frosty and clear. The shadows are black now, but this late afternoon they will turn a cold blue. The sun is pouring in the windows, and we have let the fire in the fireplace die and have turned down the electric heat. The strong rays are hot upon one's shoulders, and when we stoop to stroke the puppies lying in the sun, their fur is soft and warm. We know that by dinner time we shall feel the air becoming colder. We know that we shall build up the fire and turn up the heat and that sweaters will feel comfortable as we sit and knit. The moon tonight will light our way when we take our evening walk. The peaks will rise clear and white. The stars will be out and will shine cold and distant above us. When we turn our snowshoes toward the cabin door, we shall see through the great windows the glowing fire within and perhaps as we come closer hear the strains of Eine Kleine Nachtmusik from the stereo.

We realize that here in our Valley our lives will always be close to the weather, that the weather becomes an integral part of all existence. We know that whatever comes in the way of rain or clouds or sun there is nothing we can do to change it, and change it we never would desire. A mountain snow storm is as welcome to us as the warmth of the sun or blue, cloudless skies. One feels close to the heart of things here, and wild creatures and winds and storms and sun and stars become the warp and woof of one's being. Strength and power and peace and security lie in such an elemental existence. One soon learns to distinguish the real

79

from the unreal, the true from the superficial, the significant from the trivial, and, perhaps most important of all, what beauty and majesty really mean and the tremendous power which they wield in the life and heart of man.

February 1, 1965

A FEW DAYS AGO the atmosphere in the upper Valley was soft and white; it was difficult to distinguish trees and buildings only a few yards distant. There was a magic and unearthly feeling, and suddenly it occurred to us that we were, for the moment, living on a cloud. If people in lower parts of the Valley had happened to glance in our direction, they would have seen only a mist, and we were having the unique experience of living right in the center of it. None of us had ever had the experience of living on a cloud before—city fog, city smog, city smoke, perhaps, which on occasion may give the illusion of a cloud—but this was different. The air was clean and fresh with no city fumes and odors permeating it. This was a real cloud, and we seemed to walk lightly, speak in muffled voices, and at times be lifted right off the snowy ground to float through it. When the cloud lifted the next day and the warm rays of the sun took its place, every twig and branch had long, two-inch frost feathers brilliant in the clear air. In the rays of the sun the air gleamed with millions of diamonds floating through it. We put on our snowshoes to walk across the snow to a grove of aspen a half mile away to examine the frost feathers more closely and found they were long and white, delicate on the branches, and would silently shake to the ground at the slightest touch. That evening the sky was pink and mauve with a streak here and there of pale green, and when the cold moon appeared, it illuminated the world around us with a splintering, bright light which made the sweeping lights from the airport across the river look dim and faint.

On one of the clearest, brightest days we left early in the morning, excited, eager, expectant, for our first skiing lesson of the season. It was

80

Witty's very first lesson, and while Bill was giving her the first instructions, we practiced and tried to limber our muscles and become accustomed to our new skis. When Witty's lesson was concluded, Bill directed the two of us to get on the chair lift and meet him at the first station. We were thrilled as we stood in line for our tickets, stepped into position for the chair, saw it approaching over our shoulders, and felt it bump gently against our knees as we sat down. The first slight sway up and back as we began the ascent of the hill brought back all of the fun and joy of last year, we grinned at each other, looked over our shoulders at Bill who was following in the next chair, and sat back to enjoy the ride. The massive pine trees which we passed were heavy with snow, and occasionally under them we saw ski tracks headed toward the slope. Before we knew it, we saw the familiar sign "Tips Up" and knew we were approaching the station. We leaned forward slightly, let our skis skim over the surface of the platform, gave the chair a quick push, skied off, being careful to duck as our empty chairs passed over our heads. Bill soon joined us, gave us a few review instructions, and off we skimmed, over the incline through the short stretch of woods, out onto the open slope. We stopped again for more instructions, practiced slide-slipping for a few minutes, and down we started, turning, gliding, once in a while falling, but we made the bottom easily, and loved the feeling of the wonder of skiing, thinking happily of all the many weeks ahead of us filled with fun and excitement on the hill. We have gone to the slopes several times since our lesson, practicing, making mistakes, doing turns over again, and Witty far below us on the bunny hill has been doing valiantly, learning to feel at ease on skis, knowing as she looked up at us on the slope that it would not be long before she would join us and then truly know the joy of skiing.

Yesterday we put on our heavy Air Force pants and jackets, our hoods faced with wolverine fur which cannot frost, pulled on our insulated Korean boots and warm mittens, flew over the snow on the SkiDoo to the Jeep at the gate, and drove to the elk refuge to ride the enormous feeding sleighs. We were welcomed by Ken on the vast load of hay piled high on the sled, and the signal was given to Jim in the tractor to start. We rode slowly and ponderously over the deep snows, headed directly for the elk herd which numbers about 2700 head. The other herds we could see black in the distance against the snow. The estimate is 8,000 head in all. We saw, only a few feet from us, mighty bull elk with wide spreads of massive antlers, young bulls with antlers still small in comparison, gentle-eyed cows, and furry, large-eyed calves. All watched the movements of the sleigh carefully, knowing it was bringing fresh food to

81

them. As we drove on, the elk would run a few yards to get out of the way, then stop and look back curiously watching Ken who was tossing hay to them, and finally and speedily close in on our track to eat the fresh hay. We drove around and around in and out among the animals, amazed at their beauty, their sleek bodies, their noble heads, their grace in every movement. The elk in turn watched us, chewing contentedly on their hay, stretching their necks to peer at us as we moved in and out among them. Some would be especially daring and rise to their feet from a reclining position only as the tractor lumbered near them. Others would run off and view the sleigh from a safer distance, showing only their cream-colored rumps and stubby tails as they turned to flee. Around and around we went until the last bale of hay had been tossed off. We wondered which of the herd had been in the forests above the cabin this summer, which of the bulls we had heard bugling on frosty October nights.

We think that actually and figuratively we are living on a cloud. When to the joys of a mountain winter are added the joy of greenhouse flowers, music, books, fine friends, and the pleasure of outdoor sports at their best, we realize how lucky we are to have been able to settle on our particular cloud. This noon when we turned on the radio to get the mid-day news, we were greeted by the last snaches of an old song of which we have not thought in years and which seemed to express our mood exactly. We hummed it gaily as we prepared lunch—

> Zippety-doo-da
> Zippety-ay
> Wonderful feeling,
> Wonderful day!

March 1, 1965

ORDINARILY we have two steps down from the porch to the ground. Now we have cut into the snow eight steps going up from the porch. When we look from our windows, we see the SkiDoo perched high on its ramp, five feet or more above our heads. We catch glimpses of the puppies' legs only as they trot by the top of the windows and down to the door. As we come to the front porch, we hold onto a corner of the roof to steady ourselves for the snowy steps. Each time we go to the Jeep, we unknowingly walk right over it, buried deep beneath the snow. When we go to the wood pile for kindling or logs, we dig down into a subterranean cavern and all that can be seen from the house windows are sticks being tossed to the top of the snow, the digger herself completely hidden in the cave.

Not long ago we took our metal saucers to the saddle shed and to our neighbors' cabin just beyond, climbed to the roof of each building, got our saucers fixed comfortably to sit on, and skimmed down the roof to the continuous drifts beneath, sliding far out on the snow beyond, a-whooping and a-hollering as we whizzed down. The roofs, the snow connecting them to the wide expanse of snow at the bottom made an ideal hill for "saucering." We find our saucers of great use, too, in clearing the porch of snow. We scoop a few shovelsful onto the saucers, attach a rope to them, and easily pull them up the short hill from the edge of the porch to the snow field beyond. And then—oh joy!—we sit on the saucers and slide back to resume the process.

One sunny day recently we packed a lunch in a knapsack, drove to the road in the SkiDoo, got into the Jeep, and started to the other side of the Valley. It was warm, and before long we had peeled off our heavy parkas and hoods to ride in our shirt sleeves. We passed ranches where cattle and horses were being fed bales of hay, we drove to the parking lot near the lake where snow planes are left, watched one of them just as it was taking off over the snow, and we saw figures on the frozen lake ice-fishing. All along the highway were many moose, feeding contentedly on willows, or lying placidly in the snow while the warm rays of the sun soaked into their heavy coats. Coyotes, singly or in pairs, were running over the snow searching for food, and a pair of snowy white trumpeter swans were floating gracefully on an unfrozen creek. The tall pines were black, the willows a rosy red, the sky pure blue, and the peaks, almost entirely snow-covered, picked up lights and shadows as massive white clouds floated over them. We stopped at a place along the road where we had a fine view of the mountains, unpacked our lunches, and had our winter picnic. Picnics in the summer time are always pleasant, but nothing is quite so fine as a winter picnic, and we returned home as sunburned as if we had had a day's outing in July.

We would never dream of missing the public service announcements which come at noon over the radio each day. Of all the local radio programs, this is our favorite because of its intimacy and hominess. This is the program when anyone may tell of lost objects, announce newsy bits about the day's happenings, or make known some object recently found whose owner may recover by calling and identifying it. For quite some time a considerate person has been holding a pair of children's ski poles for identification and recovery by its owner. Not long ago someone picked up a child's mitten and is eager to have its owner claim it. We have been disturbed because someone with a cold hand has been searching for one black Mohawk glove with white trimming. We wonder if anyone has claimed the Lab puppy that a kind person is sheltering and feeding. The lost border collie puppy called Bear has probably wandered back home as there have been no recent announcements about him. We were distressed about the man who lost a roll of roofing material somewhere between his home and the lumber yard and wonder if anyone called him to tell its whereabouts. We imagine by this time someone has adopted the tiger kitten, "good with children," which was advertised as needing a good home. We were interested in the announcement that someone had returned home from a meeting the other night with two left foot rubbers and wonder if anyone discovered he had two right foot ones so that an exchange could be effected.

The snow outside may be blowing around the cabin, but we are enjoying all four seasons inside. May flowers are bursting, and, although the hyacinths have faded, the daffodils and narcissus are in full bloom, white ones, yellow ones, white ones with orange centers, and the greenhouse is fragrant with spring. The pot of fritillarias is blossoming, big white ones, hanging their fragile cups downward so we can see the delicate green vein in each petal. The sweet peas are bursting and are gay on their wire trellis, lavender, pink, red. The lemon tree has two more blossoms, the snapdragons we planted from seed are in full bloom, and there is a huge bouquet of them on the dining room table. The chrysanthemums are in their second bloom, and the pansy geranium plant is covered with saucy little faces. The new floribunda rose bushes are covered with tiny red shoots, and this morning the miniature climbing rose opened its first pink bloom. The petunias still cascade from their hanging baskets in showers of white and pink and red and purple, and the marigolds, which we thought were almost finished blooming, are covered with hundreds of new buds. We are having a difficult time keeping up with the tomatoes which are ripening fast, and we notice many new blossoms which will produce fruit in days to come. The lilies are strong and green, the asters will show buds soon, the carnations are growing large and brilliant flowers, and the first sign of life in the huge amaryllis bulbs is visible. The planters by the windows in the library downstairs are gay with coleus leaves, primroses, and daffodils which are now beginning to bloom. The three fuchsias in their great hanging baskets there have blossoms. On Valentine's Day we brought in our first pot of blossoming tulips, large double red and white ones.

We look with something of dread at the lengthening days and feel a little sad when we feel the mild chinook winds blowing over the sage flats or see the icicles dripping from the roof in the stronger rays of the sun. We look at the calendar, too, and see that winter will be officially over in a matter of a few short weeks. We cannot bear quite yet, much as we love spring and all seasons in the Valley, to see winter and snow and cold and ice slipping away and gradually, oh so gradually, the first signs of spring, feel the softer air, and notice the swelling buds on the cotton-woods. Not that we don't welcome spring—indeed we do, but we love winter here so much that we want it to last just a little longer with its snow and gusts of wind. And then we settle back comfortably to think that the best skiing is yet to come, that March can bring blizzard after blizzard, that the snows will not disappear entirely until May, that we shall still have many a roaring fire in the fireplace, and that it is much too early to pack away heavy mittens, socks, and hoods for this season. There is much of winter left, and we intend to enjoy every moment of it to the full, every run down the hill on our skis, every trip to the Jeep in the SkiDoo, every drive down the snowy road to the post office. And then when the Valley's winter really has gone for this year, we shall find joy in anticipating next winter and all it will bring. But in the meantime there will be all the delights which spring and summer and autumn will hold, making us think that each of these seasons is the best of them all.

April 1, 1965

A WEEK AGO we were invited to go to the new ski area and partici-pate in a ski movie. We were interested, of course, in being in a movie but were even more eager to see the progress which had been made in the new area since we had visited it last October. To ski down one of the new slopes promised to be the most exciting adventure of all. We had been told to dress in bright ski clothes as the movie would be in color, so we put on colorful sweaters, caps, and parkas and started for the hill to be there promptly at ten in the morning. Fifty or sixty other skiers ar-rived at the time we did, and, skis over our shoulders and poles in hand, we began the short climb to the beginners' slope. We were divided into six or seven groups, each with an instructor. As soon as we had put on our skis and had waited for a few preliminary pictures, one group at a time grabbed onto heavy ropes behind a Christi-Cat and was pulled to the top of the slope. We were given brief instructions and then we skied down, passing in front of the big cameras near the bottom of the slope. The slope where we skied was fantastically good. The snow was in per-fect condition, the terrain was varied, and the run between massive pine trees was long and wide. What a slope for beginners! What an oppor-tunity to practice turning, slide-slipping, kick turning! We raised our

85

eyes, too, to look in the direction of the intermediate and more difficult slopes higher up and knew that they would be equally spectacular.

April 15, 1965

OF ALL THE MONTHS, April is the one in the mountains when travel on foot is least possible. The snow is still several feet deep, but it is soft, and except for early morning or late at night when a crust of frozen snow covers the top, each step one takes carries him knee or hip deep beneath the surface. The SkiDoo manages well, but rides these days are bumpy. The one of us whose turn it is to ride the sled behind thumps along and sways from side to side. Twice one of us riding there has been dumped when the sled spun around a sharp curve. No damage, only hilarious laughter resulted from these mishaps, but the passenger who rides behind the driver on the SkiDoo has learned now to sit backward to warn the driver by a sharp rap on the shoulder if part of the cargo, human or otherwise, spills off, as the distressed one could never shout his predicament loudly enough to be heard above the roar of the motor. When such happens, the SkiDoo stops, and the dumped one hears the reassuring words, "We just lost Betty" or "We have spilled Witty," and knows that soon the machine will make a wide circle and she will be retrieved before the journey continues.

Witty, who has never spent an April here before, did not realize at first what could result if one stepped off the hard track made by the SkiDoo and ventured beyond it. She has complained of late that her pacs, heavy rubber knee-high boots, were tight and difficult to get off. Perhaps, she suggested, she needed another pair which laced more loosely below the knee. We all were taking our puppies for a walk the other morning, and Witty indicated a desire to break away from the hard trail and go to see how the river looked from the top of the bench. We said nothing, winked knowingly at each other, and knew that her initiation would be the same as ours had been during our first April here. Her progress was smooth at first, but then we saw one of her legs sink down. We could not get to her to help, knowing that three of us floundering there would have created a hopeless situation, so all we could do was stand and watch and shout suggestions. All three of us began to laugh uncontrollably, and before we knew it, Witty's other leg disappeared. She struggled a few minutes and got one foot out, but sock and pac were left in the deep hole. Finally the second leg appeared, also sockless and packless. She knelt over the two caverns her legs had made, bare feet waving behind. We realized how cold her feet must be when we saw her

86

take off her mittens, reach back, and put one on each foot. Then, lying flat, face down, she reached into the two deep holes and one at a time pulled up the snow-filled pacs. Our shouts and laughter were heard all over the flats. At last she managed to pull on her wet foot gear, struggled the short distance to the path, and got to the cabin. We have heard no more about the looseness of her pacs.

One day last week we took a thermos of hot coffee and a sack of sandwiches and rode the SkiDoo over the unbroken snow to the large moose ponds near Sawmill Creek. We sat on the sled in the sun, soon becoming so warm that we took off our jackets and hoods. We spent an hour or more watching flocks of ducks fly over, some of them goldeneyes who whistled shrilly as they flew. A pair of geese was swimming just below us on the pond. Soon they got out of the water and stood on the bank, stretching themselves, looking about, standing first on one leg, then the other, until both grew drowsy in the sun, turned their heads under their wings, and went to sleep. A raven rose from a nearby pine tree, uttering his raucous cry as he flew over our heads. The geese awakened and answered his call in deep, throaty cries.

The nights are frosty and calm. As one drops to sleep, the silence is profound, and the sounds of the river seem only to intensify the quiet, as do the owl's sleepy call to its mate, the honking of the geese, the cries of the coyotes. Peace is deep with only the music of the wilderness around one. But through it runs a breath of excitement, a stir of anticipation, a thrill of expectation which only these temperamental April days and nights can bring.

REMEMBRANCE OF A MOUNTAIN LAKE   *May 1, 1965*

I feel the lips of Peace are pale and mute,
I see that greed and terror stalk this land.
Yet I do know a place where Peace reigns absolute
And holds eternal beauty in her hand.
War and destruction have not touched that lake;
The air is calm and free from bombers' roar.
Only the cry of swans can such deep silence break,
Only an eagle's wings into those clouds will soar.
But each day as I slog through jungle mud,
To cringe and cower as murderous planes scream low,
And learn to deem heroic shedding human blood,

And feel this poisoned hate within me grow—
Then shall I hold in memory before my eyes
That mountain lake, those peaks, those summer skies.

June 15, 1965

LAST WEEK we hitched the trailer to the station wagon and drove to the large ranch near town where the burros spend the winters. At our approach and voices, all four came to the gate of the corral, welcomed us with friendly braying, and very obviously wanted to go home with us. We can take only two at a time, so we chose Fidelity and little Loli for the first trip. Loli protested somewhat about getting into the trailer, but a dishful of oats helped persuade her, and then Fidelity, with never a murmur, walked sedately up the ramp and stood to be tied next to her little daughter. We rode slowly back, getting out every now and then to be certain our passengers were riding comfortably and safely. Their two heads with long ears seen above the trailer sides caused much interest on the highway. Finally we turned into our road and then into the Circle H meadows where the burros will stay for a few days until our buck and rail fence is finished. They got out of the trailer easily, walked to the pasture, and seemed happy to be home. The horses soon caught sight of them and raced over to greet their old friends. The burros took off, horses after them, and the galloping procession made an exciting picture on the meadow. Soon the burros thought they had teased the horses long enough, stopped, and the eight horses and two burros gathered in a group, noses together, ears alert for all the winter gossip they were exchanging.

We remembered with longing the two gray noses of TNT and Esso lifted above the corral gate, wanting to return with Fidelity and

88

Loli, so the next day we hurried down to the big ranch with our trailer and loaded them. They were eager to join the others and we learned that they had called all that night for the two missing members of the family. When we drove up to the meadow with them, we watched to see the happy reunion. The two pairs of burros soon spotted each other, the two in the meadow came over immediately to greet the two just arrived by trailer, and they stood, all four, in a perfect circle, heads together, to discuss their brief separation and joyous home-coming. Then they raced off, single file, Fidelity leading, little Loli bringing up the rear, heads up, long ears forward, all relieved to be together again.

July 1, 1965

THESE ARE PICNIC days, and none of us needs much urging to pack sandwiches and a thermos of hot coffee in a knapsack and start off, one morning to our ranch across the river, one morning to the ponds below a neighboring butte, one morning to a favorite woodsy spot several miles up the Valley. We go on excursions through the woods and over the meadows on these days, certain always of finding innumerable surprises. In our hip boots we wade through streams and come upon water cress, fresh and crisp, growing knee deep at the edge of the cold, clear water. We pick bunches of it to put into our sandwiches, some to take home for dinner salads. We stoop to examine closely a blade of blue-eyed grass or the first Indian paint brush. In some places the ground is covered with tiny purple wood violets, and in others there are patches of tall pale blue forget-me-nots or delicate pink and white wild phlox. We pick up to keep as a book-mark a feather, brilliant orange and black, which some flicker has dropped. We stop suddenly in our tracks for fear of disturbing a white-crowned sparrow's nest, skillfully hidden in tall grasses, holding in its rounded cup four slate-blue and brown speckled eggs. As we eat our lunch we notice the bright coloring in bushes and trees of the black-headed grosbeak and the Audubon warbler. We watch climbing with difficulty through the grass on its new legs a baby toad, or we laugh as we watch a huge adult toad at the entrance to its hole, basking and blinking indolently in the warm sun.

On one of our picnic excursions Harry took us to the rookery, a solitary place near the river, and as we looked up, we saw scores of great blue herons flying above our heads, perching on branches, or sitting on the edge of their nests. The huge cottonwoods which held their nests towered above us, each tree holding at least one massive home of these birds, and in one we counted five. Probably herons have made this rookery their home for centuries. As we were leaving, we found on the ground a broken egg, freshly opened to free a long, gangly, fuzzy baby heron.

In the evenings when the lights in the cabin are turned on and the world outside is dark, hundreds of moths come to our big windows and provide for us boundless entertainment. There are tiny, dainty moths with wings of soft gray, designed in filigree patterns, there are the larger and more common sphynx moths, and every evening for the past week we have been startled by the huge cecropia which, according to our book on moths, is not supposed to live in Western areas at all. We have watched its big velvety wings, decorated with soft shades of blue and rose, its long furry antennae, and have wondered at the perfect symmetry of the patterns and designs on this beautiful insect. One evening we had five of them, one at each lighted window, coming as if on purpose to dance for us an enchanted nocturnal ballet. We shall watch carefully for their tough, brown cocoons on willow twigs and branches this winter and hope in the late spring to see one of them hatch, emerging and unfolding its great wings to a spread of five or six inches.

There is day after day of sunny summer weather in the Valley now, with bluer skies than one could ever imagine, great white cumulus clouds passing slowly through them, casting their mighty shadows as they move. There are summer nights, cool and still, always with the sound of the river rushing below, stars above incredibly big and bright, undimmed by a city's artificial lights. There are gray days, too, which bring soft and gentle rain, days when the peaks and sage flats are misty and indistinct, days when silver drops cling to every twig and blade of grass.

The lines of John Muir have been coming back to us again and again during these summer days. We have been repeating them to ourselves each time we go out of doors to see the peaks, to feel the sunshine, the soft rains, the winds—

"Climb the mountains and get their good tidings.
Nature's peace will flow into you
 as sunshine flows into trees.
The winds will blow their own freshness into you,
 and the storms their energy,
 while cares will drop off like autumn leaves."

July 15, 1965

ON A RECENT drive to our ranch across the river, Harry and Margaret and we rode over the meadowland, which seems to stretch endlessly before our eyes, on our way to the wooded area on the river bottom.

90

As we drove, we noticed a group of men at work. They were building a buck and pole fence to enclose a piece of property we had sold. As we watched, we thought of the homes that would be built soon on this Upper Meadow section and tried to imagine how it would look when families had moved into them, when children would be playing around them, when groups of people would be starting to the fishing streams in the woods with fishing rods in hand, creels over their shoulders, when horses would be grazing contentedly on the land. We all spoke of the fact that many of the people to whom we have sold home sites intend to remain in the Valley the year around.

Then we drove back over the vast meadowland to the far end of the ranch and turned at the little dirt road which leads to our favorite picnic spot. Here, at this end of the ranch, we have sold one home site and there will be a home built soon and a family moving in. There will be others, like us, we thought, who have learned to love this land, who will glance up, like us, to the mighty mountains, who will stop to examine an interesting mushroom, a wild flower, the clear, sunny streams as they bounce and sparkle over the shining stones. Like us, others will walk along this road with a picnic lunch, find a shady spot, and sit down to enjoy a simple meal made glorious by the surroundings. Like us, others will stretch back and look high into a blue sky. Like us, others will learn the silence and peace of the wilderness.

As we walked over our ranch, we stopped now and then to sit in the sun, to pick up in our fingers the fragrant warm earth, to watch a brilliant butterfly float past, and we began to realize a little wistfully that some of this beautiful ranch is no longer ours. This knowledge saddened us for a moment and made us want to envelop all of it in our arms and hold it tightly, never to relinquish it.

But then we thought of the six long years we had looked for a place to build a cabin and how we would settle for nothing but the finest. We remembered all the longing for a home of our own in the Valley and the happy days we spent in planning and then building the cabin exactly as we wanted it. We thought of how stark and new the cabin had looked at first, but how its logs soon weathered and how it seemed to settle down into its surroundings and look as if it had been here always. We spoke of all the happy times at the cabin and in the Valley, only during the summer months at first with a fleeting visit at Christmas time, and then the contentment and peace we learned when we realized at last that we were here for good and never had to leave. We have learned, too, that there are others, just like us, who feel the same way, and we remembered a few short years ago when all of us bought the ranch how we decided that our first purpose would be to provide a very few home sites, spaced widely apart, where others, like us, would find the same happiness, peace, freedom, and security which we have found.

We have come to the conclusion that to find the land, one must sometimes lose it, and we feel that our greatest joy in the ranch may be still to come. It is not in owning and possessing land—one can never really do that anyway—but in providing a place where others may find the same joy as ours and hold in lease for a brief time their own land surrounded eternally by forests and rivers and streams and meadows and mountains, unspoiled, untouched as they have been for ages past and will be for ages to come.

August 1, 1965

THERE HAVE BEEN several barbecue parties lately. One at the Circle H last week provided all that any gourmet could wish. As we sat on the patio, steaks, sizzling juicily on the open-air grill, we watched the horses, just released from the corral, playing in the meadow, galloping, bucking, chasing each other like a herd of wild horses. The sun dipped behind the mountains and the sky became a soft gray, streaked with banners of pink and crimson which illuminated the snow-capped peaks. Someone put on the recording of Mahler's Fifth Symphony. The first star appeared in the nearest canyon. A shy deer came from the forest to the salt lick in the meadow. Even the children's voices became hushed, and we sat in silence during the enchanted moments before dark.

Another barbecue with Katie and the Elbo guests started beautifully, and we all had been served our ears of freshly roasted sweet corn as the steaks were put on the big grill. The children sat on one side telling stories, and the adults sat around the camp fire visiting. Katie and Peavie were supervising the cooking and all seemed calm, when without any warning the sky grew black, fierce gusts of wind furiously chased twigs and leaves, paper napkins and cups, and blew the flames higher. Then with no further announcement, the skies opened and the rain fell. With never a word, the guests grabbed flying hats and jackets, plates of salad and corn, and flew over logs and sage bushes to find haven in the nearest cabins. In an instant the barbecue grounds were deserted, the steaks continued to cook by themselves, and the cabin which we had chosen for shelter became more crowded with laughing people by the minute. More and more children and adults came in, rain dripping from their hair, their noses, their chins. Plates of salad were put on dressers and

92

desks, what little there was left of salad after the wind had carried off leaves of lettuce, cucumbers, tomatoes. One hungry guest appeared with a morsel of steak on his plate which he promptly cut into small pieces with his fishing knife and gallantly shared with all of us. Just as quickly as the flash storm had started, it ended. All became still, the clouds passed, and the stars came out. We found our way back to the fire and steak grill, resumed our meal, laughing and enjoying the excitement. The party concluded as calmly as it had begun, Peavie cutting two big cakes in honor of Katie's birthday. The air was fresh and fragrant with wet sage and pine. The log seats and chairs soon dried, and all of us were exhilarated by the brief tempest which for a moment had threatened to upset the party entirely. Nature, we agreed, can afford more entertainment than man.

On Sunday we were invited to the christening of Kathryn Sue at the little chapel a few miles away. There was a flurry of preparation at the cabin. It had been so long since any of us had worn dresses that we had to search in the attic long and carefully in order to assemble three suitable outfits. One by one each of us went to examine and choose from what the various suitcases and wardrobes had to offer, one by one each went to her respective room to array herself in what attire had been found, and then one by one each appeared before the others to see if her appearance was right. Several of the hats chosen were claimed by one or both of the others as hers. It was difficult to find three pairs of nylon stockings as we had donated most of them to Steve and Bill to wear over their heads at night to assure that their new butch hair cuts would stand up stiffly. When Sunday came, we wobbled to the car in our high heels, had a difficult time with tight skirts getting onto the high seats of the Jeep, but finally settled back, white gloves and all, to ride in style to the chapel. We met several friends on the way, all of whom recognized the bright red car, but none of whom seemed to find familiar the passengers, so they passed us by and looked back questioningly.

We were the first to arrive at the chapel, but soon the family came, last of all Harry, Sr., carrying little Kathy, happy and smiling, dressed in her christening robes. She laughed and chuckled at her brothers and sister, and seemed most content in Harry Sr.'s arms when he walked around with her before the ceremony. Her sister Ann, dressed all in pink, was proud of her and every once in a while, seated next to us, would glance up, eyes shining, and grin at us, showing two great gaps where she recently had lost two front teeth, the picture of a happy six-year-old. Only once did Ann's exuberance carry her away, when in the midst of the ceremony she suddenly and for no apparent reason reached over the pew

93

and hit her brother Steven as he was standing in front of her. Steven turned around in a dignified manner, scowled fiercely at her, but Ann, knowing she was out of reach, simply looked up at us, smiled, angelic-appearing and a model of propriety.

The service progressed, simple, dignified, and impressive, with proud parents, proud grandfather and grandmother, proud uncle and aunt, happy brothers and sister, all surrounding, on her first important day, a joyous and laughing baby.

September 1, 1965

Summer is relinquishing her spell: rustling, dry leaves of balsam root;
The first hint of ruddy shades on huckleberry leaves,
Ripe huckleberries, fragrant on the bush in the hot sun,
Fragrant in a kettle on the stove, bubbling in purple sweetness.
Silent, cool mornings, a trace of white frost on roofs and tall grasses.
Gray skies and blue mists; cool rains and white ribbons of cloud
Against green hills; warm, sunny days when all living things sense
The approach of autumn: burros cavorting and racing down the road and
Over the sage flats in joyful, senseless antics; horses eager for rides
Through cool and shady forests, over open, sunny flats, snatching
In their mouths the last blue lupin flowers and goldeneyes, happy to
Stand with their riders on high crests, looking over the silent lands
Below, the winding river, the green buttes, soon to be brilliant
With the rosy yellow of quaking aspens; the drone of bees gathering
The last few drops of summer sweetness from the fading flowers; the
Scampering flash of squirrels and chipmunks racing to store
Late seeds and berries; the harsh call of wild geese and ducks
Over ponds. Woodgathering in late afternoons, piling up carefully
One by one, or armful by armful,
The smooth, gray sticks which sound soft and gentle
As they strike one another on the growing piles;
The fragrance of cold earth on gnarled, dead roots;
Shorter days which imperceptibly fade into evening
In clouds of pink and apricot
Against a blue and apple green sky;
Clouds enveloping the snow-capped peaks, turning soon
From brilliance to soft grays
As the silver crescent moon appears
And the first bright star above the canyon.

Crackling logs in the fireplace,
Outside the wailing howl of a lone coyote
And the long and mournful hoot of an owl.
Hushed and frosty autumn darkness descends
Upon a silent, sleeping valley.

September 15, 1965

WE WERE JUST sitting down to dinner four or five days ago when the phone rang and Harry reported that our burros had escaped and were wandering down the road several miles away. We left our dinner in the oven, and away we went with oats and halters to bring them back. We rode and rode, but there was no sign of the familiar gray bodies or long, dark ears. We left the car by the side of the road, searched for them on foot, and finally, becoming discouraged, we were just ready to turn our back when we caught a glimpse in the growing darkness of their small hoof prints in the dust beside the road. We followed them until we came to a narrow bridge over a roaring mountain stream, stooped to examine the tracks more closely, and found that they had turned and started back. We tried to follow but by this time it was too dark to see, so back we drove, slowly, fearfully, ever watching for the big ears, ever listening for a lonesome bray. We had almost decided to leave our search until morning when suddenly our headlights picked out first one little body ahead, then another, and another, and another. There they were, all four, standing at the gate leading into the meadow, glad to be home, happy to hear our voices, delighted with the oats we had brought, and resolved never to take any unchaperoned excursions again. Since then they have not once left the vicinity of the cabin, and we feel that their adventure down the road in strange and unfamiliar territory taught them that home is the best place after all.

October 1, 1965

IT IS NOT EASY to find an organist who is willing to come many miles to a remote French town to dedicate a new organ, not even if the church which houses the organ is four centuries old. There are many churches in France four centuries old, and there are many organs to be dedicated. No one in this particular French Huguenot church knew of such an organist, no one in the congregation, not even the minister himself. But a twelve-year-old girl who sang in the choir, suddenly remembered some one she had met a few months before while visiting two school friends in Alsace. With all the confidence of a child, she suggested that she write to this organist she had met in Strasbourg and she was

95

quite certain, she said, that he would accept the invitation, even though the church funds were insufficient to pay him. The members of the church indulged her and permitted her to write but in the meantime searched further for someone else as they doubted that this man, never heard of by any of them, would care to come a full day's trip unless he would be paid. The little girl remembered how in Strasbourg her two friends had introduced her to one of their favorite people, an artist, tall, gaunt, raw-boned, with a happy face and laughing eyes. Uncle Hansi, as he was called, was full of tricks to delight children and had told many of his favorite jokes to the three little girls. At last he invited all of them to visit his studio. After the visit, he suggested that they might like to meet an old friend of his, an organist, just released as a prisoner of war, who at that moment was playing at the big cathedral. The two little Alsatians already knew him, but as a special treat they wanted their visitor to meet him, too, so off the three went with Uncle Hansi who sat with the children in the dark church and listened to the sublime playing of a Bach toccata and fugue. After the concert the children met their friend, the organist, and he talked to them and joked with them before they had to leave for home. This was the organist whom the twelve-year-old French child remembered and who, she was certain would accept her invitation to come and play for her church.

Much to the church congregation's astonishment, but not at all to the twelve-year-old girl's, a letter arrived from the Strasbourg organist a few days later saying he would be happy to come to dedicate the new organ. The child was certain her friend would play beautifully—hadn't she heard him?—but there was misgiving in the hearts of the minister and choir members. Time was growing short, however, no one else had been suggested, so it was decided to make the best of it, take the little girl's word that all would be well, and go ahead with final plans.

The minister and the little girl were at the railroad station when the organist's train was due, and all three would walk the mile from there to the church. The train arrived, the passengers got off, and the child, immediately recognizing her friend, ran up to a disheveled figure in crumpled clothes, battered hat, with untrimmed mustaches drooping around his mouth. The minister's heart sank. Never, he thought, could this unkempt person have the sensitivity, the power to play the organ. The child talked to her friend on the way to the church; the minister kept strangely silent, fearing what the evening would bring. Upon arrival at the church a few minutes before eight when the concert was to begin, the three entering the church, saw all heads turn, all eyes fasten upon them, then a look of dismay spread over all faces. The organist was led up the circular stairway to the organ and choir loft above. The members

96

of the choir, eager to see what the soloist was like, peered curiously over the top rail. Their faces fell. Everyone in the church was reproaching himself for having listened to a child who had insisted her friend was the best organist of them all. The man sat down at the organ, moved his feet over the pedals, let his fine, strong fingers run over the keys. A glance at the minister and the choir indicated that he was ready. The first great notes sounded firm, strong, powerful. The choir and audience began to relax. At least the playing would be acceptable. The music continued, magnificent, true, breathtakingly beautiful. The accompaniment for the choir was sure and accurate. Never had the choir sung so well, never had an organ responded so sublimely. The solo numbers were flawless. The little church resounded with the superb playing, particularly with the music of Bach. Everyone was held under the spell; even those most ignorant of music knew that this was playing such as is heard once in a lifetime and only then if one is fortunate.

Finally the last powerful strains died away, the concert was concluded, the congregation sat silent for a few moments before leaving the church, the twelve-year-old girl and the minister took the organist back to the station where he was to catch a late train for Strasbourg. The organ had been dedicated, the ceremony was over, but not one member of the audience who had heard the playing would ever forget it, although the organist's name most had not bothered to ask.

And the little twelve-year-old girl who had been responsible for bringing the great organist to her French town? None other than Witty, who lives with us now and is affectionately called by those who know her here, "one of the Bettys." We have heard her tell this story many, many times and, never tiring of it, hope we shall hear her tell it many, many more. We asked her to tell it to us again on the evening of September 5 when the world had just received the news of the death of this organist friend of hers, death which came quietly and peacefully to him, then ninety years old.

And the organist? Of course you have guessed. It was Dr. Albert Schweitzer. The three of us here would like to share this story with all of you and let it be our small tribute to a man who accomplished tremendous things in his long lifetime, became world famous as a doctor, musician, philosopher, writer, theologian, benefactor of all living things, winner of the Nobel Peace Prize. But his greatest accomplishment, out of his own life and thought, through his own reverence for life, was in showing every man whether in Asia, Europe, America, Africa, or anywhere on earth, the way to make his own life, too, one of service and love for his fellow beings everywhere.

THESE ARE THE days we love best for riding, amid the golden willows on the river bottom, high on mountain trails to mountain lakes where we see no human being and hear nothing but feel the deep silences of the forests and mountains. On a recent ride a great bull moose crossed our path and watched us as we disappeared into the trees along the trail. We saw four deer on another ride who stood motionless, watching us with curious eyes until we had passed. Almost always we see, walking with dignity and majesty, a ruffed grouse or two, refusing to be disturbed or hurried by anything so ordinary as a horse and rider.

A week or so ago when we awoke we saw the first covering of snow on the ground and in the chill winds that blew we felt the first icy breath of winter. The burros and horses were as excited as we and raced, bucking and kicking over the flats and meadows. The puppies, too, became weather-intoxicated and rolled and played and romped in the new fallen snow, coming in finally to the warm house with white snow balls on the tips of their noses. But the snow soon melted, the winds died away, the skies became clear and blue again, and the sun shone with all its customary autumn warmth.

This is the time of year when horses become restless and want to be on their way to winter pastures. The other night a tree blew across the buck fence at the Circle H meadow, and Margaret phoned us the next day telling us the horses, one and all, had disappeared. We thought they were grazing in the river bottom and would soon find their way back to the meadow, but when we looked for them, no sign, no track did we find. We drove along the road a way and soon caught sight of their tracks in the soft dirt, so off we started in pursuit. We rode for several miles, watching tracks as we went and finally came to the conclusion that the horses could not possibly have traveled so far in so short a time. But the tracks continued and so did we, beyond the dirt road, onto the highway, beyond the new ski area. At last we saw in the distance six horses grazing unconcernedly in an open field. As we approached, we recognized them as ours, pulled up to the side of the road, calling them by name. One by one startled heads were raised and we could tell by their attitude and appearance that they knew their escapade was over. We had a bridle in the car but no saddle, so we rounded them up, bridled Royalty, and one of us stayed to ride him bareback, wrangling the others along the road, while the second one of us returned home for a saddle. All went well and finally where the road narrowed we could bring them along simply by driving behind them in the car. About dark six sheepish horses were driven into their home meadow.

These are blue and golden days in the Valley, days of leisure when one can absorb all that each sunny day and starry night bring. Days and nights, too, of music, the background music of the river, the call of wild ducks and geese flying over the ponds, the bugling of the elk on the bench above, the rustlings of dry leaves on the ground. Muted music it is, accented only by the sharp, raucous cry of an occasional magpie or raven circling above.

November 1, 1965

THE FIFTEEN HUNDRED bulbs we ordered have arrived and are now in the ground, all varieties of tulips and daffodils which we planted in the back of the cabin over the bench. The road to the post office has been poled so when heavy snows come, the plows can more easily find where the road is and not wander too far from the track. People are asking each other, "Are you ready for winter?" The suppressed excitement grows.

Frank phoned us from the Whitegrass Ranch one afternoon last week and said the trucks would arrive early the next morning to take the horses to their winter pastures 200 miles east. We set our alarm clocks, got up the next morning while it was still dark, ate a hurried breakfast, and went to the corral for our last ride of the season. The horses sensed that something unusual was happening in the early morning light. They shivered a little in the frosty air as we put their cold saddle blankets and saddles on them and slipped the icy bits into their mouths. No sooner had we mounted than we felt the eagerness of the horses and their desire to be on the way. We rode through fog and mists on an unaccustomed trail, and at each upturned stump and root the horses pricked their ears, looked at them quizzically, and shied from them as though they hid behind their dead branches and trunks some ferocious beast ready to pounce out. As we rode out of the woods and to the upper sage flats, the mists became more dense. We rode on in silence, feeling like characters on Egdon Heath in *The Return of the Native* or from the sinister depths of some other Hardy novel or Brontë story. The horses grew more spooky, saw larger and fiercer figures in the mists, transformed in their imaginations innocent piles of logs or ordinary culverts over streams into monsters of fearful mien. At last we approached the Whitegrass Ranch and rode the horses to the corral where their shoes were to be pulled. We took off their saddles and bridles, gave them each a farewell pat and hug, and went into the warm cabin for hot coffee.

The burros have stayed close to the cabin during the past days, knowing that each morning and evening they would be given hay and

99

oats near the saddle shed. Almost always they have been within sight and have come frequently to the buck fence, looking between the poles and braying to be fed. One afternoon we were planting bulbs in front of the cabin, the burros watching us just on the other side of the fence. We were conscious of unusual metallic sounds which persisted. We paid no attention, thinking it was the burros finding something interesting on the Jeep or scratching their noses on the metal gates. Suddenly we looked up, saw the gate swing slowly inward, and four burros walk sedately into the yard in single file. They headed directly for some of our choice plants, intending to pull them up and play with them. We rushed over and whisked them out. Now that they have learned to open the gate into forbidden territory, we shall have to devise some burro-proof means of latching it more firmly. We have felt that the new buck fence hurt their feelings a little as they no longer can come to peer into our windows, but, much as we love to see their curious eyes looking in, shrubbery must be preserved.

A few days later we saw a magnificent bull moose walking slowly over the sage flats. At first we were so engrossed in seeing his gigantic size, and his enormous spread of antlers that we noticed nothing else. Soon, however, we looked behind him and saw, walking in his footsteps with exactly the same dignity and self-possession, four little burros, ears alert and bodies moving in precisely his deliberate motion. Before long the moose came to a fence which he stepped over easily and majestically, but the fence was too much for the burros. They lined up along it to watch the moose move over the flats and finally disappear into the timber. It had been a strange procession, and probably the moose himself had no idea he was being followed and emulated by such unusual long-eared creatures.

November 15, 1965

"BUT WHAT do you do for culture?" some of our city friends have asked, friends who have never visited this Valley. "You gather rose hips for jelly, you gather kindling wood for fires, you ride, you ski," they continue, "but are there no challenges to one's intellect? Are your days composed entirely of physical activities?"

We have pondered this question many times, not because it is difficult to describe activities of the mind, but rather because it is difficult to classify and categorize them in any intelligible fashion. One cannot classify the air he breathes. One cannot categorize the human atmosphere which surrounds him.

100

Long before we came to this Valley as permanent residents, when we were here for only a few short weeks in the summer, for even shorter vacations at Christmas, we began to feel something unique about the atmosphere in the Valley and about the people whom we met. Many times we felt a little disturbed when conversations turned to subjects about which we knew we should have some knowledge but didn't. In other words, we were beginning to realize our own deficiencies in many branches of learning, be a little startled by such lack, and begin, maybe for the first time, to think we were missing something. For the first time perhaps we felt eager to learn, not for the sake of grades or advanced degrees but because we suspected that such learning might be challenging and stimulating. It seemed to be so to others, and we began to understand that the acquisition of new knowledge *per se* might hold attractions for us, too.

Before we left our city homes, we went to a college bookstore and loaded up with armsful of texts on anthropology, biology, botany, zoology, music, art, comparative religion, geography, geology. We were eager to fill as best we could the abysmal gaps in our educational backgrounds, and as soon as we were settled here, we began. Such individual study is not so effective perhaps as courses under learned professors, but it is better than nothing. Each time we begin a new book and discuss it, we find our horizons creaking rustily outward and our desire to learn becoming more acute. Best of all, we are with people here who are interested in the same things, whose ideas challenge ours, whose learning is an inspiration to us. So it was with many of our city friends, but there never seemed to be enough time to hear what they were thinking and learning. An appointment or a class or a conference always seemed to interfere.

The people who are natives of this Valley, who have lived here most or all of their lives have a culture unique and highly developed. They are, for the most part, gentle folk and soft-spoken. Their sense of refinement, hospitality, plain goodness and kindness is instinctive. They possess the noblest of courtesy, the greatest of wisdom. Their tales of early life in the West and their songs to the accompaniment of guitars hold one enthralled for hours on end. Their culture is undoubtedly the most unusual and fascinating of all the Valley has to offer.

The other, the more cosmopolitan, sophisticated culture is found here, too. On the street in town the other day we met a friend who said, "I understand you enjoy Mahler's Second Symphony. Have you heard his Ninth?" We hadn't but sent for it and when we heard it, were transported. Another friend whom we met shopping recently said she

had been reading Bronson Alcott and the other American transcenden-
talists and had finally turned, through growing interest, to a study of
Plato. We attended a few days ago a meeting in which an interested
group is learning about the great religions of the world and then beginning a study of art, poetry, music, the dance—a course built around the
theme of "man's relationship to that which transcends him." Be it said
to our discredit, we had never cared for, simply because we had never
understood, the music of Bach. The former conductor of the summer
Fine Arts Symphony in the Valley told us what to look for in Bach, advised us to listen to his music over and over again as it is the most satisfying ever written. We took his advice and have learned to appreciate the
Brandenburg Concertos, the St. Matthew Passion, the great Mass in B
Minor, the toccatas, the fugues.

And so we say to our friends who are concerned about what the
Valley has to offer in an intellectual way—the outdoor life is tremendously important. Living with all kinds of weather, enjoying the out of
doors in sun, snow, rain, and wind, finding stimulation and wonder and
knowledge and joy in nature is a life we love. On the other hand, feeling
within us a stirring for greater and more knowledge from books and
music and art is a life we love, too. In such a life one is never lonely in
this Valley. There are many others who find it a fascinating pursuit to
search for the knowledge and wisdom which has elevated mankind
through the ages to his finest potential. We are surrounded by such
people on all sides. The Valley has had them here for many years and is
attracting them from all parts of the world. We have discovered, as they
have, that a background of mountains and trees and streams and stars,
a background of peace and silence and congeniality among people is the
finest of all for learning and for following the needs of mind and spirit.

December 1, 1965

THE DAY BEFORE Thanksgiving, we were watching the snow flurries
and recalling last year at this time when we were struck by one of the
most furious blizzards of all. People had told us no heavy snows were
expected until December, and suddenly it occurred to us that it was
almost that month now. But there was no precipitation all day except a
few wet snow flakes which melted almost as soon as they reached the
ground. After dinner we were sitting in the living room playing cribbage
when one of the dogs came in and we noticed her coat was covered with
thick snow. We rushed to the windows and saw that visibility was poor
and that the air was filled with snow flakes as large as silver dollars. We

102

thought nothing much of it, hardly daring to hope that this was really a snow-in storm, and returned to our game. Shortly after eight o'clock we thought we would like to get out in the snow for a while and decided that just for fun we'd drive the SkiDoo around the sage flats and maybe even take the Jeep to the road if the snow seemed heavy. We put on ski pants, parkas, warm pacs, and got the snow shoes from the basement. We stepped onto the porch into a foot or more of snow, and then we realized that this was a full-blown storm. We began to move a little faster. We took flashlights and a snow shovel and stopped at the saddle shed for the SkiDoo, happy to hear the familiar roar of its little engine. One of us started down the road with it while the other two followed slowly in the Jeep. The one in the SkiDoo rode down the main road, noticing with delight the trees heavy with snow on either side, thinking of course the other two would follow immediately in the car. She stopped the SkiDoo at the Circle H gate where the Jeep would be left and sat there expecting the lights of the Jeep to appear around the bend at any moment. The only fear on that dark, snowy night was that a moose might appear suddenly from the trees. At that moment a branch snapped, and the one on the SkiDoo felt her heart beat a little faster as she glanced up to see which tree would be the best to climb in case her fears were realized. But nothing further happened, and it was apparent that the crackling branch had been broken by too heavy a load of snow. No sign of lights. No sign of the Jeep. Just deep, deep silence, as deep as the ever falling snows. Finally a light appeared far away, coming closer, but slowly, and looking like an enormous star in the distance. It moved too slowly for a car, and as it came closer, the one on the SkiDoo·called and discovered it was Witty, walking down the road with a flashlight. The Jeep had slowed down, stopped, and stubbornly refused to start, and she had walked to tell the news and help bring the SkiDoo back. First, groans. Then, laughter. And back went the SkiDoo. All of a sudden there was a queer click, and the SkiDoo stopped, too, right in the middle of the road. Our third member who had started walking up the road, too, by this time reached the disabled SkiDoo, and all of us did all we knew to get it started, but not a cough of encouragement did it give. Headlights appeared on the road, and a pick-up truck slowed as it saw us with flashlights in the road. It was Dennis with his family. After the hood of the motor had been removed, a twist given here and there with a pair of pliers, we touched the starter button, and the SkiDoo once again roared into action. Then Dennis insisted on going back with us to pull the Jeep out before the snows completely covered it. Back we all went to the stalled car, and with the help of a powerful winch, the Jeep began to move, the pick-up going backward all the way to the gate where our car was left. As we drove home, we felt great appreciation and gratitude to Dennis who had given us such willing and expert help. As we approached the cabin, a little cold and wet but laughing at our plight, the lights from the living room shone gaily in welcome. As we got closer, the lights began to blink on then off, on then off, and we thought, "How nice! The cabin is urging us on just a little further where there will be dry clothes and a warm fire." And then we realized what the blinking lights really meant. Sure enough. They gave one last feeble blink, and then all was total darkness. A power failure. We covered the SkiDoo with the big tarp, stumbled up the steps, now completely invisible under the snow, onto the porch, groped for the door knob, and went in. We managed to get into dry clothes, found candles, threw heavy logs on the fire, and started another fire in the library downstairs. Then, warm and dry and comfortable, watching the flickering lights from the candles and fire on the walls and ceiling, we sat down and began to laugh and laugh at our experience. We became weak from laughter, and as each of us recalled the next funny incident, we'd start off again into peals of hilarity. All was ready for our Thanksgiving guests the next day, the pies had been baked, the table set, and we knew by morning at the latest the power would be on and the turkey could be roasted. We knew, too, that the Jeep would be quickly fixed by service men from town, and that if anything serious was wrong with the SkiDoo, that could be remedied, too. Finally at midnight, the lights came on, the pump began to churn, and the heaters in the greenhouse to whirr. All was well, and we started for bed.

The great day has come. The snows are here for good. As we went to sleep, we happily thought of the weeks and weeks of this glorious weather which lie ahead. We are more snug and comfortable and safe in our wilderness home than anyone in the world. No panic, no confusion, no fear, no deprivation, no real inconvenience. Just fun, good, clean, wholesome fun if one learns to respect weather and does not try to fight or outwit or conquer it but just rolls easily and wisely with all of nature's moods, the wild as well as the gentle.

1966

NEVER HAVE WE SEEN so much wild life near the cabin. Each morning and evening as we look over the flats, there are elk and moose, and on our way to the post office we usually spot a half dozen deer. They seem troubled not at all by their proximity to human life and habitation, but wander complacently about, nibbling willow twigs and any grasses which still poke through the snow. Their coats are thick, and they are fat and well fed. The fawns play about their mothers, and we see them racing over the bench and back again in great glee. A bald eagle flies about the cabin and often perches on a tall pine on the island below. We picked out with the binoculars a kitten-faced marten and are watching carefully for the reappearance of a family of otters.

The birds were given a new swinging feeder for Christmas, filled with delicious sunflower seeds. They swing from the wire which attaches it to the eaves, peer down with their sharp, black little eyes, but as yet have not ventured to the feeder itself. We know that will come soon. Another natural feeder holds greater interest for them at the moment. Wasps built a gigantic nest last summer under the eaves, and the chickadees are finding it fascinating to investigate and profitable to peck. They hang upside down as they poke large holes at the bottom of the nest and apparently are eating the hibernating wasps and insects inside. Already the nest is half demolished, and we know the sleeping and unsuspecting inmates are being devoured by the dozens each day.

The greenhouse is flourishing and each night as we have dinner in the dining room, the flood lights are turned on the tubs of crimson, white, and pink geraniums, the white and lavender cascading petunias, the carnations, and snapdragons. The violets are beginning to bud, the new snapdragons are growing straight and tall, the pansy seedlings are strong, and the sweet peas are climbing their trellises so rapidly that last night as we looked at them, we decided we would train them over the ceiling of the greenhouse as well as up either side. The chrysanthemums are in bloom, too, and with their yellow and bronze colored flowers bring light and sunshine into the house even on the grayest days. No matter what the weather may be or how deep the snows, there is always a part of the cabin which is fragrant spring.

We have discovered a new joy in wilderness living. Splitting wood. We have a light sledge hammer and two wedges. We have learned just the right place to drive the wedge in with easy strokes until it takes hold, firm and steady, and then the big crack through the center of the log appears. Another blow, and deeper goes the wedge, and we begin to catch the first fragrance of the wood at the center of the log. The wedge has almost disappeared by this time, and then comes the final clang of the metal, and the log splits straight through the center, falls, and exposes the clean, white wood in the middle. We stoop to pick up the fallen wedge and to catch even more closely the strong fragrance of pine. Log after log is tossed onto the pile. They seem to burn more warmly and brightly when we have split them ourselves.

February 1, 1966

OUR HEARTS SING at all seasons here, but there is something special about winter, special from the moment the sun rises until deep cold night settles down under starry skies. No one had ever told us how delightful the winters in the Valley are. All we had heard were reports of cabin fever among people who wanted to get out but couldn't because of icy highways, bitter cold, deep, deep snows. We had never heard about the bright, sunny days, the sparkling air, the heavy frost feathers on the trees and shrubs. But now we know, and there is no lure of ocean beaches, palm trees, roses growing out of doors in January, or searching for shells on hot sands that can tempt us.

Our thoughts turn to skiing these days, and many times we have been to the fantastic new ski area. The delight and joy to ride up, up through the trees, over mountain streams, to the various stations, skim or tumble down the getting off places, turn, and see stretching before our eyes miles and miles of valley floor, mountains on all sides, and immediately ahead the long, smooth slopes of the ski hills! We catch our breath as we look around, adjusting our ski pole straps to our wrists, before we begin the delicious descent. Clear, cold air, warm, bright sun, long, winding slopes between mighty trees—why would we ever want to exchange one moment of this joy for anything else? A delicious hot lunch at one of the fine restaurants, or a cup of coffee or hot chocolate if it is mid-afternoon, and away we go again for one more swoop down the hill, loving the silences all around us, the only sound being the soft swishing of our skis through the snow.

As we drive home, our faces burn from the sun and the wind, and we know that soon we shall have a coat of tan which will be far darker than anything the summer sun produces. Gradually all of us are taking on the appearance of owls because of the great white circles around our eyes, the marks of our ski goggles. We drive into the home parking area, leave the Jeep, and go to the waiting Ski Doo. We whip over the hard track which its treads have made. We look up to the mighty, snowy mountains, down to the steaming river, and see behind us as though a signature to the glorious day, the pure rays of the sinking sun, pouring through the clouds and mists in showers of gold upon the Valley below.

We hum as we get ready for bed—

Who could ask for anything more?
Who could ask for ANYTHING more!

March 1, 1966

ONE CLEAR, SUNNY morning recently, Katie phoned us from the Elbo Ranch across the Valley and suggested that we drive over to see her and Peavie that afternoon. The minute we entered the ranch kitchen, warm and sunny, we knew that Peavie had been baking fresh bread. We sniffed hungrily the delicious fragrance and soon we were all gathered around the table enjoying hot rolls and coffee. We talked about Valley happenings for a while, and then Katie said it was time to feed the horses. One of us offered to go with her and help, and the other two of us went with Peavie to the front porch, then waded through deep snow to the top rail of the buck fence, the only one visible above the snow, and sat there to watch. The horses sensed that their dinner time was near and crowded closer to the lodge, watching intently what was going on in back. We could not see the feeding preparations in back, but we could tell by the excited eagerness of the horses, all twenty-three of them with the burro Tonto in their midst, that Katie's SkiDoo was about to roar into action, proceed down the road, carrying on the sled in back their bales of hay. Finally we heard the motor start and come nearer, and as the two on the SkiDoo passed the lodge and went down the road, the horses turned, moving slowly at first with admirable restraint and good manners and headed toward their feeding lot. Then, knowing that dinner was almost ready, they began to move faster, racing and bucking in delightful anticipation of the good hay.

We could hear from the fence the voices of the two doing the feeding, see the SkiDoo pass around in a large circle and the one on back opening the bales of hay and tossing great armsful of it to the waiting horses. Each one seemed to have a special place in the great circle, and soon all were still, munching their dinners contentedly. A last few armsful of hay were scattered, and then the SkiDoo turned around, came back down the road, and disappeared behind the lodge where more bales of hay were loaded in preparation for the early feeding the next morning. We all went in, warmed our fingers in front of the kitchen stove, and after a little more visiting, started back, noticing as we left the last rays of the sun dipping behind the mountains.

April 1, 1966

WE KNEW the Valley would be spectacular after the snow, and we wanted to see as much of it as possible, so we made reservations for an over the snow trip, along the river and to near-by lakes, far from roads and highways. There were ten of us who left in mid-morning in the large and comfortable snowmobile from the place where the snow plows turn back and leave the highway unplowed for the winter. We took off over the snowy sage flats and headed directly for the river, riding along the top of the bench from which point we could see numerous ducks and geese swimming in the water or flying overhead, great black moose sunning themselves near the willows, and an eagles' nest high in the top of a dead pine tree. We caught a flash in the sun of the white head of the bald eagle who was sitting on her eggs in the nest. There were no tracks ahead of us, and the tremendous skis on the front of the machine and the large treads cut the only path. We saw the peaks from various angles, each one seeming more superb than the one before. Snow and silence, white peaks and blue skies with only a few misty clouds floating close to the mountains. Soon the snowmobile turned and we drove straight through a pine forest, the trees heavy with the new snow. We stopped for lunch on the shore of one of the lakes, now completely frozen and snow covered with only occasional breaks to indicate where fishermen had cut holes and dropped their lines through the ice. We took off our parkas in the warm sun and sat on them in the snow and enjoyed a winter picnic, concluded with hot spiced cider. As we drove back, we realized we had seen places where even summer visitors rarely go.

May 1, 1966

OH, THE WONDER of this Valley! And the glory of this Valley! Within the past two weeks we have had more miracles around us than could be imagined. We have experienced excitement, beauty, surprise, calm, violence, and have stood in awe before it all.

One sunny, warm afternoon we shed our jackets and worked in our shirt sleeves, uncovering the lilacs to see the green swelling buds on each one. We hilled in some strawberry plants until we could put them into their permanent bed, planted a dozen or so black raspberry bushes, and found a cool, shady place on the north side of the cabin where we set out a hundred lily-of-the-valley pips. We felt hot after our work as we sat in the sun on the porch for a few minutes before going in to prepare dinner. The next day we picked the first bouquet from our outdoor garden—snowdrops and blue squills. One of our puppies was playing with something in the front yard, and when we approached to investigate, we discovered it was the first spring wild flower, a minute salt and pepper blossom. A few days later, the ground was covered with them, and we found, too, the first shiny yellow buttercup. Along the road and in the river bottom below, the willows have turned a bright rosy orange. Our first tulip bloomed over the bench, bright red and yellow, and opened its petals to the warmth of the sun but closed them tightly again as the sun went down behind the mountains in the evening.

Spring is really here, we thought, and called to have Charlie come with his big V plow to dig out the road to the cabin. We could see him on his way, his plow sending up tons of snow as he approached. Later when we drove the Jeep to the cabin, the snow on either side of the road was so high, it seemed like driving through a tunnel. We realized then how deeply we had been snowed in since last December. The SkiDoo can still be used, but the track is bumpy, the snow soft and hollow around the sage bushes. We sink to precarious levels, and the going is a little rough, so we are happy to have the car so near at last.

And then—and then! The day after the road had been plowed, the skies grew dark, a terrific wind came, and when we went to bed that night, we noticed a few flakes, large as silver dollars, falling and blowing in gusts around the front door. We thought that the storm would not amount to much and in the morning we thought the spring sun would be shining with its accustomed warmth on all our spring flowers and budding trees. That's what we thought. But when we awoke the next morning, a familiar silence pervaded the whole out-of-doors, the peaks were not in sight, and fifteen inches of new snow had fallen and blown in deep drifts around the cabin and in the newly plowed road. We tried to move the Jeep, but it stuck, firm and fast, in a four foot drift. We knew any shoveling would be useless. We waited all that day and the next; the snows continued, and the wind abated only momentarily. We resorted again to the SkiDoo which seemed perkier than ever and not a little pleased and proud that its use for this season was not over yet. After the snows had stopped, we again called Charlie to come and plow us out, and this time he brought his big rotary and sent the new snow showering in cascades for many yards beyond the road. He pulled out the Jeep and once more we covered the SkiDoo. We watched our new flower shoots anxiously, but no harm had been done. We swept the snow from the wood pile and again brought in armsful of logs and kindling wood, again built big fires, and brought down from the attic some of the sweaters we had prematurely packed away.

The warm sun soon melted most of the snow, and the spring wild flowers continued to bloom. The wild animals are crossing the river to reach higher feeding grounds, and one evening as we drove to town, we counted twelve elk and thirteen moose, all on their trek to spring and summer pastures. One morning early the dogs set up such a howl that we were roused to see what had excited them and saw three cow moose and two big bulls on their way through our front property to the bench above. The white trumpeter swans fly over the cabin daily, trumpeting as they go. We held our breath when we saw ten white and black pelicans drifting with the air currents high above the canyon. We have finally attracted a pair of Steller's jays at the feeding station. Their brilliant royal blue plumage and coal black heads shine against the snow, their raucous cries echo all day from the feeder as they peck greedily at the seeds and suet there. Hordes of white-crowned sparrows and rosy Rufous-crowned sparrows and juncos swarm over the yard, pecking for seeds and sand, and at night the eerie call of the owl, the honking of the geese, and the quacking of the ducks continue to rise from the river bottom and ponds.

May 15, 1966

ON OCTOBER 26, 1853, Thoreau wrote in his Journal that he had heard the dream of the toads. After a spell of raw, cold weather, there had come the last warm, sunny days before winter set in. In walking by a shallow pool, Thoreau heard, ringing through the air, the dream of the toads, although his companion with him plodded on, noticing it not at all. If there was the dream of the toads in late autumn in Concord, here in our high wilderness living, we listen each spring for the dream of the frogs. For the past few days we have been catching it, faintly at first, but as the sun grows warmer and living things under the earth begin to stir, we hear the dream, growing stronger and clearer.

We hear the dream of the frogs as we walk through the sage and see the grass growing tall and green. After a spring rain, when we step out at night, we hear the dream of the frogs in the fragrance of the sage and the budding cottonwoods. The yard and porches are covered now with the catkins of the cottonwoods, and often the dogs sweep them up with their long tails and come in festooned with the long, reddish tassels. There is the dream in the yellow fritillarias and the white and pink spring beauties which now are covering the sage flats.

A cow moose who stays in the vicinity of the cabin the year around gives birth every other spring to twin calves, and the other day we saw them, small, brown creatures, following their mother as she disappeared into the willows, capering and playing with each other as they trotted behind. Each evening about dinner time we are assured of a spectacle from our living room windows as elk, moose, and deer move up the bench to the forests above. One day, Witty, as she returned from town, saw four fat, sleek brown bears clambering awkwardly up the slope. All of these sights give strength to the melody of the dream of the frogs.

The snow is almost gone, except for isolated patches here and there, and we have spent many hours in the garden, tilling the soil with our new roto-tiller, preparing beds for vegetables, roses, strawberries, and raspberries. We watch each day for new shoots of flowers to appear. The firefly tulips are brilliant and gay just outside our windows, and the bench below the cabin is already covered with a variety of daffodils, each golden trumpet holding tenderly the dream of the frogs. Our delight and excitement knew no bounds when we spotted the first spears of asparagus, and we hurried to get into the ground the lettuce, carrots, beets, peas, onions, garlic, and leek. With the careful planting of each row and with the fragrance of the spring earth, we heard the dream of the frogs, promising miracles to come.

Harry spotted the first Morel mushroom the other day on his ranch. The first was enough for us, and we have baskets in readiness to go in search of more. Surely the dream of the frogs is heard very clearly in every tiny mushroom growing in the damp woods.

There are appaloosa horses in a pasture on the way to town, and lately we have noticed that the mares, about to foal, have been isolated in one section. Each time we drive past them, we strain our eyes to look for colts and fillies. A week ago, we saw the first one, a tiny black thing with a white speckled rump. A few days later we saw five, and yesterday when we stopped the car near the fence, we counted fourteen. Two of them had discovered what their long, spindly legs were for, and found tremendous joy in running about their mothers, chasing each other, and bucking playfully. We heard the dream of the frogs in the foals' tiny bodies, their wobbly walk, their happy playing.

Each morning when the sun touches the daffodils over the bench, each noon, after a morning of gardening, when we take our lunch to the porch, each late afternoon when we bring in logs for fires on chilly spring evenings, and each night as we go out to breathe the clear and fresh air, we hear the dream of the frogs. If we listen carefully and are very still, we can hear the frogs themselves from nearby pools, discussing their dreams in deep, throaty tones, and we know these dreams are not so very different from our own.

June 1, 1966

WITH THIS ISSUE, Cabin Comments is celebrating its third birthday. We look back to three years ago today and remember that we mimeographed only thirty copies of our first few issues and had twenty names on our mailing list. Now we have over four hundred on our mailing list and send our paper to readers in every state except six. We also have subscribers in Europe, the South Sea Islands, and the Orient. If our readers find pleasure in our little paper, that pleasure cannot be any greater than ours in composing it. Often when one begins a venture such as this, the results are unexpected. So it has been with us. The aspect of Cabin Comments which we value most is the many new friends we have made because of it, many of whom we have never met. We want to take this opportunity on our third anniversary to thank all of you for your generous reception of Cabin Comments and to say that we hope sometime to meet our many new friends here in this happy Valley.

Cabin Comments and we, too, are entering upon our fourth year in the Valley. It is comforting to know that never again shall we have to leave, that no longer will duties and obligations in the city call us away. As we have said many times before, this kind of life would not appeal to all. But we know surely what we want and are among the fortunate few who have it. Perhaps that is why we can now look at life with a more steady, level gaze.

June 15, 1966

"THE HORSES will be in tomorrow!" Harry phoned one night. The next day we put on our boots, took a bowlful of oats, our saddles and bridles, and were on our way. Our excitement rose as we approached the ranch, and as we drove nearer the corral, we strained our eyes to catch the first glimpse of our horses. There they were, and as we called each one by name, three pairs of ears pricked forward, and three heads were lifted. We approached them, noticing how well they looked, and they came eagerly to greet us. They nibbled on the handful of oats we had for them and stood quietly as we patted them and slipped the reins over their necks, the bits into their mouths, and fastened the throat straps. We led them out of the corral and after walking them around for a minute, saddled them, got on, and headed for home. As our horses left the ranch property and their horse friends with whom they had spent the winter, they all turned and whinnied a farewell till fall and then started off in earnest for their summer pastures. We rode along the old trail, probably the first riders of the season there, being careful to avoid rocky places as horses had no shoes and we did not want them to bruise their feet. Finally we crossed the road and opened the big gate leading home. The horses paused a minute and looked around to see that everything was the same as it had always been. As we came near the home corral, they stopped in the usual place, let us get off and unsaddle them, and then galloped off to examine their old haunts and stop for a drink at the creek. The next day we had them shod, and the following day took our first real ride of the season. We rode up the draw, noticing the "sarvis" blossoms in full bloom, seeing the trunks of several trees where porcupines had recently gnawed the bark, pausing for a minute to examine the huckleberry bushes to see if there might be plentiful fruit in late summer, and thrilling to see several tiny purple calliope orchids in the forest. The horses remembered each turn, each boulder, each fallen tree. They stopped occasionally to listen to a tree creaking in the wind or a bird singing from a nearby branch. It was a good ride.

The seeds we planted in the garden are up and thriving. The Russell Lupines are growing taller each day and so are the peonies and delphinium. The red and black raspberries and the strawberries look healthy, and we have hopes of fruit this summer. The greenhouse soil has been removed, the greenhouse itself completely scrubbed and cleaned, and fresh, rich earth has been put into the benches.

We want to conclude this issue with a story of a mother robin. When we hitched the burro trailer to the car and drove off with it, we had no idea that we were participating in a thrilling drama, fearful at first but with a happy ending. When we lowered the tail gate at the ranch and were ready to load the first two burros, we walked into the trailer to put a few oats into the trough in front. There before our startled eyes we found a robin's nest with three eggs! We thought of the poor robin left behind who had undoubtedly watched with frantic heart her home and babies disappearing down the road. We carefully lifted the nest out, deposited it in the sun in the car, hoping to return with it before the mother had become completely distraught with fear and anxiety. We left the nest in the car until all burros had been returned and the trailer put exactly where it had been. The mother robin was waiting for us, chirping nervously as she flew from the electric wire overhead to the post of the corral. Carefully, carefully we lifted the little bird home with its precious contents back into the trough precisely where it had been. We feared for the eggs, however, as we thought the mother might have become too alarmed ever to return to them. We tiptoed off and did not dare return to look until evening. But when we went to put the burros in for the night, we walked noiselessly to the edge of the trailer, peeked in, and there sat the mother, one shiny eye watching us closely. We tiptoed off again, happy that all was well, and when we go to the corral now, we listen for the chirp of tiny birds and watch for the mother appearing with worms and insects in her bill. We hope all will go well with the family and that the forty mile ride of the eggs without the protecting wings of the mother will have done no damage.

July 15, 1966

A FRIEND of ours who had just bought property in the Valley asked us the other day what he could expect in the way of annoyances and exasperations in wilderness living. He had heard our enthusiastic tales of life here and wondered if we had anything to say on the other side. What unpleasantness, in other words, had we met? When were the times we became frustrated? At the time, we had no definite answer for him, but perhaps if he had asked his question during the past week, we might have been able to enlighten him.

This has been a week of exasperations, one building swiftly upon the last. First, one of our horses was stung by a vicious wasp, gave a cry of pain, a mighty buck, and his rider went flying through the air and landed with a thud on the ground. The parts for the repair of one of our cars did not arrive and the car still stands idle. The timer on our washing machine gave out, and the replacement is slow in arriving. Laundry is accumulating in the basement. Business papers which were promised us were forgotten and are late. The greenhouse zinnias are doing poorly and we can find no remedy for their ills. The plumbing in the kitchen sink has gone awry and water from the garbage disposal gurgles back into the drain in the second sink. When we thought we had that drain clear, we watched with horror the water bubbling back into the disposal. Back and forth it goes, but never out. Washing dishes seemed an insurmountable problem and we invested in dozens of paper plates. The burros found their way out of the pasture, started gaily down the road in search of adventure, and we were frantic for several hours. We discovered a wasp nest under our eaves near the front door and had visions of being stung as we went in and out. The hinge on the top of our stereo broke, and the top flops down in an infuriating manner whenever we try to put on or take off records. We tried a new recipe for home-baked bread, confident that our loaves would be as golden brown, light, and appetizing as the pictures in the cook book. Our loaves were flat and soggy. Such has been our week.

But—after the injured one who had been bucked off her horse had been taken to the hospital, carefully examined and X-rayed, it was happily discovered that no bones were broken, no damage done except for a few severe bruises which were crippling for only a few days. After a long distance phone call, we were assured the washing machine timer was on its way. Business in town is settled and is proceeding on schedule. A book propped under the stereo top does the job until a new hinge is installed. The plumber arrives tomorrow to administer aid to our ailing pipes and drains. Harry, Sr., happened to see our gypsy burros on the road, turned them toward home, and now they are happy and safe from further wandering. Last night Harry, Jr., lit a flaming torch and burned out the wasps, their egg cone, and their nest.

In addition to these quick remedies for our ills, things of a happy nature have occurred this week, too. The artist Touraine who is in the Valley prepared a delicious Mexican meal for us and some of our friends. Her friend, Phil, entertained us afterward with his beautiful singing and guitar playing. Clarence, Glenn, and Eddie brought in their folding organ and added their fine act to the program. We bought several of Touraine's glorious animal paintings, and she presented us with another, a lovely thing portraying a faun lying in the forest in a shaft of sunlight. She also did a beautiful water color portrait of our dog Bitters which is fantastic in its resemblance to him. Two more portraits of our little girl dogs will follow later. If the zinnias are not thriving, the roses are, and most are in bud. Soon we shall have fresh vegetables from our garden. A few of the new peonies are ready to burst into white and pink blooms, and the yellow and orange poppies are gay against the logs at the front of the cabin. A pair of green-tailed towhees have adopted the bench in back of the cabin as home. A dozen or more new records arrived two days ago and are furnishing delightful evening concerts.

Last night in reviewing our misfortunes of the week, we thought of the easy solutions to our problems and began to think of all the nice things that had happened as antidotes to our ills. Before we went to bed, our unanimous conclusion was that there really were no grounds for complaints, all was working out beautifully, and the week, having begun badly had the happiest of endings.

SUMMER MIRACLES   *August 1, 1966*

A bluebird family lined up on the buck fence, the mother and father hurrying to find enough food to poke down the hungry, squawking throats of the babies.

A spider web just outside the window, sparkling with morning dew and catching in its delicate strands a prism in the sun.

The white laciness of water hemlock cascading like waterfalls over the bench.

A bright-eyed otter watching us curiously from a meadow near the pond.

Four trumpeter swan cygnets swimming happily after their mother on a creek near town.

Twin baby moose romping after their mother across the sage flats.

The first fresh peas and carrots from our kitchen garden.

A tiny wren singing gaily all day long from the top of one of the bucks in the fence as she rests momentarily before continuing to feed her brood in a nest under the eaves.

A summer storm in the west, sweeping with power and majesty over the peaks, gray and black clouds broken only by swift streaks of jagged lightning, while the sky in the north-east remains calm and blue with pink clouds reflecting the last rays of the setting sun.

Gentle rains falling on hot, parched earth, visibly refreshing all living things.

The leaves of the cottonwoods nodding and discussing affairs of the wilderness as the summer breeze passes through them.

A flash of green and magenta as a humming bird pauses briefly near a Sweet William flower.

The opening to the sun of the petals of the first pink climbing rose.

The joy of floating on an inner tube on a quiet mountain lake or river, becoming hypnotized by the flow of water all around till the peaks in the distance seem to move while the floater remains motionless and still.

The happiness of the burros trotting over the sage flats in the late afternoon, headed for their home corral.

The muddy feet and legs of the puppies and the puppy joy after an evening's swim in the pond.

Sweet night fragrances of wild roses, damp earth, and dripping sage
bushes.

A slender, crescent moon above the pines, and someone's turning you to
get the first glimpse of it over your left shoulder.

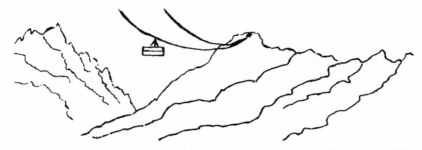

August 15, 1966

FIRST, A MAN must have a dream.

Then, no matter what the obstacles, if his determination, faith, and
courage are great enough, he will see that dream become reality.

On a clear, sunny morning, we started for the new ski area, not a
little excited and tremendously eager to see the new developments. As
we approached the parking area, we noticed that it was full of cars with
license plates from all over the country. We went to the ticket windows
where last winter we used to check in for skiing. We got our tickets,
this time not for the chair lifts, but for the new aerial tramway which
had been in operation for less than a week. We went to the deck to wait
and then looked high above to the summit of Rendezvous Peak, over
four thousand feet above our heads, rising to an elevation of 10,446 feet.
We held our breath, we knew that in a matter of minutes we would be
traveling to that peak. And then—and then—we saw coming slowly,
steadily, smoothly toward us the tram itself, approaching nearer and
nearer by the second. We felt much as people do when they witness the
docking of a mighty ocean liner on her maiden voyage. Then the tram,
filled with excited passengers, slowly moved into the slip, doors were
opened, and the people left, some talking eagerly about the trip, some
exclaiming about the wonders they had seen, some silent with awe.

In a few minutes, trembling with excitement, we stepped into the
tram, the doors were closed, and we began to move very slowly at first,
gaining speed as we progressed, passing over the tops of nearby buildings, rising above the trees, and we, too, had started our voyage to
the clouds.

117

Up, up we went, easily, incredibly smoothly and noiselessly, seeing first the aspen tree tops, then moving still higher over the tips of mighty pines. We moved over the roofs of new homes, passed the second tower, and began to see the Valley open below. Up, up still higher until the trees became fewer and fewer, and we passed over rocky cliffs, deep canyons, huge boulders, and patches of snow. We closed our eyes for a second, felt hardly any sensation of moving, and marveled at the magnificent engineering feat which had made this ride possible. We saw pass by the summits of mountains we had viewed hundreds of times from the Valley floor, noticed the soft grays and pinks of the rocks, and were startled suddenly to see the second tram pass us on its way down. Up, up still further, still climbing, we were lifted with almost no motion at all to the very last tower where the tram came to a slow and easy stop, doors were opened, and we went onto the deck at the top of the world, with a two hundred mile wonderland visible all about us. We paused a moment, then went down the steps to look around to the Valley floor miles and miles below, to the highest mountain in the range almost on a level with us, to peak after peak in the distance, topped by white and apricot-colored clouds. "The purple mountain majesties" stood not above us but all around us. We projected ourselves several months ahead when we knew these windy heights would be under many, many feet of snow and people from all parts of the globe would be thronging in to enjoy the ultimate in skiing. There are many bowls where the skiing will be unsurpassed, steep and swift trails for expert competition, and many less precipitous slopes for the less experienced. We turned in every direction, amazed. We knew that in dozens and dozens of trips on the tram we could not possibly exhaust all the fascinations of peaks and lakes and canyons and clouds.

On the way down we looked for miles and miles into the distance, saw other ranges of mountains on the far side of the Valley, the blue river winding its way back and forth, our ranch on the other side, our cabin hardly perceptible from this distance. Again we moved over the tops of trees, saw high altitude flowers, green Indian paint brush, brilliant yellow blossoms, star-like white ones. Again we passed above the massive boulders, saw the steep and rocky cliff we had watched so often from the cabin windows, down, down, back over the pines and aspens until in an unbelievably short time we felt the tram slow down, and we had moved into the slip and were ready to disembark.

We know what tremendous time and planning have gone into this smooth and safe journey we took. We know, too, the inevitable set-backs and disappointments which came before the tram was pronounced ready

118

to take its first load of passengers. We know the defeatist attitude which many expressed. But, more powerful than all, we know, too, the perseverance, the courage, and the dream which urged on the planners of this gigantic undertaking, urged them on to continue in the face of everything, undaunted, impervious to discouragements. We had just witnessed the result, victory at last and the thrill of knowing that they had built, out of dreams and discouragements, out of hopes and disappointments, the very finest of its kind in the world.

First, a man must have a dream.

Then, no matter what the obstacles, if his determination, faith, and courage are great enough, he will see that dream become reality.

October 1, 1966

COME SPEND a day with us! An autumn day, a golden day! See with us things of wonder. Tiny things, immense, magnificent things. Come spend a day with us!

First, early in the morning, we shall walk the half mile to the Circle H meadow, in our pockets four carrots, freshly pulled from the garden. We shall take the little path at the top of the bench, see the blue river below, the yellow cottonwoods beyond, and feel the fresh morning breezes on our faces. As we approach the meadow, we shall call to the burros and be answered by lusty brays. As we come near the fence, all four little animals will trot to meet us and we shall divide our carrots equally among them. We shall spend a few minutes there, scratching their ears, currying their coats, talking to them of the lovely day ahead. Then we shall start back, this time through the sage, noticing the brilliant red of the Oregon grape, the gold and orange of the aspens on the upper bench, the white of the snow on the peaks. We shall smell the fragrances of the sage, the earth, the purity of the air.

We shall pack a lunch in our knapsack and a little before noon be in the Jeep, headed for the red hills on the other side of the Valley. We shall pass ranches and see the hay cut, baled, and piled in enormous stacks. We shall see cattle beginning to come down to lower pastures. We shall see three horses near the highway, unconcernedly grazing, looking up in mild curiosity at passersby.

We shall turn by the little creek and begin our journey upward, driving through groves of golden aspens, seeing many more on the gentle slopes, made more brilliant by contrast with the dark green pines growing among them. We shall stop often as we round one bend after another to see the river or a mountain lake, green and shining in the sun.

119

We shall look high above us and see another grove of aspens, each leaf quaking in the breeze, each leaf a gold piece, only more precious and more wonderful by far. Soon we shall approach the red, red hills and see more aspens, more pines, and notice a bright orange splash of color here and there of hawthorne and mountain maple. We shall drive over an old wooden bridge, hear the river beneath, see the white water where the current rushes fast over rocky ledges, and know we are near our favorite picnic spot.

As we eat our lunch, we shall look up to the red slope above us, the sparse pines, bent and twisted by strong winds, and perhaps see a mountain sheep or two. Our eyes will come slowly down, and we shall catch a glimpse of a mink darting in and out of the underbrush across the river. Right beside us, we shall notice a swarm of ants among the crumbs we have dropped, see one snatch a piece of bread twice his size, and turn and twirl over twigs and pebbles to carry it away to some secret cache.

On the way back, we shall see the autumn coloring from the other direction, the same winding road, the same lakes and river and mountain slopes, but this time completely different in the more slanting sunlight of afternoon which makes the aspens a deeper yellow, the splashes of undergrowth a darker red. Perhaps we shall hear a honking overhead, and lift our eyes to see a flock of wild geese flying above in perfect V formation. And there in the distance, as we make a sharp curve down, we shall see coming into view the tops of the mighty peaks, silent, majestic, overlooking the entire Valley.

As we turn toward the cabin, two bluebirds will fly just ahead of the car to lead us in, and as we stop, we shall hear the joyful barks of the puppies, welcoming us home.

In the late afternoon we shall saw to proper lengths a load of fine dry kindling wood, stacking it neatly on the wood pile, enjoying the sight of the clean, white sawdust, the fragrance of the freshly cut branches. We shall feel frost in the air as the sun dips behind the peaks, and we shall go to the garden for armsful of multi-colored sweet peas and asters, for some tender green lettuce, and a big, solid head of cabbage.

During dinner, startled by the sharp, frantic barking of the dogs, we shall look from the dining room window, and there, near the basement door, we shall see a fat brown bear, lumbering along the top of the bench. After a short stop to sniff for food, he will be on his way, his bulky body soon disappearing from sight.

In the evening as the autumn moon shines upon the river and we have lit a fire in the living room, we shall listen to music. This evening our concert may be two or three of the Brandenburg Concertos, perhaps a Mozart symphony. The stars come out, the moon rises higher, and we can hear as always the rushing of the river below.

Come spend an autumn day with us!

November 1, 1966

THERE'S SOMETHING about a pair of blue jeans. Certainly they are not handsome. To those who wear jeans for the first time, they seem stiff and uncomfortable. Nothing is hotter in summer or colder in winter. After wearing them out of doors in wintry weather, one shudders when his bare leg touches their iciness. After standing in front of the fire, one cannot bear to touch the great heat which they have accumulated. One snowy day, Harry stood in front of our fire for a minute or two, then jumped away, a pained expression on his face, and, putting his hand to his hip pocket, exclaimed, "A hot rivet on my jeans!" Nevertheless, with all their disadvantages, there's something about a pair of jeans.

As guests at a dude ranch before we had the cabin, we discovered that each of us who stayed longer than a week or so was expected to make his own napkin clip, the more original in design, the better. Some guests carved boats, guns, horses' heads, or cowboy hats. The idea was suggested to us that we take a clothes pin, use the two pins as legs, and fashion a pair of blue jeans. We cut a long tail from one of our blue denim shirts, sewed it in the form of legs, tied a thin leather thong around the waist for a belt, and made a tiny pocket on the hip into which we put a diminutive red bandana. We have been told our blue jeans clothes pin went down in history, but it so completely captured the fancy of one of the children that it mysteriously disappeared when she left.

Margaret told us laughingly an experience she had in ironing Harry's jeans. When they were first married, she wanted to prove herself a meticulous and exemplary wife, doing everything properly and with loving attention. When she ironed his jeans, she tried to press a crease in them. "Try pressing a crease in them," she continued, "and see what happens to the seams!" But she said she has learned much over the years, and now simply hangs them on the line after they have been laundered and leaves the rest to the Western breezes.

A city friend of ours came to one of the guest ranches in the Valley, and seeing the high esteem in which blue jeans were held, bought herself a pair for riding. The cowboys and wranglers at the corral were startled when they saw her appear in her new jeans with the fly zippered in the back instead of the front. One of them approached her quietly and suggested that perhaps she might have her jeans on backward which, much to her chagrin, she did. But, she explained, as she disappeared into her cabin to turn them around, that is the only way women's pants should be worn!

One really becomes attached to jeans only after they have been worn for some time. Then they grow faded and soft, although usually the pockets are hopelessly frayed. It is only then that they become a part of one's self and feel homey and comfortable. They may look disreputable so far as pockets and knees are concerned, but that only increases one's strong attachment to them. Witty had a pair of such jeans. There was a hole in one leg, the knees were threadbare, and the pockets hardly existed. We had long been after her to get some new ones and, hard as we knew it would be, to discard the old. Even with blue jeans there comes a time. But she continued to wear them, explaining apologetically that she would do so only in the garden. One day she, too, must have become convinced that their day had come, and we saw her with a rueful, sad expression on her face, her beloved jeans tucked under her arm, as she headed toward the trash box.

Jeans are useful for sliding down a rocky slope after an illusive but especially juicy cluster of choke cherries. One can walk waist deep through wild rose brambles while gathering rose hips and never feel a scratch. Jeans serve as comfortable pillows when rolled up neatly and tucked under one's head in a sleeping bag. A person can kneel and sit while gardening, and the dirt which accumulates is easily brushed off and does not penetrate the heavy denim. If cut to bermuda short length, they are fine to wear if one wants to float a stream or lake on an inner tube.

There are elegant slacks of wool, soft mole skin slacks, corduroy ones, and fine combed cotton ones which we wear for entertaining and for informal parties. There are attractive cotton and heavy wool ones which we wear in the afternoons and evenings at home. There are knickers and ski pants for winter weather, and even leder hosen knickers for especially elegant ski excursions, but when all is said and done, blue jeans have won our hearts.

January 1, 1967

NEW YEAR'S RESOLUTIONS MADE IN THE WILDERNESS

Living in a wilderness area, beautiful beyond compare, majestic, stately, though violent at times, may we never forget

To protect and revere all living things;

To help maintain the beauty which lies around us, refusing to violate or deface it in any way;

To keep our own dwelling and property in order that they may not inject discordant notes into the order and clean wholesomeness of nature;

To be prudent and cautious when on mountain or stream that no other may have to risk his life to rescue us from danger;

To try to make our own lives more worthy of the splendor which surrounds us;

To meet the dawn of each new day and the evening of each approaching night with gratitude, appreciation, reverence.

January 15, 1967

AT NIGHT we heard a loud crack, almost like the report of a gun. We rushed to the greenhouse, fearful lest one of the glass panes had broken, but when no damage was apparent and the sharp snaps continued, we concluded it must be one of the logs in the wall cracking from the cold. From the back windows we saw the brilliance of the full moon rising behind the butte, and as we awakened early enough the next day, saw it again, just as brilliant, setting in the early morning blue of the sky behind the snowy mountains. We saw the river steam at night and in the morning held our breath at a real snow rainbow, distinct prisms made by the sun above the river as its rays caught the sparkling of the heavy frost feathers. We saw the snow, not too heavy yet, as we drove the

SkiDoo to the road. Winter at last, we thought, but still we scanned the skies eagerly for signs of clouds which might bring a real mountain snow storm. And then, one night, it was New Year's Eve, we noticed that the barometer had dropped, the thermometer had risen, and we smiled happily, knowing precisely what would happen.

Before we went to bed that night, we saw great white flakes of snow in the air. We looked at the porch, at the logs stacked there, and saw that everything was already covered with white. The wind had risen, the skies were dark and starless, and we knew what sights would greet us when we awoke the next morning.

The minute we opened our eyes, we sensed the silence, broken only by gusts of wind. When we went to the windows in back of the cabin, we saw the sills buried in snow, the bare trees with long lines of heavy snow tracing their twigs and branches, the slope leading to the bench an expanse of unbroken white. From the front windows we could scarcely see the saddle shed and corral as the snows whirled and swept over the sage flats. It was with difficulty that we opened the doors, so deep lay the white fluff on the porches. There was no break in the clouds; the barometer was still falling.

As we were preparing breakfast, we ran from one window to the next, happy as children, and watched the snow pile higher and deeper, the fences seeming to sink out of sight before our eyes. We made a pretense at pushing the snow from the porches, but knew our efforts were useless as no sooner would we go indoors than our paths would be completely obliterated. We brushed off and brought in more firewood, built a big fire, made quick mental notes to be certain we had all the provisions we needed, and then settled back to enjoy a real "sock in" storm.

All that day, that night, the next day and night, the following day and night, the snows continued. We made no attempt to get out, even for the mail. The farthest we got from the cabin were the few feet to the woodpile where we floundered, shrieking and laughing, felt one foot and leg sink, then the other, pulled ourselves out, only to sink deep again. The SkiDoo was buried, the snow on the roof accumulated to three feet, and still the storms continued. We phoned a hardware store in town and ordered a snow blowing machine as we knew the cars at the parking lot would require more than hand shoveling if we hoped to dig them out before spring. Harry picked up our machine in town for us and kept it in his car until we could unbury the SkiDoo, make a track, and get out.

One morning the snows had stopped, the skies had grown blue

124

again, and we thought we would be wise to get to the car if we could and at least begin the shoveling we knew would be imperative before we could move the Jeep. We made a track with the SkiDoo and skimmed over the flats, the sage now completely buried, noticing moose and deer tracks on the way. When we got to our car, Harry was there ahead of us, digging out his car. All we could see of our Jeep was a narrow red line we judged to be somewhere near the top. We began shoveling, an easy job as the snow was so light, and then tried out the snow blower. A release of the choke, a tug at the rope, and away she went, whirring along, throwing the snow high all around. Harry had a thermos of coffee with him, and we all stopped occasionally for a coffee break, sitting on the SkiDoo and sled, enjoying the fine winter scene, the mighty snow laden pine trees, the mountains in the distance, rising white and gleaming through the clouds. We had no trouble, and with our snow blower saw the form of the Jeep come into sight much more quickly than we had expected.

Our wish had been granted—the mountain snows had come.

WINTER DESIGNS   *February 15, 1967*

Rare and exquisite embroidery fashioned by bare trees against the brilliant blue of wintry skies;

Bird and animal tracks—tiny footprints of mice; deep and ponderous steps of moose; delicate marks of weasel and marten; dainty feet of chickadees;

Firm and intricate marks of snowshoes; slender, long traces of skis with pointed pole marks on either side;

Sweeps and ripples of snow left by wind on hardened snow, like tracings of waves on white sand shores;

Showers of snow, cascades of bridal veils, the rotary plows fling up as they move like fountains down the road;

Long, tapering icicles which the sun strikes, lighting them one by one, and changing them to nature's glowing candles;

Fences transformed by soft, white fluff from commonplace wire and rail to finest lace;

Whorls and swirls the wind cuts sharply into drifts of snow;

Sparkling frost feathers clinging with airy grace to twigs and branches.

125

IF WE HAD BEEN living in a city, we would have discarded the defective part and gone to buy a new one at once. But we don't live in a city; we live in the wilderness, and when a part of a household appliance breaks down, we try to fix it ourselves before calling for help. We took the vacuum cleaner to the library downstairs to clean the wood shavings a workman had left when he had to remove two or three of the slabs from the ceiling in order to re-set a pipe. We knew we could accomplish the job of cleaning in a few minutes and were eager to see the library neat and livable once again. The vacuum cleaner sounded all right, but did not seem to pick up even the smallest shaving. We put our hands over the nozzle and felt no pull at all, so we realized there was no suction and something was probably clogging the hose. One of us said, "You take one end of the hose, I'll take the other, and we'll look through it. If I can't see your eye and you can't see mine, then we'll be certain it's clogged." One of us moved to the far corner of the room, the other to the other corner, we held up the hose, and each put an eye to it. "Can you see my eye?" said one. "No," was the reply. The same response came from the other, so we began to look around for an instrument long enough to go through the hose and pry out the clogging. We saw a fishing rod and thought it would be just the thing. One of us jammed it through one end of the hose, it struck something within, but failed to move it. "Let me try," said the other and she seized the rod and gave it a mighty poke, but nothing moved. She jiggled it around, jammed it in again, twisted, and turned it, but no success. So hard, however, did she push it that it snapped into three pieces and had to be shaken loose. She looked around for a second and stronger rod, but the owner of the first remonstrated and said we had already broken her eighty dollar rod and under no circumstance were we to experiment with the second. Then our eye fell upon the carpet sweeper handle. That could be screwed loose and would be much stronger and surely would jam out the wedge. We gave the carpet sweeper handle one powerful poke, and before we knew it, it had completely disappeared into the vacuum cleaner hose. The problem now was how to get it out. One of us stood at one end of the room, the other at the other end, each holding an end of the hose, but how to tip it high enough to recover the handle was the problem. As we lifted the hose high, the low end hit two flower pots on the window ledge and knocked them over, adding moist earth, petals, leaves to the shavings on the carpet. Still we could not raise it high enough to get the handle loose. We got chairs and ladders and finally one of us,

126

bumping her head on the ceiling at every move, managed to tip it far enough so the handle slid out. By this time, after so much poking and pushing, the hose resembled nothing so much as the drawing St. Exupery made for the little prince of a boa constrictor in the process of digesting an elephant.

Then we thought of the pickle fork. True, it was short, only five or six inches long, but it had a hook on the end and, if attached firmly to something, could reach down, grab onto the wedge, and pull it out. We got the fork, wired it to a piece of baling wire, and poked it down the hose. Sure enough, we felt it hook onto something, and with our combined strengths, we gave a tug. The baling wire came loose and left the pickle fork in the hose. We soon shook it out, rewired it more securely, jammed it in the hose, felt it catch to something, and then we pulled again. Something was giving! But the fork came loose again, and out it came a second time, having dislodged nothing. "You get out of the way," one of us said, "and I'm going to blow. Maybe that will shoot the lump out the other end." The one stood back, the other pressed the end of the hose to her lips and gave a tremendous puff, turning purple in the face before she caught her breath. Nothing happened. "Maybe if we take it to a filling station, it can be blown out with the air pump," one of us feebly suggested. So frantic were we, that we felt ourselves becoming completely unrealistic and foolish. But it was the pickle fork, we both agreed, that would do the job if anything could, so we resolved to try once again. By this time, we were hot, completely exhausted, frustrated, and utterly helpless. What we thought would be a simple job had proved more difficult than we had ever dreamed. Nevertheless, we were determined. If the job took all night, we would finish it. We reattached the fork to the wire and then began poking with vengeance. Something was moving inside the hose, and we felt that this time we might be victorious. Not a word did we say, we both got on the end of the baling wire again and pulled with all the strength we could muster. The lump was moving! But we did not notice, so great was our excitement, that the vacuum cleaner hose above the lump had grown limp. We continued to tug and pull and were ready to shout with triumph when out came a piece of wire, not baling wire, but another kind of wire. "We've got it!" cried one of us, "But how did all this wire get into the hose in the first place?" And then the ghastly truth dawned. We looked at each other, speechless and horror stricken. "We've pulled out all the insides of the hose!" we cried. "And look at the hose *now!*" There it was, limp as a piece of spaghetti, completely eviscerated! Our efforts at moving the clogged part had been so successful that not only

127

had the lump come loose but all the insides of the hose with it! We were discouraged, disgusted with ourselves, and unhappy about the condition of the library carpet which would have to wait, heaven knew how long, before we could clean it. To say nothing of a completely ruined vacuum cleaner hose! We went to bed with a new low in our confidence in ourselves in the "do it yourself" line.

The first thing next morning we phoned the nearest large city to the company which services our make of vacuum cleaner. We still were cross, frustrated, distraught with our own helplessness. A calm voice at the other end of the wire made us feel more comfortable and reassured. It said that of course the hose could be replaced and another would be in the mail for us that very day. The cost would be $10.87, postpaid.

So—repairing a damaged part of a household appliance in the wilderness area is just as simple as that. See?

April 1, 1967

A JOURNEY through the Valley takes one to magic places he would never guess existed. He may see in the hazy distance, hidden almost from view, a lake called Emma Mathilda. It is difficult to find a thin flow of water down the wispy creek called Horse's Tail. If one travels far enough through mountain meadows, there is a place for quiet thought at Two Ocean Lake. Any number of treasures lie for the seeking at the end of Cache Creek. Windy Point feels the icy breath of unbroken gales, and Timber Island is a deep, dark forest set by some miracle in the wide expanse of flat sage land. If one strains his eyes and is very quiet, he sees graceful forms leaping at incredible speed over Antelope Flats, and one's bucket is filled to overflowing with wild, sweet fruit on Huckleberry Ridge. Great pine forests rise dark and steep along the sides of Black Tail Butte. Wolverine Creek is a wild, lonely spot, but what mountain peace for dipping, bobbing birds at Ouzel Falls! Black Rock is dark and forbidding, but how high and clean is Goose Wing!

Wilderness Falls is the habitation only of animals and birds, untamed and free. Wraith-like beings chant weird cries as they move in solemn steps on the moon-lit shores of Owl Creek. Freshness and purity and fragrance are found at Columbine Cascade, and only after hours of hard and rocky trails should one be rewarded by the cool sapphire blue of Surprise Lake. What apprehension one would feel if lost alone near Rolling Thunder Mountain. Silences deep and peaceful lie at Snowshoe Canyon and Snowdrift Lake, but ear-piercing crashes and rolls at Falling Ice Glacier. The peaks rise through clouds and mists more majestically

128

at Cloudveil Dome, and what eerie and unearthly dreams might one expect after visiting Mystic Isle. Relics of tragedy and violence should be sought at Burned Wagon Gulch, and anything at all can happen at Dead Man's Bar. A maze of animal tracks winds to the shores of Mink Lake and Grizzly Bear Lake. Airy sprites dance by the light of the moon and sing fragments of wistful songs at Forget-Me-Not Lake. Through early morning summer mists appear the blue and lavender beauties of Lupine Meadows.

And what could be lovelier than to come at evening over creeks and trails, through mountain meadows and down steep canyons to the lights of a log cabin on the outskirts of a little Western settlement called Moose?

_April 15, 1967

ON THESE EARLY spring days when we walk over unbroken snow in back of the cabin, we look upon land and river and mountains which show no sign of man. The tall pines reach in pointed spires toward the sky, the snow breaks in huge chunks around the edges of the ponds until there are ever wider expanses of black water where ducks swim, disturbed only by the quick movement of a muskrat or a beaver. Among the ruddy colored willows beyond, we can almost always see two or three moose whose tremendous black forms are prominent against the white of the snow. Coyotes lope through the trees toward the river's edge, and wild geese honk as they fly above our heads. No sign of man, no indication that he has ever been here. Just as it must have been, untouched and unspoiled, for centuries past.

Our thoughts wander, and we muse about what this river bottom, these ponds, these trees, these animals were millions of years ago. Did the same trill of the first spring red wing sound through trees like this centuries ago, we wonder. Did a robin, like this plump one nearby, peck and cock his head to cold earth? Did another flock of juncos or a Hepburn's rosy finch like the one that just flew by, or noisy jays such as these we hear now—did their ancestors alight on a cottonwood similar to this one but long since fallen and gone? A smooth gray rock like this we hold in our hand might have broken the silence millions of years ago and tumbled down the steep slope to splash in the pond below. Squirrels and chipmunks, like these just out of hibernation, must have scampered among bushes and up trees in search of food.

Just like this, perhaps, thousands of years ago. Wild animals, birds, signs of spring. It set us to wondering.

129

We read that the earth, according to modern scientific studies, is four and a half billion years old. Trees such as these we now see, earth such as this we are sifting between our fingers, mountains like those in the distance, birds, animals—all have existed for millions and millions of years. Modern man, we read further, in comparison with the age of the earth, is but two and a half seconds old. Is an age of two and a half seconds in all eternity long enough to learn wisdom and peace? This thought set us to wondering even more.

We read of modern man, unhappy with his work, troubled by his nation's politics, worried about pollution of air and water, harried by noises of civilization, discontent with how he lives, what he has, but uncertain about what he really wants.

We wonder.

May 1, 1967

A COLD, clear morning in April. The sun's first golden shafts were beginning to light the butte in the east. Five o'clock and plenty of time to eat a hearty breakfast, dress in warm clothing, meet the others, and drive with the big rubber floats to the starting point. There was frost in the air and a chilly wind was blowing, but the sun grew warmer, the higher it rose. We knew we had plenty of hot coffee in thermos jugs, nourishing sandwiches, and we could imagine nothing more glorious than floating the river, snow still on the ground, river low, and we hoped plenty of game to see on the shores.

The minute the float had been put into the water and all of us had climbed in, our voices instinctively became hushed. Most of the time we sat in silence, watching, ever watching, for the first sign of wild life on the snows near the river, in the forests bordering it. There was the familiar lap of the waves on the float, an occasional soft bump of an oar in its lock, the dip of an oar into the water, but aside from these sounds, all was quiet. Suddenly someone raised a hand to motion toward a tree, cut down recently, another like it a little farther off—the work of beavers. Then a whispered voice said, "An elk!" and there, unperturbed, was a massive cow elk, standing motionless on the shore. As we came nearer, with a toss of her head, she turned, noiselessly, moved back, then trotted into the brush, showing only her light rump, looking as she disappeared like a gigantic powder puff. Ducks flew about us, mallards, mergansers, golden eyes, the latter making a thin whistling sound with their wings as they flew low over the water. Rarely were we out of sound of the honking of geese, some in the air, others strolling peacefully on shore.

130

Once we laughed to see a pair walking companionably over the pebbles at the edge of the river. The male urged the female on, nipping at her from behind to hurry her along, complaining all the while in typical masculine fashion of her dilatory feminine ways.

On, on we floated, slowly, easily, taking our time, eager to see all the animal life possible. More work of beavers was seen on shore, and several times we saw the large black holes which led to their houses. The wind blew fresh, and we were grateful for every stitch of warm clothing we had worn and for the carpeting on the floor of the float which kept out chill dampness from the river. But the sun was warm, and we could feel ourselves becoming more burned and brown by the minute.

Around a bend we saw what looked like seven gigantic mushrooms growing on inordinately long, slender stems. As we rounded the bend, our mushrooms proved to be the heads and long necks of seven white trumpeter swans. They continued to swim peacefully until they eyed the approaching float and then with one sweep, their wings lifted them gracefully into the air, and we saw them fly off, then circle back, and disappear at last into the blue of the sky.

A massive bald eagle perched on a dead tree just ahead of us, and as we drew nearer, he, too, took to the air, but he and several others like him were overcome by curiosity and followed the float for several miles down the river. Once, around another bend, we spotted a herd of elk drinking from the river. They looked up as we came near, watched for several minutes as the float approached their watering place. Then one, more timid than the rest, turned, the entire herd with him, and trotted in a dignified, sedate manner over the meadow into the sheltering forest beyond. Many large, awkward moose peered at us from the shore, then turned, and moved toward the brush and trees. We noticed how they were shedding their winter coats, looking shaggy, unkempt, and tousled.

A pair of coyotes came swiftly over the crest of the steep cliff above the river, raced down the snowy slope, and romped on the shore. They had startled a herd of fifteen or twenty deer who ran quickly up the side of the slope to the very top where they collected in a group, turned, and watched the coyotes below.

To our right as we moved on, we saw the snowy mountains, clear in the bright sunlight, impressive, rising tall and majestic. The snow glistened on their slopes and farther down, the trees showed black against the white. The sky above was blue, a few white clouds curled around their peaks and moved slowly down to their base, casting shadows of interesting and fleeting shapes.

POETRY LIES about us these spring days, poetry spoken in the rhythm of the winds, the songs of the birds, the chatter of chipmunks and squirrels, poetry chanted in the slow blossoming of wild flowers, the fragrance of earth released from winter's cold, the hum of bees, the grace of a butterfly. We feel it and hear it everywhere—

In the daffodils, white and yellow, brilliant in the sun by day, shining like stars by night under the moon;

In the silence of a mountain lake as we canoe over its clear depths and catch the smell of pine needles in the sun;

In the joyful note of the wren back to her old nesting place, perched on the fence post, tail feathers perkily upright, throat filled with song;

In the fresh spring scent of the first violets;

In the tender shoots of early peas and radishes in the kitchen garden;

In the green laciness of young leaves on tall and slender aspens;

In the delightful odor of sticky cottonwood buds;

In all young things, wobbly newborn colts, white-faced calves, looking upon a world, fresh and new, made purely for their delight;

In the inquisitive kitten face of a marten looking from the fence into our picnic party and then scampering up a tree from which vantage point it could have a better view;

In the song of frogs at dusk;

In the blue sky of evening, swept by apricot-colored clouds;

In the full moon sending a path of silver across the river and into the ponds;

In the flames of a bonfire after dark, the snap of twigs, the fragrance of wood smoke, the taste of hot toasted marshmallows held on the end of long forks over the last glowing coals;

In the silence of a starry sky, the last sleepy chirp of a restless bird settling down for the night.

THE LATIN NAME for a Morel mushroom is *esculenta* which means edible. Morels come only in the spring, and, we read further in our mushroom book, like best a limestone country, a loamy soil which is rich in humus. They grow in deciduous forests and in grassy spots. The cap of this mushroom resembles a small sponge.

For weeks before Morel mushroom time, we watch the weather carefully rejoicing when there are soft, warm rains alternating with hot, sunny spells. We become dejected when the spring is dry or too cold, and no matter how much it rains, if the skies clear only occasionally and the warm sun shines through the clouds even briefly, we say to each other, "Good Morel weather—when shall we plan to take our baskets and go in search of them?"

To us, Morels mean starting early in the morning, well prepared for damp earth and wet grasses. They mean taking empty baskets with the hopes that in a short while they will be filled to overflowing with our fragrant harvest. The delight of searching for such treasures! If we knew precisely where to find them each year, if they grew abundantly each spring, part of the fun would be lost. It is their mystery and perversity which is part of their charm. We may look for a long, long time and not find one, but always we have the delicious feeling of anticipation that just around the next big cottonwood or in that grassy place just beyond the stream, we shall find a whole bed of them, some growing six or eight in one cluster. No treasure of precious jewels could bring us more thrill than first one tiny sponge-like growth, then another, then two or three more. We find ourselves breathing more rapidly, our hearts tripping like hammers because we are certain that if we find one, there surely must be hundreds of others close by if only we have the patience and the sharp eyes to spy them.

And as we search, there are hundreds of other treasures to see. The last time we went on a Morel expedition, one of us called, "Look what I found!" We rushed over to see, and there, hidden almost from sight in the tall grasses, was a perfect bronze-colored mission bell, one of the prize wild flowers, petals still wet with the last rain. A little farther on, one of called, "An elk!" and as we looked up, we heard thundering hooves. Through the forest, within feet of us, raced a beautiful cow elk, startled by strange figures in her home territory. Once very near us a doe sped out of the trees, leaped over the fence, and disappeared into the woods across the creek. We knew a fawn was lying near, motionless and still.

Equipped with sturdy sticks and dressed in our hip boots, we cross rocky mountain streams. Once, in such a crossing, we heard a strange sound which we discovered was a mother duck, talking softly to eight little yellow balls of fuzz, swimming saucily after her downstream. We

133

tramp tirelessly over miles of grassy, open spots and through forests. We rarely raise our eyes from the ground, so fearful are we that we may miss a hidden Morel. Certainly we must resemble Mammon with his eyes cast down constantly on the golden streets of heaven.

We are happy if we see the spotted coralroot, a member of the orchid family, or, even rarer, the tiny, delicate calypso orchid growing at the foot of some mighty tree. We notice the pure white of the wild strawberry blossoms. We start as we see a flash of orange through the trees and realize the Western tanager is near. His clear, sweet note as we pass is one of the loveliest solos in the forest symphony.

We must work fast and pick all we can, because the Morels do not last. All else is forgotten during these days in June when our attention is given to looking for these little sponge-like mushrooms. But, find them or not, a good year for them or not, the search for them has been thrilling and there is so much to see and hear as we wander, baskets in hand, eyes to the ground, looking.

The Latin name for a Morel mushroom is *esculenta* which means edible. They come early in the spring and prefer a limestone country, a loamy soil which is rich in humus. We know they come early in the spring and what kind of soil they like best. But the book never tells all the other things we know about Morel mushrooms. All the joy and excitement we feel when we plan a day of searching, all the thrill when we come upon them. The book on mushrooms doesn't mention these things at all, and we think that however musical the Latin name of *esculenta* may be, it does not begin to carry the magic which these sponge-like mushrooms hold in their funny little pointed caps.

July 15, 1967

PERHAPS it's our incurable love of gadgets that makes us devotees of the catalogs that come to us by the dozen from mail order houses all over the country. Whatever the reason, when such a catalog arrives, there is deep silence in the cabin as each one of us turns the pages thoughtfully, dog-earing those which show things we simply must order. And then the joy when, a few days later, we see a notice of a package in our mail box and know that our order has arrived!

We have all kinds of silver cleaner, most of which promised to keep silver tarnish-free for incredibly long periods of time. But ours, for some unknown reason, continues to tarnish badly and recently, tired of the frequent polishing and rubbing, we bought a set of stainless steel silverware which we know needs no attention at all. But we have on the shelf five bottles of silver polish as yet unopened. We have a miniature vacuum cleaner with a tiny bag for catching dust. It runs on a small battery and although it doesn't have enough suction to pick up a crumb, we think it is too cute to discard and some day we may find a use for it. We have all kinds of garden equipment—a sprinkler which will soak or spray, a two-way faucet with twin controls which makes one outdoor faucet into two, but the controls are in the back, and it is frustrating to feel for them without being able to see them. Usually, when trying to direct the flow of water, we manage to succeed, but we get well drenched in the process. We have two long canvas hoses which soak the rose garden admirably; when they are draped over the buck fence to dry, they give an ornamental look of festoons and garlands. We have tiny rolls of cedar wood paper for clothes hangers. When we first opened their box, they were fragrant as a pine forest in the sun, but, alas, the fragrance soon wore off and now they are nothing but nuisances bobbing at the top of the hangers. We have a windproof napkin stand for our picnic table, but so fragile is it that we hang on for dear life to the napkins and it, too, whenever a gust of wind blows our way.

We have always had trouble moving our heavy refrigerator so we could clean behind it, but, oh joy, there was the answer to our problem—four easy-glide teflon casters. We ordered two sets, but never thought of the problem of lifting the ponderous appliance onto them. The easy-gliders remain in a drawer. We got two comb cleaners but were dismayed when we opened the box as they looked exactly like the cut off ends of bottle brushes. They do not work efficiently and we have returned, sadder but wiser, to our old brush for cleaning combs. To the one of us who is responsible for most of the house work, the panacea for dusting has been reached at last—dust mops with short handles which looked in the catalog as if they would swish lightly around furniture legs and lamp shades. In her elation, she ordered six. When they arrived, they were stiff and could never slip easily into difficult places. They are firm and practically indestructible and we shall be using them to paddle naughty puppies for centuries. A "broom bloomer" came next, a contrivance for putting on the end of a broom to sweep cobwebs from ceilings and high places. This is quite elegant as it has a lovely mink trim at one end. We were carried away by advertisements of furniture polish, guaranteed to magnetize a cloth so it would easily pick up all particles of dust with one swipe. We have seven cans of this wondrous stuff, but so ardent did we become in spraying the liquid polish onto the cloth that it gave too heavy a coating to the furniture and now the tables and chairs have

135

become magnetized. Only one who has seen our dusty furniture can imagine the dire result.

One of us is deplorably poor in arithmetic, still counts on her fingers when no one is looking, and she delighted in ordering a pocket-sized adding machine which multiples and subtracts, too. So complicated is the gadget, however, that she tossed it disdainfully aside and has returned to the more simple and, as she says, accurate method of finger counting. We were appalled when a new laundry gadget arrived, a gallon plastic jar with ribbed sides. If you douse woolens or delicate fabrics in it for 1 to 3 minutes, the advertisement said, the clothes come out spotlessly clean. It looks, too, as if the clothes might be well agitated if one squeezed the jar in and out as he would an accordion. The advertisement said further that when not in use as a washing device, the jar is valuable for carrying cold lemonade to picnics. We have put it to neither use as yet but have an eye on it for use in the winter to carry gasoline for our SkiDoos. We have not as yet tried any of the beauty aids advertized in our catalogs, eye lash curlers, girdles which produce slimming effects, braces for straightening stooped shoulders, or straps to hold up sagging chins, although once we were tempted to order three wigs to startle our friends in the Valley.

There is one more thing we have ordered and at the moment are impatiently awaiting its arrival. It is a packet of 24 wondrous seeds, quick germinating, producing brilliant flowers. These, when dried, turn into sponges. The transformation must be miraculous and we can hardly wait to watch. We are assured the flowers will produce a five years' supply of sponges for us, and in that case, such cleanliness we shall know! We can then discard all our floor mops, dust mops, furniture polish, and live in a state of purity for five long years simply by swishing one of our homegrown sponges over furniture, windows, and floors. And all this for only 49 cents! The economy of this is amazing and we just know it will work—it couldn't possibly fail us.

MID-SUMMER JOURNAL   *August 1, 1967*

Wild flowers as far as eye can see, red of the scarlet gilia and Indian
    paintbrush, blue of the lupin, flax, and harebell, pink of the wild
    geranium, eglantine, and wild hollyhock, gold of the sun flower
    and butter-and-eggs, white of the water hemlock and daisies, cream
    of wild buckwheat, mauve of flea bane;

Wisps of cotton from the cottonwood trees floating through the air and
    drifting to the roadsides, reminders of the first light snow;

A baby moose, fat and brown, following its mother over sage flats and river bottoms; a gentle-eyed fawn, peeping shyly through the trees as a doe nearby keeps apprehensive but courageous guard;

Hot, bright sun at midday, fresh, cool mornings and evenings;

Songs of myriads of birds; cheep of ravenous chipmunks and pine squirrels, tails a-quiver with ecstasy, as they devour melon seeds at the bird feeder;

A row of baby bluebirds perched on the fence being fed succulent insects by their parents;

Fragrance of wet sage and clover after a summer shower;

Sharp streaks of lightning over the mountains followed by the rumbling complaint of distant thunder;

The drone of bees and the whirr of humming bird wings among the honey-filled blossoms;

The green beauty of a kitchen garden, the taste of its first spinach, lettuce, and radishes; the reward of labors realized in blossoming peas and heading cabbages;

Taste of early garden strawberries, sweet and warm from the sun;

Fast disappearing snows from the peaks; brown mountain creeks; white water rushing over jagged boulders in swelling streams;

Burros' ears visible in lush feeding grounds, their sleek, plump bodies hidden in tall meadow grasses;

Riders on the bench above, moving slowly through the trees along narrow mountain trails;

Puddles in the road after rain, edged with the gold of pollen;

Mourning doves sitting in pairs on the electric wires, murmuring soft, plaintive cries;

Sunlight through wet leaves, a rainbow spanning the heavens, and a world washed green and pure.

August 15, 1967

EVERY CAMPER who packs into the hills has some favorite piece of equipment to which he remains steadfastly loyal in spite of its age or outmoded attributes. Trips deep into wilderness areas are unthinkable without this old standby. Sometimes it is a favorite axe, sometimes a duffle bag, sometimes a panier, sometimes a sleeping bag. Such an esteemed piece of equipment was Delilah, and we are not about to desert her now for something new and more modern.

137

Delilah is not attractive, especially now as her glossy black exterior is bent and rusted, and her sides are pitifully caved in. Her stove pipes are dented, and when put into place present an appearance of untold age. She gives forth mysterious creaks when her doors are opened and shut. But we love her in spite of her present decrepitude because we remember the glory which once was hers.

Delilah is a camp stove who gave unsurpassed service in her day. If on damp, rainy days in the hills, she refused to light into roaring fires and produce hot breakfasts immediately, she always came around eventually, and those who loved her understood how to humor her and bring out her best. On sunny, warm days, she performed to perfection, so one's only recourse against her occasional temperamental ways was to remain loyal, wait patiently, and, above all, understand and know how to coax her vagaries out of her.

Delilah experienced all manner of excitement on her many camping trips; she was there when from the top of Huckleberry Mountain we saw five forest fires crown in the distance. She provided heat and comfort when campers were cold and wet. She was there when we had to rush one unfortunate camper back to civilization for an emergency appendectomy. She shivered fearfully in rain storms when, dripping and cold, she was put on a pack horse, led along slick clay roads, and felt the horse's hooves under her take one step forward only to slip back two. She was there on sunny days when campers spent the day fishing on mountain streams and lakes, and it was always Delilah who provided a hot fire to fry the fish crisp and brown for dinner. It was Delilah's miniature oven that turned forth hot huckleberry muffins and cakes, something no ordinary camp stove would dream of attempting. Delilah was the first thing to be unpacked when camp was set up, the last thing to be stowed away when camp broke up. She was given the place of honor on the pack horse. She was given more care and attention than the campers themselves. She became famous in the hills and has produced hot sustenance for numberless cowboys, wranglers, and campers.

It had been years since we had seen Delilah. We had spoken of her often with affection and happy memories. We had laughed indulgently when we remembered her capricious ways. We never thought we should see her again, but she remained in our thoughts as one of the chief reasons why we loved pack trips and cook-outs.

The ranch where Delilah spent her retirement was recently sold, and much of the equipment there was for sale before the new owners took over. We went to see what we could buy and decided upon a crowbar, a strong towing chain for the new Jeepster, two handsome benches for the porches, a couple of Dutch ovens. One of us said hopefully but a little fearfully, "You don't happen to have Delilah, do you?" "Indeed we do," was the answer, "but she has not been used in years and perhaps she is hardly worth carrying away." We were led to the saddle shed and, after stepping over saddles, tarps, kegs of nails, there in a far, dark corner, we spied our love. True, she was covered with dust and looked extremely forlorn, but we exclaimed with joy and said at once that we would take her. She was lifted out of her dark and cobwebby nook, piece by piece of her old black and familiar shape coming into sight, her crooked stove pipes appearing last. Breathless with excitement, we loaded her into the back of the Jeep and drove her home, being careful to take the bumps and ruts on the way with great caution lest we jolt her unmercifully and see her dear sides fall to pieces entirely.

That same evening, so eager were we, we took Delilah to our picnic area, set her up with trembling hands, gathered twigs and dry branches, and lit the fire, the first, we are certain, she had experienced in many a year. We held our breath as we heard the twigs begin to crackle. When the first curl of smoke rose from her twisted stove pipe, we cheered lustily and performed a ceremonial dance around her. But, alas, there were many leaks in Delilah, smoke escaped where it shouldn't, heat was lost through her many rusty holes. She tried her best, but could not produce sufficient heat to cook our dinner, so, hoping she would not despair and give up entirely in feeble collapse, we prepared dinner on our new grills.

But the story has a happy ending after all. Delilah still stands at our picnic area in the place of honor. Birds once again sing about her, she hears the familiar murmur of a mountain stream nearby, and the trees whisper in gentle conversation above her. We have paid a visit to Jim's Welding Shop in town, and this winter she will be worked on and given new sides, top, and pipes. Her oven will be sealed tight to produce muffins and cakes once again. We shall call for her in the spring, set her up again under the trees and close to the stream. She will regain her lost beauty and dignity and once more resume her coveted position as queen of the grills and Dutch ovens. We love her as dearly as ever, and if she lapses into moments of perversity, as we know she will, we shall only smile and understand. We are very happy and pleased to have her as ours, and all those who knew her may be assured that Delilah will cook again.

September 15, 1967

WE WERE JIGGLED and joggled until our teeth chattered as we guided our roto tiller through the earth to prepare it for spring planting.

In late May we raked the dirt smooth and dug straight and shallow trenches for the planting of seeds. We spent hours of back-breaking work dropping into their dark, moist beds the carrot seeds, the lettuce seeds, the cauliflower plants, the onion sets, and many more. We enjoyed the work, but we must admit that at times we thought how cheaply and easily we could buy lettuce at the store or frozen and canned vegetables, and we wondered if perhaps this wasn't all an expenditure of needless time and effort.

But then came the thrill when we first spied the Alaska peas in almost imperceptible green rows, the first shoots of asparagus, the leaves of the early radishes, and we began to realize that never would we find such pleasure as lay ahead of us in our garden in any boxes of frozen vegetables commercially prepared. Soon it was time to sprinkle the garden and keep the tiny seedlings wet and fresh. Then came weeding, and we became so accustomed to going on our hands and knees through the rows of vegetables that it was difficult to straighten our backs and walk erect. We remember the first snowy white blossoms of the peas, the red blossoms of the Chinese peas, the delicate sprays of the first carrot tops, and the silvery green of the kohlrabi. We watched the plants growing bigger and healthier by the day. We had our first meal of beets, our first salads made with our own lettuce, and what a banquet when we served the first tender green peas! On cool nights we watched the thermometer anxiously and listened for radio weather reports. On these nights we went out with flashlights and covered the more tender plants with protective sheets and cardboard boxes as we apprehended frost.

Then, all of a sudden, everything matured at once. We had bushels of lettuce, green lettuce, red lettuce, and small, firm heads of the Boston variety. We had quantities of radishes, red ones and the long, slender icicles. We had green string beans and yellow wax ones. We ate vegetables at most meals, and finally, so abundantly did the garden produce, that we began to freeze the overflow. By the last count we have enough in the freezer for over sixty meals. As we walk through the garden, we realize there is much more to come. The parsnips, carrots, and beets will be left in the ground, having been carefully planted where we know the snow will not drift too heavily. We shall mark these rows with tall poles and all winter dig through the snow and find root vegetables as fresh and crisp as they are in summer. The potato plants yielded a bumper crop, and in the cellar we have crate after wooden crate of them.

In addition to the meals our vegetable garden has furnished, there is plenty of aesthetic pleasure there, too. The vegetables, growing in neat, even rows, are as attractive in their way as the flowers—the green and red of the lettuce, the shiny red stems and broad, green leaves of the Swiss chard, the feathery asparagus plants ornamented with bright green berries, the misty green of the broccoli. The parsley adds attraction to the border of the garden, and the leek and white and red onions add fragrance. The French shallots, so good in pork roasts and pork chops, wonderful when used to flavor spinach, are all laid out in rows to dry on the ground, and soon will be gathered into baskets for winter keeping. The red and green cabbages are massive with leaves as big as elephant ears, and cupped in the center of each plant is a firm, large head. The heads of the cauliflower are fine and white.

We know now that all our concern about frost, all the labor which went into the garden have been well worth it, and if there were moments of fatigue or discouragement, all are now forgotten as we look through seed catalogs and begin to plan our kitchen garden for next year.

We are not the only ones who think our kitchen garden is a fine addition to the cabin. Night before last as we were eating dinner, one of us glanced toward the garden and called the others to look quickly. There, crawling clumsily through the rails of the buck fence was a fat brown bear. After he had managed to squeeze his chubby body through, he dropped to all fours and started down the garden path, walking slowly and sedately and sniffing the air as he went. He stopped to admire the red petunias along the edge and the multi-colored pansies, sweet peas, and asters. He stuck his nose into the Canterbury bells. He smelled the cabbages, he looked at the golden poppies, he sniffed the onions. On he went, never once stepping from the path, deliberately, appreciatively, until he had surveyed the entire garden, looking with pleasure at the flowers, with fascination at the vegetables. Having made the tour, he went back to the fence, found the same place through which he had entered, looked back once more, gave a shake of his head which indicated approval, and lumbered over the edge of the bench out of sight.

October 1, 1967

WE HAVE FINISHED our Christmas shopping. We realize that we are obnoxiously efficient, obnoxiously far-sighted, obnoxiously smug about this, but the advantages of being able to look at packages ready for Christmas wrappings, to have checked off, one by one, the various presents we are giving, to feel no dread of last minute rush—these advantages are significant. We think, too, it's nice to be able to stretch the holiday spirit into several months instead of a few frenzied days. Also, and perhaps this is the most important reason we do our Christmas shopping early, we sometimes like to succumb to temptation and say, "Here's a gift I picked up in town for you today." That way the fun can be even more prolonged as we know we shall have to choose another gift to take the place on Christmas morning of the original one.

But unforeseen troubles may occur because of such early shopping. The other day one of us was fretting because she had nothing to read. She had finished the current magazines, the newspaper, and the book which had occupied her for the past few days. "Nothing to read!" she wailed as she wandered aimlessly about, picking up this book, then that, putting them down as not quite appealing for the moment. Another member of the family went quietly to her bedroom and returned with a package which she handed to the restless one. "Here's something to keep you occupied for quite a while," she said. "I had intended to give it to you for Christmas, but you might just as well have it now." It was Harold Nicolson's Diaries and Letters which was fallen upon immediately, and the fretful one has been quiet ever since.

Last week one of us went to town and during her shopping expedition had to phone home to ask an important question of the other two. The question to be answered by the two at home was the size shoe each wore. That evening after dinner there was a discussion between the two about what kind of shoes they would find under the tree on Christmas morning. "Do you suppose they are for summer wear or winter wear?" asked one. "What color do you think they will be?" asked the other. "I hope they'll have sturdy soles as thin ones are not good for this rocky ground." The one who had made the purchase overhead the discussion, smiled slyly and asked, "Whatever in the world makes you think my gift to you will be, of all things, shoes?"

One of us came from town recently and happily announced, "I got a Christmas present for each of you today!" The curiosity of the others was insatiable and finally the information was extorted from the first that the gifts were articles of wearing apparel. She said to one of us, "I hope you like yours—it's wild and gaudy." Something wild and gaudy to anticipate for three whole months! What a delight! Further hints will be forthcoming if only we employ patience, and we wager that by the time a few more days have passed, we'll not only know what the wild and gaudy object is but very possibly even be wearing it.

One of us is devoted to St. Francis. Simply and for no other reason than that he loved animals. Many times she has threatened to buy a statue of St. Francis. She already has one, a tiny one, beautifully carved in wood, and brought to her by friends who visited Assisi. But each time she speaks of getting a larger one, the other two protest violently and say they have not seen one lovely enough. Most are garish, modern, unattractive, poorly done. A week ago two of us went to a very fine gift shop on the other side of the Valley. There in the show case, prominently displayed was a remarkable statue of the saint, done in soft brown and white ceramic, the cowl on his robe gently draped over his head, a beatific expression on his face, two small birds at his feet, another on his shoulder. Resistance to this extraordinary statue was impossible, so our animal lover bought him, had him wrapped carefully and, much to her surprise, found no opposition from the other. At home when the statue was apprehensively unwrapped and shown to the third member of the family, something strange and unexpected happened. A look of horror then a cry of dismay from the third one who had not been present at the statue's purchase. She went quickly to her room, returned with a wan look, holding a box which looked suspiciously like the one just unwrapped. "Merry Christmas," she said weakly.

Then there was the beautiful portrait of the one hundred year old Indian woman, Princess Angeline, daughter of Chief Seattle. We all had stopped at the very elegant art gallery in town many, many times to admire her. Each secretly longed for her—but the price! We all had decided that we would find something else less expensive, but we could not forget Princess Angeline, and knew that anything else would be only second best. Only hours before the gallery closed for the season, when the owners were packing in big crates paintings, antiques, exquisite objects of art, one of us decided it would be now or never. She phoned the gallery and learned that Princess Angeline was still there but ready to be packed and taken for display to another gallery on the west coast. Before she could argue with herself and possibly talk herself out of such a rash act, she was in the car and away, her check book tucked into the back pocket of her blue jeans, just in case. When she arrived at the gallery, there was the Princess waiting for her, as magnificent as ever. She explained to her friends, owners of the gallery, that she wanted her for a Christmas gift to the cabin. Right now you want her? Right now?" they asked incredulously. "Yes," was the answer. "Right now before I have a chance to change my mind." "Now, Betty," they said as they wrapped her carefully and prepared the bill of sale for insurance purposes, "don't tell. Don't say a word to the others. Just put her away and have a lovely surprise on Christmas morning." "Oh, I wouldn't tell for the world. This must be kept a secret," she answered, but already she felt qualms about being able to keep quiet about it. She became more excited the nearer home she got. She stepped on the gas to get there more quickly. "What a pity to hide Princess Angeline for three whole months. Think

143

of all the enjoyment we shall be missing. But I musn't. I mustn't," she thought. When she arrived at the cabin, the other two, not knowing where she had gone, were waiting for her on the porch. "What in the world do you have?" they asked as she moved the large treasure from the back seat. "What can it possibly be?" And then she could stand the suspense and excitement no longer. Waiting for three months to tell the secret would be asking something beyond human endurance. So she bounded up the porch steps with the package and cried, "Merry Christmas to the cabin! This is Princess Angeline!" Breathlessly, we hung her in the most appropriate place, turned on the light above her, and all stood back, thrilled to goose flesh and tears. Already she dominates the entire cabin, our eyes wander to her all day long and all evening long, too, as we sit around the fire. Are we happy we did not pack Princess Angeline away until Christmas? The answer is yours.

A merry Christmas shopping to all of you, too!

October 15, 1967

FROM THE BACK windows of the cabin we look across to our ranch on the other side of the river and see the cottonwoods a deep gold with patches of ruddy underbrush near the shore. We stand under the cottonwoods which shade the back of the cabin, look up, and if there is a wind, see showering around us pure gold pieces. The aspens on the bench above are yellow, and as the sun touches them, they glow like festive candles. Some are rosy tipped, some are solid yellow, some, not having turned completely yet, still carry leaves of summer green. A straight, even row of them with slender, young trunks are girls in ballet dresses of bright autumn gold and in the wind they move in graceful, airy dance steps.

A group of us took our canoes and went for a gala picnic to a near-by mountain lake. We were the only ones for miles around, and the deep silences which surrounded us bespoke the departure of summer visitors and the arrival of autumn to the Valley. The trails around the lake were silent—only the chattering of a squirrel in the high pines and his dropping of cones from above were heard. Once the sharp cry of a Clark's nutcracker and the glimpse of gray feathers in the sun came to us, but nothing more. We walked over mountain trails made soft by age old pine needles, past rosy huckleberry bushes, down to the lake, silent and smooth. We saw as we paddled quietly near the shore, a massive bull moose and near him a cow. The cow looked at the gay canoes and then vanished into the underbrush, but the bull, in a gallant spirit, snorted and blew at us and tossed his head, mighty and powerful.

We see the sun rise from behind the butte. We see fresh snow on the peaks and the early rays of the sun touch each one with a rosy glow. We see in the early morning the autumn mists rising from the river. We see the blue smoke curling from our chimney and catch its fragrance in the clear air. Once again we take turns at the joyful task of splitting wood and carrying it in, ready for the next fire. We hear in the evening the elk bugling from the bench above, crystal clear in the frosty air. We listen as one elk after another takes up the mating cry, sending clarion chimes from one end of the bench to the other. And there, as the skies grow darker, against a gray cloud hugging the side of the mountain and accentuating this October splendor, is a perfect V as the black forms of wild geese, honking as they go, fly out of sight into the autumn skies.

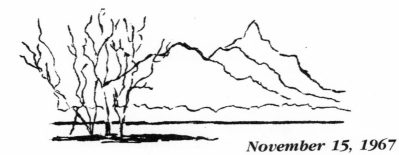

November 15, 1967

The brilliance of nature vanished with the last golden aspen leaves;
The fading yellow November dandelions, huddling close to earth for protection,
The tall wild hollyhocks, the graceful water balsam, now only bunches of dried branches and brown leaves.
But there is life, there is color yet, muted, more subdued, giving proof that summer splendors
Do not perish, but give evidence always
Of re-created life and growth and strength
Nourished by cold earth, fallen leaves, snow and winds and winter sun—

Rough, bare cottonwood trees, straight or gnarled,
As snows and winds have fashioned them;
A golden eagle, a-top one,
Silhouetted, stark and ominous, against the sky;
Silver of aspen trunks; green-black of pines against
First dusting of snows;
Gray-green sage crowned with tawny seeds;

145

The purity of wild white swans against a blue and wintry sky.

Slender, blond grasses, bent low by buffeting November winds;
By creeks and streams
Red willows, silvery purple in the distance;
Shiny pinks and browns and striped grays of stones, cold and wet;
The sharp black outline of a massive moose, moving deliberately
Through fresh, clean snow;
The purity of wild white swans against a blue and wintry sky.

Flash of green and iridescent purple of ducks in ponds;
Red of woodpeckers' heads
Bobbing and pecking at suet;
Delicate grays and whites, accented by black,
On wings of chickadees and nutcrackers;
A streak of black and white—a magpie skimming low
Over dark ponds;
The redness of rose hips, clinging bravely
To bare and thorny branches;
Late afternoon's gray clouds,
Edged with mauve and rose and fiery red, enshrouding the peaks;
The purity of wild white swans against
The silvery mist
Of a rising moon.

December 1, 1967

IT STARTED with the bazaar given by the ladies of the LDS church
the Saturday before Thanksgiving. We realized we had finished most of
our Christmas shopping, but, since we had weakly succumbed to temptation and distributed many of our family gifts soon after we brought
them home, there were still things to buy to replace them, surprises to
plan, mysteries to keep to ourselves if we could muster the required will
power. We started to the bazaar in high holiday spirits which mounted
the minute we entered the doors of the church, smelled the fresh aroma
of home-baked bread, cinnamon rolls, cakes, pies, and saw the old-
fashioned ice cream parlor near the entrance where hand-cranked ice
cream was being sold in cones. We became even more imbued with the
Christmas spirit when we saw the hand-made quilts, mittens, dolls'
clothes, all the other handicraft items displayed amid gay Christmas
decorations. We walked slowly around the various tables and finally left

with our arms full of some of the delights we had seen, in our hands elegant chocolate ice cream cones.

Holiday shopping in town is pure fun. No one is rushed, everyone takes his time, no one is too busy to stop for a visit, and everyone enjoys the gaiety and the excitement and the joyful anticipation of the Christmas season. The stores are busy but not crowded, there is plenty of opportunity to visit with the shop owners, and one can buy things with the greatest leisure as there are no high-pressured sales people, no harassed shoppers. In many of the shops there are trays of coffee, hot mulled cider, Christmas cookies, fruit cakes, candy, to which customers may help themselves as they walk through the stores to make their holiday purchases. Sometimes we stop for lunch at one of the restaurants where we are certain to meet others who are enjoying the pre-holiday festivities, too, and we visit and compare notes on the surprises in our many bags and boxes. We stop for a minute at the entrance to the park in the center of town to watch the huge arches of elk antlers being decorated with bright lights, and we catch the strains of a Christmas carol as it comes over the loud speakers along the streets.

One of the happiest things about this year's pre-holiday festivities was the return from town, the back of the car laden with our many purchases. As we cut through a back road, we saw ahead of us a herd of cattle, slowly, meditatively coming down the road toward us. The cowboys on their horses were dressed warmly in heavy caps, scarves, gloves, and leather chaps. There were cattle dogs running beside the cows and calves to keep them from wandering. We slowed the car until we could make our way through the mass of moving animals, stopped to wave to the cowboys, exchange holiday greetings with them, and when the herd had passed, we moved on. Where, we asked ourselves, could one return from Christmas shopping and be delayed, not by heavy traffic of cars and buses, but by a herd of cattle? It was all so simple and right, just the necessary Western touch to our Western holiday.

1968

WE REMEMBER 1967—

In January riding the chair lifts above animal tracks in fresh snow, above mountain streams, above pines, sliding off the lifts, taking deep breaths, skiing down snowy slopes in bright sun.

In February carrying in wood for fires, glancing at the sun's first rays touching the peaks with rose and gold.

In March buzzing over deep snow on the SkiDoos, through the big meadow, into the pine forest, feeling occasional bumps as the SkiDoo sank into melting snows around sage bushes.

In April feeling the warm chinook winds, looking at enormous icicles dripping at the edge of the roof, seeing patches of black road through disappearing ice, watching the massive rotary ponderously clearing our road of snow.

In May watching the daffodils and tulips over the back bench growing taller and stronger in the warm air, seeing the fat, multi-colored buds swelling until they burst, opening their chalices and trumpets to the spring sun.

In June waiting for the return of each bird, searching the ground for the opening of each wild flower, until all were there—bluebirds, robins, humming birds, fritillarias, spring beauties, showers of white choke cherry blossoms making fragrant the winding road to the cabin.

In July slipping our canoe into the lake and, silent with excitement, taking her on her maiden voyage into inlets, around wooded bends, through reflections of the peaks in calm waters.

In August riding over quiet mountain trails, fishing in rivers and streams, smelling steaks or chicken or hot cakes cooking on our grills at the picnic area.

In September watching green aspens slowly turning yellow, cottonwoods sending golden leaves to the ground, feeling the first frost on our

148

finger tips, harvesting garden crops, setting out bird seeds and suet on the feeders.

In October seeing the Valley's brilliant garb fading slowly, grasses becoming tawny and brown, trees standing bare, taking one last canoe trip, having one last picnic, one last ride, splitting the last huge logs for the wood pile—all before the arrival of cold air and snow.

In November tingling to sharp winds, thrilling to the first real snow fall, enjoying a Thanksgiving goose, regretfully taking the burros to their winter pasture, having the SkiDoos checked, anti-freeze and engine heaters put into the Jeeps, bringing out snowshoes and skis.

In December seeing the full moon on white peaks above, the steaming river below, following at dusk the path into the cabin, leaving cold, blue footprints behind us in the snow, to the bright Christmas tree lights, crackling fires, books, and music beckoning us in.

February 1, 1968

MANY OF OUR city friends have wondered what we would do in case of emergency during the winter months when we are snowed in and dependent upon SkiDoos to get us the mile and a half over the snow to the parked cars at the road. Sometimes, we must confess, we have wondered ourselves, although we knew the over-the-snow machines were entirely trustworthy and that the Jeeps, with engine heaters plugged into the power line, would start quickly. But we could not know, for certain until we were put to the test. We have been put to the test, and we think we managed the emergency well. Now all our apprehensive friends may put their minds at rest. We have done it once and know we can do it any time in the future if the necessity should arise.

One night just before bed-time, Witty decided that the snow had piled against the front door too heavily, so, she went out the front door, took the shovel, and began to scoop a little snow from the door. Horror of horrors, she had on leather-soled shoes, treacherous on slippery snow. We saw her turn to come in, slip, swing to one side, and go down. When she did not recover her balance at once, the other two of us watching from the window, rushed to her aid. We brought her in, sat her on the bench in the entry hall, and noticed she was as white as the snow she had been shoveling. We saw beads of perspiration appear on her forehead and upper lip. She could not move her foot, and we immediately feared a badly sprained ankle. After a minute or two, we gave her a drink of whisky, and helped her hobble on one foot to bed where we warmed her with hot water bottles and electric blankets. The pain was intense, the

149

swelling around the ankle had started, and we decided to take her the first thing in the morning to the hospital for X-rays. She was very brave, but we could tell she was in great pain. Before long, however, her color returned, she grew warmer, and with her leg propped up and encased in ice bags, she managed to get a little sleep.

The next morning the pain was no better, so we phoned our very fine orthopedic surgeon in the Valley and made an appointment. Then we began to get her ready, wondering what in the world we could do to support the injured leg. Finally we hit upon an idea. We wrapped small terry cloth towels around it, and then one of us found some fine-meshed wire we use for suet on the bird feeder. With our wire cutters we fashioned a large shoe-shaped cage, and put that on her foot. We wound ace bandages around that, and there we had it—an effective, neat looking splint. We dressed the patient in her bright red SkiDoo suit, all in one piece, made of nylon on the outside, thus extremely slippery. She hopped on one leg to the front hall and out the door. Then we sat her gently on the snow. We got her up the heap of snow in front of the porch, turned her, and she put both legs straight in front of her. We took her by the collar of her suit and pulled her swiftly along the snow, she sliding easily in her nylon suit, even laughing at the strange appearance all of us made. Then to the small hill of snow in front of the gate, one foot held high and looking most professional in our home made splint. One more incline, we gave one last tug, and got her up the slope on the other side of the gate to the waiting SkiBoose. She stood on one foot, and we lifted her easily into the little sled. We were ready to go. All went well at the car, we got her into the back seat where she could stretch her aching leg, and away we went to the doctor.

The X-rays showed one broken leg bone just above the ankle, a cracked leg bone on the other side, so she really had done the job well, and our ideas of a minor sprained ankle became ridiculous. But there was no bone misplacement, and after a professional cast had been put on and three days spent in the hospital, we brought her back, a wheel chair and crutches sticking from the sides of the Ski Doo, Witty following gaily in the SkiBoose. Again we dragged her over the snow in her slippery suit, brought her into the house, and knew that all was well. At the moment she is doing beautifully, feels less pain every day, and is able to move about quite comfortably. Before too long the cast will be removed and she will be as good as new.

One evening before the fire we thought over the entire incident, re-living each painful, each funny part of it. We all joined in singing

Witty's broken bone song, she herself stomping time with one crutch—

Should a crisis now arise,
Will it take us by surprise?
Helpless look and hopeless wail?
Fevered brows and faces pale?
Splints or slings or home-made crutch,
We know how to cope with such.
Ho, Ho, Ho—we've practiced much.
No one now need have a fear,
We have proved it crystal clear,
If we have a like contingency,
We shall meet that next emergency.
Ho, Ho, Ho—we feel so proud,
We'll proclaim our feat aloud.
Witty's fine and on the mend,
Thus our story finds an end.

March 1, 1968

FOR THE SAKE of convenience to our readers, we shall name the three characters in this issue The One Who Takes Care of the Greenhouse, The One Who Does Not Take Care of the Greenhouse, and The One with the Broken Leg. Now we can proceed.

The One Who Takes Care of the Greenhouse decided a short time ago that she would spend the month of February in Arizona with Fran and JB, she and Fran with the prime purpose of taking art lessons. The One with the Broken Leg knows a great deal about the care of plants and normally would have been chosen by The One Who Takes Care of the Greenhouse to carry on in her place. But it is difficult to maneuver a wheel chair and crutches in a narrow area with sprinkling cans, hoses, spray guns impeding the path. The One Who Does Not Take Care of the Greenhouse, a poor substitute, was chosen as the only alternative.

The One Who Does Not Take Care of the Greenhouse enjoys flowers tremendously, but only in their finished state. She knows little about caring for them or raising them. She thought her job as temporary caretaker of the greenhouse would be an easy one and she could breeze through the work triumphantly. The first day she assumed her unaccustomed duties with complete confidence, not to say vanity. She knew that she would do the work with no fuss, no mess, no trouble. For instance, when *she* did the sprinkling, not a drop of water would be spilled and the

151

floor would remain clean and dry. Water would go only where it was supposed to go, on the benches, into the flower pots, and into the hanging baskets. She took out the hose, turned on the water, and began. La de da! she thought; this is easy. I'm doing famously—not a spray, not a sprinkle except on the plants themselves. La de da! and she danced from bench to bench, from pot to pot, from hanging basket to hanging basket. Suddenly she felt her feet becoming cold and damp; she looked down to find herself ankle-deep in water, rivers of water, oceans of water, streaming all over the floor, dripping from the benches, leaking from the pots, pouring from the hanging baskets. Everything, including the wiser and more humble One Who Does Not Take Care of the Greenhouse, was drenched, drowned. The flowers seemed to cast reproachful looks at her as she ran for the mop. The rest of that morning was spent in swabbing, mopping, slopping through the flood, and for a while she feared she would have to call in the entire household, dogs included, and set them to drinking to make the waters recede.

First lesson in tending a greenhouse, and the second followed fast on its heels.

If the earth in the greenhouse is too wet, hundreds and thousands of tiny angle worms emerge and stretch their full length on the dirt. There they lie until the soil becomes drier. Occasionally the worms will fall over the edge of the benches to the floor where they writhe in agony. The One Who Does Not Take Care of the Greenhouse felt such pity for these blind, helpless reptiles that every few minutes she would rush to the greenhouse, scoop the hapless ones from the floor and put them back onto their home territory. In two days she counted she had rescued 319 of these creatures, so she soon learned not to sprinkle so heavily and thus keep the worms where they belonged.

But the last lesson in the greenhouse was the most difficult and terrifying of all. Aphids. The One Who Takes Care of the Greenhouse had warned about them before she left for Arizona, saying they were the most destructive thing possible to plants. They seemed to appear from nowhere, would attach themselves with fierce tenacity to leaves, stems, blossoms, and then, horror of horrors, like deadly vampires, would suck all the life from a plant. The One Who Does Not Take Care of the Greenhouse was shown an aphid, a dead one, and then, dreadful to see, a live one, wriggling on a stem, waving its repugnant front legs in the air, waiting to begin its deadly feast. It seems they never appear singly, always in hordes. Harry told us about carrying an infested plant through the orchid section of his greenhouse and in that split second, the beasts slithered or flew or crawled or whatever they do, from the sick plant to a healthy orchid plant, and the trouble began. The One Who Does Not Take Care of the Greenhouse did a little research on her own on aphids and found there are thousands of varieties, all equally malevolent. She became obsessed with aphids. When she dusted the house, she looked under everything for fear a band of them might be hiding, ready to leap out and attack whatever might be passing. When she brought in logs for the fire, she examined each piece of wood meticulously for fear an innocent looking log might be harboring the vicious creatures. Even a harmless beetle scuttling across the floor caused alarm in the heart of The One Who Does Not Take Care of the Greenhouse as she was afraid it might be an over-sized aphid on the loose. Pure terror when one day The One with the Broken Leg announced from her wheel chair as she was looking through the glass doors to the greenhouse, "That tulip over there is covered with aphids!" Quickly the spray gun was filled with its lethal solution, speedily gusts of it were sent in the direction of the suffering tulip, and the evil things began to drop.

One morning The One Who Does Not Take Care of the Greenhouse came to breakfast, visibly shaken and wan. "I had the most awful dream," she announced, shaking her head vigorously as if to rid her mind of the fright she had suffered. "That's what you get," said The One with the Broken Leg, "for reading Alfred Hitchcock stories before you go to bed." "It wasn't anything so mild as Alfred Hitchcock," was the answer. "It was far worse. I saw the greenhouse completely flooded, full of water like a swimming pool. Then the water disappeared. From the slime that was left rose enormous, repulsive creatures, giant aphids, each waving its front legs before its face, each with a ravenous look in its great, stupid eyes. They pounced mercilessly upon the sweet peas, then the yellow oxalis, then the geraniums, the carnations, the calendulas, the stock, the nasturtiums. Each flower in turn was devoured as the beasts licked their chops and continued their vile destruction. Nothing was left of a single plant. All were chewed to the roots. And then, and then," she continued, reliving every horrible minute, "they turned on *us* with leers and hot breath. But then I awoke and after a few dreadful seconds realized it was a dream. Or was it?" she asked in terror.

But as she glanced fearfully toward the greenhouse, the tall, healthy snapdragons, the gay oxalis, the fragrant sweet peas and stock, the geraniums, the tiny pansy plants—all looked happy and well and nodded reassurance. It was obvious that the aphid solution and the spraying had done their job, that lessons about oversprinkling and dashing the hose about helter-skelter had been mastered. The One Who Does Not Take Care of the Greenhouse deservedly has earned a new name—The One

Who Has Learned—the Hard Way. And while her thumb isn't exactly emerald colored yet, there are decided and definite shades of pale green beginning to show.

April 15, 1968

Light snows; porches and logs, frosted; fences, a marvel of white lace,
But close to the cabin white crocuses and snowdrops budding.
Winds blowing chill, snow pecking sharp,
But slender, green spears of daffodils and tulips appearing on bare hill-
    sides.
The melody of red-wings in ponds below,
Two sedate moose in the warm sun nibbling on willows in the river
    bottom,
The first new-born colt romping about its mother,
Birds in flocks hovering about the feeders,
Interrupted now by scampering chipmunks and pine squirrels.
Banks of snow surrounding the ponds,
But pond lilies showing green spikes in dark waters.
Trees standing bare and stark,
But willows red with renewed life, cottonwoods with swelling buds,
    furry pussies creeping along bare branches.
Snow still lying deep on sage flats,
But dark spots, edged with feathery ice, revealing the first tip of reappear-
    ing sage.
Silence of nights now broken by cries of ducks and geese and swans.
Nature holding her breath as winter slowly, slowly withdraws,
Bowing out to spring in meadows, ponds, streams, deep forests.
Sleeping things stir
As Persephone emerges from dark regions below,
To set foot lightly on an expectant earth.

May 1, 1968

WE KNOW nothing at all about the nation's finances and its economy. We only know that we have been reading everywhere about a possible tax increase. If an individual spends more money than he earns, trouble results. We suppose it is the same with the United States government. But a tax raise sounds grim; no citizen would welcome it. If the treasury of this country needs money, what is the quickest, simplest, surest way of raising it? We would like to offer a humble suggestion.

The other day we attended a bake sale in town. Cars were parked

154

in every available space. Women, a look of bright anticipation on their faces, were racing into the sale, empty baskets in hand. We joined the happy throng, equally expectant, knowing we would have a gay time choosing which pies, cakes, cookies, bread we would buy to take home. A steady stream of buyers for the baked goods continued as more cakes, more pies, more bread were put on display to take the place of those which had so speedily disappeared. It was fun for everyone, those giving the sale as well as those buying, and we understand that the money realized was most gratifying.

This experience made us remember school bake sales. In schools every organization needs money—the Athletic Association, the Glee Club, the athletic teams, the Student Council, and all the rest. None seems to have the affluence needed to continue activities effectively. None, however, seems to remain in a state of impoverishment for long. A bake sale never failed to solve the problems of the treasury. A student whose favorite organization is giving a bake sale may neglect his Latin grammar or his English theme the night before, but always there is time to bake a cake, a batch of cookies or fudge.

We propose a national bake sale to solve the problems of government finances and make the tax increase unnecessary. We would have every family in the country contribute something. A day would be set aside for the sale and be declared a national holiday. Schools, banks, stores, post offices would be closed, and the full concentration of the nation would be on the bake sales sweeping the country from coast to coast. Proceeds from each sale would be sent immediately to the United States Treasury, and it might be most satisfying to learn of the possible billions of dollars which had rolled in as a result of the industry and ingenuity of the nation's housewives. We suggest that this entire project be in the hands of the women of the country; men would be most welcome to buy at the sales, but it would be the feminine element of the nation who would instigate the plan and carry it to a triumphant conclusion. It would be enormous fun for all; no staggering sums need be spent; all would work together in close cooperation; the participants would have a great feeling of satisfaction in knowing they had helped lift the nation's finances from the doldrums.

And, who knows, the national bake sale might grow until it becomes international in scope. We understand that right now the Japanese, from tiny tots to kimonoed grandmothers, are experiencing excited delight over imported American ice cream, hot dogs, and pizzas. Americans and people from other countries might find equally appetizing favorite dishes from their foreign neighbors. Imagine the delirium of

155

excitement if the women of the world began to exchange recipes! It could lead to almost anything.

At least we think our idea is better than a tax raise. What joy is there in relinquishing a little more of one's income on four dreary dates of the year? But a bake sale! That would be fun and highly profitable from its earliest inception to the devouring of the last tasty crumb. We remember one of our former students who had participated actively in dozens of bake sales. In a history class she was told how women of certain countries in ancient times had to give a few months of their early womanhood to the world's oldest profession in order to raise money for the local temples. She thought a minute, looked at her teacher with wide, startled eyes, and said simply and firmly, "I'd rather have a bake sale." The people of America when faced with something as distasteful as higher taxes and economic troubles might well feel quite like Betsy and say earnestly and eagerly, "We'd rather have a bake sale."

May 15, 1968

FOR A LONG TIME we have suspected that the housing problem in the neighborhood of the cabin was acute, but we did not realize until recently how serious it really was. Newcomers to the Valley or others who are returning from a winter in other parts have arrived, and all are concerned at the present time with only one thing: establishing themselves in an attractive, comfortable home which will be suitable for raising a family. We watch the process of house hunting and are happy when we see each home seeker finding an appealing and satisfactory place to settle.

The excitement usually begins at daybreak and continues during the entire day and even into the night. It is interesting to watch what kind of surroundings, what kind of establishment each newcomer desires. All sites are attractive and all command a fine view as the spring flowers are now beginning to bloom, and the ponds below the cabin are open and full of large spikes which soon will unfurl into yellow pond lilies. Any home site for our newcomers is pleasant, but something more than beauty is necessary, too. We have noticed that some families prefer height and choose homes at the top of the bench. Others enjoy a life near the ponds and like to be close to trees. Others want suburban living with no close neighbors, while some enjoy apartment living. Others want complete seclusion. Some favor large houses, while others settle for more modest, smaller homes. We have watched with interest the male member of a family examine a possible home while his wife remained patiently to one side. After the masculine inspection had concluded, the feminine began, and there followed a discussion of the relative merits and disadvantages of what had been seen.

The couples differ greatly in appearance and characteristics. Some are large and some are small. Some are shy and some are audacious, even slightly aggressive. Some are red-headed, some have dark backs and handsome red vests; some are brilliant blue and carry, as Thoreau said, the sky on their backs. Some are gray with bold, black markings, some flamboyant in their yellow, orange, and black coloring. The family which often arrives near the end of the house hunting season is perhaps the most colorful of all, being a bright iridescent green with a sole ornament in the form of a magnificent magenta necklace. But in spite of their great differences in appearance and temperament, there seems to be no disagreement at all among the house hunting couples. Each apparently has its own requirements for a home, its own needs for raising a family, and these in no way interfere with what the others are seeking.

Once a home has been found, a scurry of activity follows; old homes must be renovated, new ones made inviting. Building materials are plentiful, and since the husband and wife both work industriously, a house can be put into good shape in a very short time. Some couples, it is true, are more fastidious and particular than others. One couple with an adolescent child, for instance, looked hard and long before it found exactly what it wanted, deciding finally upon a home it had occupied once before. After the home has been settled, we have noticed, there is much bustle and hurry in looking for food and the places where it is most abundant. Some of our families find sustenance very close to their own door steps; others have to travel abroad to find the delicacies which to them are the most appetizing.

We have had great fun watching our little community around the cabin become established. We know that we shall enjoy having such congenial and pleasant families living nearby.

June 15, 1968

IN JUNE we pause to re-live the wonders of

A tuft of yellow violets by the road;
Fragrance of purple shooting stars, wet with rain;
Blue of a robin's egg, broken on the ground,
Telling of a brood in trees above;
A stately and indifferent bull moose,
Antlers in velvet,
Followed by a timid but designing cow;

157

Sound of Morel mushrooms gently bumping
Into tin pails;
Fresh watercress in cold mountain springs;
Meadows turned golden with dandelions;
Orange and yellow of tanagers
Shyly pecking at crumbs on the feeders;
Delicate scent of sticky cottonwood leaves
Unfolding to the sun;
Chatter of pine squirrels and chipmunks,
Their solitude disturbed;
Shiny white petals of wild strawberries;
Soft burro noses and eager mouths
Reaching over the fence
For a feast of carrots;
Full mountain creeks
Dancing over brown pebbles;
Iridescence of the first humming bird
Poised above a sprig of larkspur;
The new moon's silver crescent
Dipping behind snowy peaks;
The long, lone cry of a coyote;
Faint twitter of birds
Through the dark;
Lullaby of spring rains
Soothing and sending to sleep
All creatures of wood and stream.

July 1, 1968

WHEN WE TOOK a canoe trip last week, we enjoyed a leisurely paddle across the lake, found a pleasant place on a wooded bank to spread out our food, and had barely started our lunch when one of us said quietly, "I think we had better leave here at once." The rest of us looked up in wonder and noticed a bull moose standing only a few feet from us. One look was enough; we dropped our sandwiches, our plates, our cups of coffee, and in the flash of an eye scrambled over underbrush to reach the canoes before the moose decided to sit down and join us. We climbed into the canoes and turned to watch the drama. Then we saw not only one moose but two, both bulls. They came closer and closer to our picnic, looked over the thermos jugs, the partially eaten food, and continued to graze as we sat in the canoes, fascinated, but ready to paddle away in a hurry should they come any nearer. They were not in the least perturbed and continued to eat their lunch close to ours. We were hungry and wanted to continue our meal, but we waited until first one and then the second moved slowly on, hearing the snap of branches under their hooves as they disappeared from sight. The sight of moose is common, and we expect to see several in the course of a day's canoeing, but we hardly expect to have two of them drop in uninvited for a picnic lunch.

On another canoe trip recently, this time to a more distant and wilder mountain lake, we launched the canoes, paddled slowly in the silence, hearing only the dip of our paddles in the water. We rounded a bend and on the shore of the lake saw five pairs of snowy white trumpeter swans swimming placidly in the calm waters. One pair of trumpeters is not an unusual sight here, but five pairs is completely unexpected and thrilling. As we turned the canoes, we noticed near us in the reeds and marshes on shore six white birds walking sand-piper fashion on the pebbles near the edge of the water. They rose in flight, dipping like swallows. They came closer and we were astonished by their rosy heads and necks and the striking black markings in perfect geometrical figures on their white backs and wings. Avocets, we exclaimed—we had never seen them before and marveled at their beauty and grace. Herons we see often, even eagles high above us perched on a dead tree. Gulls and ducks and geese are in abundance on mountain lakes, but avocets were something entirely unexpected and exciting, and they and the ten trumpeters had turned what we thought would be one of our usual canoe trips into true adventure.

Early last May we ordered some porch furniture, sight unseen, but were assured by the very polite clerk that it was nice. We were told we could expect the furniture within four weeks at the latest. We alerted the local delivery truck here to be looking for it, and sat and waited for the elegant chairs, tables, and chaise to arrive. June came and went, the weather was warm, and we wanted to sit on our new porch chairs and have lunch at the new tables. We sat on the porch steps with our plates on our laps into July, took to the porch railings in early August, and then one day decided to phone the summer furniture department to see what had happened. Yes, we were assured, our order would be checked at once, and soon we would hear. August faded into September, the weather became cool, and we telephoned again. Yes, we were courteously promised, our order would be traced at once and we could expect a phone call about it the next day. When the phone rang in the morning, we all raced to hear the news. Sad, sad. No record had been made of our order at all, but our store would phone the furniture factory in Florida to see what could be done. We could expect, madam, another phone call in the morning. We were told this time that the furniture would be shipped at once from Florida and since we had been inconvenienced, our store would pay the freight on it from Florida to our store in the Mid West. We could take it from there. Things were beginning to move and we thought our store was behaving with characteristic fairness. The next morning we received a third call, saying that the store had re-considered. Since we had been *so* inconvenienced, we would have to pay no freight charges at all, and, since, madam, the furniture is all-weather furniture, you can leave it out and use it all winter. The idea of a mid-January lunch on the porch made our blood congeal, and we knew the clerk at our store had not the faintest idea what happens here in the Valley in the winter time. The local truck finally drove up, unloaded our furniture, and we had at least a day or two to use and admire it before we had to pack it away in the saddle shed.

In the early spring we ordered a set of Spode Christmas china. We knew that this had to be ordered by our store specially from England. We understood that the order would take three or four months to fill, but we said we didn't need it until Thanksgiving, so there was no hurry. Fatal mistake on our part! We were told by the clerk who took our order that soon we would receive a number. What for she didn't say, but we waited and waited and no magic number came. We wrote eight letters and made half a dozen phone calls, always being assured, madam, that everything was all right—our order would be checked. Finally, having had no word by late October, we phoned once more and asked for the head or the assistant head of the department. Both were gone, would not return until mid-November. "But," asked the clerk to whom we were speaking, "can I help you, madam?" We told our tale of woe, and her voice brightened. "Oh," she said, "I know all about your order. The whole department does. Miss Kaminski and Miss Hadley have been working on it. There was a slight delay (gross understatement, we thought), and you will have the entire set by Thanksgiving. Everything came from the Spode company in England except the creamer and sugar. Those had been forgotten, so we cabled, the company is flying them in, and the minute they arrive, they will be on their way to you, madam." The other day, thrill of thrills, our china arrived and is more beautiful than we had ever dreamed. At the bottom of the big box we found a plaintive little note, "You can expect your creamer and sugar in 30 days to three weeks." It took us quite a while to figure that one out, but something surely would happen, we just knew, between 30 days and three weeks. It did, madam. The creamer and sugar arrived the very next day.

Recently we ordered a dozen finger tip guest towels. Soon after, we received a tiny package, so very light that we could not believe all twelve of our towels, small as they were, could possibly be therein. When we opened the package, we found *one* towel. Not daring to risk the complications of writing our store about the other eleven, we decided to sit tight and wait. A wise decision. Two days later we received another small box, this one containing *two* towels. Three down and nine to go. Excitement mounts. A package of sheets we had ordered arrived soon after, and, tucked in among them as a wonderful surprise, were three more towels. We were becoming hysterical with the mystery, and our trips to the post office were filled with high suspense. In two days came another box, this one containing two more. Joy! This was like an Agatha Christie serial. Four more to come. Before long, they, too, came tagging along. Now we have the complete dozen, appreciate them even more than if they had arrived all together in a dull fashion, but it took eight mailings on the part of our store to get them here.

Not long ago, we phoned the bed linen department for some special sheets; we wanted printed patterns on them, and told the clerk who answered our call to make them as wild and gay as possible. There was a long silence on the other end of the phone. Then came a chuckle and a loud "Wow!" We repeated our request. Another even louder "Wow!" And then—we could almost see the clerk recover his equanimity and customary dignity—he said, "Madam, this is a very conservative store." Conservative or not, when our order arrived, the sheets were indeed gay and wild. One was a gorgeous leopard print with black hem, another a giraffe pattern in brown and brilliant gold. Our clerk had sent us what we wanted.

We love the things we buy there, and wouldn't for the world, madam, give up the hilarity and frantic hysteria which we experience each time we place an order.

August 15, 1968

SINCE LAST WEEK'S hilarious adventure at the drive-in near town, we have been told that when children are taken there to eat, one must be very firm. It is better, we were advised, to insist that all people under ten years of age get out of the car for their meal.

We knew that two young friends of ours love to have lunch at the drive-in, so when we had a little shopping to do, we invited them to

161

accompany us with the promise of a drive-in lunch on the way home. When we called for our guests, we were impressed by their spotless appearance—snow white blouses, clean slacks, immaculate white shoes, scrubbed faces and hands, and shining, well-combed hair. Oh, dear!

The children had been planning all morning what they would order for lunch—one papaburger with catsup, one babyburger with catsup, French fries with catsup, a root beer float, and a cherry milk shake. The lunch arrived on its tray and was snapped to the front window of the Jeep. Quickly we emptied the contents from the two large paper bags on the back seat and spread the bags out as makeshift table cloths. Eager hands reached for the food, and the plates and drinks were passed shakily along. The cherry milk shake was the pièce de résistance, a dream of thick pink goo. Adult eyes kept careful watch during its journey from one small hand to the next. Finally it was suggested that the floor would be the safest place to set it. At least if it spilled, we wouldn't have to sit in the sweet, thick puddles. The celophane containers of salt and catsup were opened, and the banquet began. Kathy, the three-year-old, was interested in nothing at first but her cherry milk shake, and with an ecstatic expression on her face, she sucked on the straw as the delicious thickness rose to her lips. She soon set aside her dessert, however, and wanted to put catsup on the French fries. Tiny fingers squeezed the celophane bag and out spurted the red contents, over paper bags, over the car seat, over clean slacks and blouses. The same fingers, eager to retrieve all that was left, scraped the improvised table cloth, the car seat, the clean clothes onto which it had squirted. Ann, her older sister, seeing the excitement and predicament, wanted to help and leaned forward quickly. Whoops! The cherry milk shake tipped, and four little hands reached down and tried valiantly to scoop up the flowing pinkness. Finally this attempt was forsaken, and all we could do was watch the pink flow creep slowly under the brakes and settle into the rubber cup holding the four-wheel drive shift. While all of us, fascinated, watched the pink river, Ann's blouse and slacks parted as she leaned over, exposing her bare, sun-burned back. Kathy, upset at this immodesty, reached over, knocking one hamburger to the floor in the process, and with fingers covered with catsup, hamburger, and milk shake, vigorously pulled down Ann's blouse, leaving marks of the entire lunch not only on Ann's clean clothes but on her back as well. The front seat of the Jeep tilts back slightly, and by this time all the salt and remaining catsup had slid back, so we had to poke the potatoes between the seat and the back of the seat in order to dip them into their seasoning. We noticed that each time we did this, some of the French fries stuck fast in the crack.

162

Finally all of us were not only well fed but well covered with lunch, and the hop girl came to carry away the debris. We ourselves brushed straws, crumbs, and plates from the front seat, put the paper bags on the floor to absorb as much of the milk shake as they could, and were ready to depart. The children thought they would like to finish the whole thing off with an ice cream cone each, ten cent cones, the huge kind, one chocolate, one half and half, chocolate and vanilla. When the girl brought them out, we were struck speechless. Each looked at least a foot high, and both were already beginning to drip away in the hot sun. As we pulled out of the drive-in, Ann remarked, "Oh, here comes a car with *eight* children for lunch!" We hurried away, hating even to imagine what that lunch would be. Down the highway we started, each child licking frantically on her cone before it disappeared in the heat. First one side would be licked, then the whole thing would be squeezed desperately, turned, and the drips and streams would be caught on the other side. Both faces were plunged, hair deep, into the cones; both tongues continued to lap. Drips, hundreds of chocolate drips, trickled between fingers. More drips trickled in rivers down arms to elbows. Finally the cones had been squeezed so hard that they became soft and wet and began to disintegrate. All of us are well aware of litter laws, but in this case there was no alternative. Out the window the cones went, leaving streams of sticky dribbles on the window, the outside of the door, the inside of the door, until all of us, looking at each other in silence, burst into gales of laughter at the mess. Ann said, to assuage her conscience about throwing litter out the window, "Some hungry bird will surely find our cones and have a feast." It is fortunate the road home is fairly straight. It would have been impossible to lift our fingers from the steering wheel to turn it for corners, so firmly were our hands stuck to it with milk shake, chocolate ice cream, onions, and catsup.

When we arrived at the children's home, we thought we would remain in the car rather than face their mother when she saw the sticky daughters we were returning to her, but when Margaret came out to meet them, looked at their chocolate covered faces and hair, saw their clothes smeared with much of their lunch, she laughed good-naturedly and said the clothes could easily be washed. She called Nanny, the children's greatgrandmother to come and see. As we drove away, we heard two tubs of water being drawn.

At home when we stepped out of the car on our way to get the hose, something made our walking difficult and unnatural. It was as if we had broad swimming fins on our feet. We looked down and there were the two paper bag table cloths, one stuck firmly to each shoe by a thick, pink mass.

Several other suggestions of our own we would now like to add to those mentioned earlier about being firm and evacuating the car of children before lunch is served at a drive-in. Next time, we chuckled to ourselves, we will be certain to take several old sheets to serve as floor and seat covers, a pan of water, soap, and wash cloths, cleaning fluid, window spray, a tube of shampoo, and a change of clothes for each child. Perhaps even more simple would be the insistence that each child wear a bathing suit and be well dunked on the way home in the nearest large body of water.

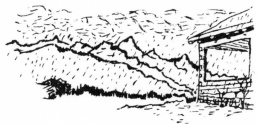

September 1, 1968

Sick of drip, drip, drip.
Need a ship, ship, ship
To go out for needed groceries
And mail.
Sick of rain, rain, rain
On the pane, pane, pane.
Soon our Jeep will grow a rudder and
A sail.
Yard is mud, mud, mud,
Road's a flood, flood, flood.
We'll grow webs upon our feet just like
A duck.
Still more clouds, clouds, clouds,
Peaks in shrouds, shrouds, shrouds.
The barometer is down and really
Stuck.
Where's the sun, sun, sun?
We want fun, fun, fun
With canoes and rides and hikes along

164

The trails.
We just sit, sit, sit,
Fingers knit, knit, knit,
And our voices rise in protests and
In wails.
Turn it off, off, off!
We just cough, cough, cough,
And we're getting colds in eyes and
Also nose.
Stop the rain, rain, rain,
Minds insane, sane, sane.
We'll never need again our garden
Hose.
We are cross, cross, cross,
At a loss, loss, loss
How best to mend our soggy, dampened
Mood.
We just mope, mope, mope,
Try to hope, hope, hope
That ere long this soppy weather will
Conclude.
It's a mess, mess, mess,
Can depress, press, press.
And when next our little paper comes
To you,
We will bet, bet, bet
In this wet, wet, wet,
Each copy will arrive in
A canoe.

September 15, 1968

IT TAKES only one golden aspen to tell us.

Most of the trees are still green, but here and there stands one of pure gold. We look into the branches of the cottonwoods and see that they, too, carry a few yellow leaves in their topmost branches. The underbrush is turning ruddy, and along the road we see a flaming branch of hawthorne. The mountains are misty. There is sharpness in the wind.

165

It takes only one golden aspen.

We see no more colorful wild flowers in the yard, only bright yellow leaves on the "sarvis" berry bushes. A cluster of wild asters or goldenrod still lingers.

It takes only one golden aspen.

The chipmunks dash up and down the bird feeder all day, whisking their tails as their nervous little paws snatch bits of crumbs or nuts. Then, cheeks bulging, they rush through the underbrush to some hole in a tree where their winter cache is stored.

It takes only one golden aspen.

After dark on these frosty evenings we put on sweaters and jackets and stand on the porch, listening for the bugling of the elk from the bench above. First one bull begins and is soon answered by many others, their chime-like call heard from all parts of the deep, silent forest.

And it takes only one golden aspen, quaking in the wind, to tell us.

October 1, 1968

TWO ADDITIONS at the cabin we would like to announce. Both were acquired in their completed form within the past three weeks, both are permanent, both designed to bring enjoyment and satisfaction. A short six months ago we did not dream of having either, but here they are in all their shining new glory.

The first mentioned acquisition is a thirty-two foot breezeway connecting a large, one room studio with the main cabin. The breezeway will have porch furniture and be used for home picnics, as well as for a place to sit and look over the river and moose ponds in back of the cabin. Under its roof in winter will be stored fire wood, so that no longer will we have to dig into deep snows to extract buried logs. The studio will be used, with its special lighting and display boards, by the two of us who paint. Cabin Comments will be assembled there on special tables for the production machinery. We shall keep our photographic equipment in the studio, cameras, special lenses, projector, and a large, permanent screen.

The second acquisition to the cabin is a piano which came as a complete birthday surprise to the third member of our group from the two artists. Knowing only where to find middle C, this member is starting her learning from the very beginning. In the past three weeks some progress has been made. She has progressed as far as "Old Mac-Donald Had a Farm" which she plays with fervor and abandon. Alternating with this old gem is "I Wish I Were an Oscar Mayer Wiener" which calls for real flourish. Two lessons from now comes "The Londonderry Air" which will be greeted with relief by our entire group. By peeking ahead to future lessons, our virtuoso is alternately thrilled and chilled by seeing a selection of Chopin, another of Mozart, but the happy day when she begins those, unfortunately, will be months away.

The pleasures derived from our new additions have already been tremendous, and any discouragements and frustrations we experience in the time to come will serve only as a challenge. It is sadly inevitable that all of us will keep the tune of Old MacDonald in our ears for a long, long time. We shall work in the studio with a brush stroke here, a brush stroke there, splashes of color everywhere, and in the library a sharp note here, a flat note there, and, at least for some time, discord everywhere. But whatever the results of our new acquisitions may be, we know we shall have unimaginable fun with them as we disprove daily the ancient adage about old dogs and new tricks.

LATE AUTUMN POTPOURRI   *November 1, 1968*

Fragrant smoke from an early morning fire of aspen branches;
Strong odor of pitch from pine logs freshly split and piled high;
Pungent mold, late fall mushrooms, damp leaves in dark forests;
Armloads of dried laundry, cold and clean from sun and wind;
The fragrance rising again under a hot iron;
A harvest casserole simmering in the oven;
Vegetable soup bubbling on the stove;
Heat first turned on, giving occasional clicks in baseboard heaters;
Bushel baskets of red and golden apples;
Misty purple of Concord grapes, dark acorn squash; bright suns of
    pumpkins;
Cold soft burro noses reaching to sniff carrots and peppermint kisses;
Blue jeans and woolen jackets, smoky with aromas of camp fires;
Pots of chrysanthemums, yellow and white and bronze;
Sweetness of new-mown hay, baled and stacked for winter feed;

Sharp tang of sage on cold nights under frosty stars;
An inquisitive cow moose and twin calves peering over the buck fence;
Brassy trumpeting of white swans from the ponds—
Autumn composing her farewell medley
Before being puffed away on a gust of cold and snowy wind.

November 15, 1968

"STAND UP on this Thanksgiving Day...Believe in your own time and place. There is not, and there never has been, a better time or a better place to live in." So spoke Phillips Brooks about his own time and place. And at this later Thanksgiving Day we are repeating his words for the truth and faith they carry today. These are the reasons for our convictions:

The miraculous discoveries not only on land, but under vast bodies of water and in outer space;

The phenomenal advances in the realm of science, particularly in medicine;

The shrinking of the world because of modern transportation until any nation can be reached by any other in a matter of brief hours;

The consequent knowledge by one nation of all others and the concern which is felt for all;

The constant search for means to achieve world peace;

The growing opportunities for all people for education and learning;

The greater amount of time allotted to man for leisure and recreation;

The increased appreciation by more people for the miracles of nature and the desire to preserve them for future generations;

The serious concern for children of all nations that their lives be healthful, happy, and secure;

The earnest desire that all peoples of the earth be able to lead lives of dignity, security, and freedom;

The vast numbers of young people who are working seriously, intelligently, industriously, and honorably to make their world a great one.

There is gratitude, of course, for all the fine and good things which have entered our own lives, but this Thanksgiving Day we are expressing our deepest appreciation for all the noble accomplishments of great and often unnamed people everywhere who have brought tremendous blessings to all of mankind and are ceaselessly striving to bring even more.

We stand to proclaim this is the best of times and the best place to live since the history of man began.

December 1, 1968

OCCASIONALLY we still use our charge account at our favorite city store, one of the most famous department stores in the world, with which we have been familiar since early childhood. We remember being taken there as a child and being delighted by the toy department, land of wonder and enchantment, by the Christmas decorations, by luncheons in one of the very beautiful tea rooms where we always ordered the very same thing—stuffed chicken legs and orange sherbet that contained luscious candied cherries. We have always thought that the things we get at our store are unique and lovely, but sometimes we must admit the entanglements we experience in having our orders filled cause us many a frustratration and desperate annoyance. When our orders finally do arrive, however, they are always worth the pain; we have learned to expect delays, misunderstandings, confusions, and be simply amused. After all, we have no alternative. And always, always our store outdoes itself in fair dealings with its customers.

We have a favorite kind of soap which is made by our store; indeed it has been a favorite of ours all our lives; as a baby, one of us used to eat the delectable, fragrant, pink almond bars. We saw in the paper one time an advertisement of this soap at an incredibly low price, twenty-five cents a bar instead of the usual one dollar. We immediately phoned our store and ordered a large quantity of it, as probably did customers all over the country. Soon after we learned that a mistake had been made in the advertising department and the sale had intended to offer the soap at seventy-five cents a bar. We fully intended to pay that for our soap, but when our bill came, the soap was, as the advertisement had stated, only twenty-five cents. We wrote the store and said that a mistake had been made in our bill, but were told that we were to pay only the amount given. The store was standing behind the mistake which it had made.

Just before fall housecleaning one year, we ordered one of our favorite mops. To our amazement we received two mop handles, but no mop. We wrote the household department about the error, returning one of the handles, saying we could do no cleaning without the mop. After much correspondence and when fall housecleaning was long since over and it was nearly time for the spring upheaval, we received, with a very gracious, apologetic letter two mops, sent air mail. We sighed, looked at each other, grinned, and without more ado, returned the extra mop and again began a lengthy and fascinating correspondence with our store.

169

1969

WILDERNESS HIGHLIGHTS OF 1968 **_January 1, 1969_**

Most beautiful sights: An eagle soaring high above, the sun catching its snow white head and tail; avocets in flight; thick, sparkling frost feathers on trees and shrubs;

Most wonderful fragrances: sticky cottonwood buds in early spring; pine forests in hot sun; sage flats after rain; smoke from picnic fires;

Most delectable tastes: choke cherry syrup on hot cakes; rose hip jelly; mountain trout sizzling on camp fire coals;

Most noteworthy books: *Harold Nicolsen's Diaries and Letters;* Mochulsky's *Dostoevsky;* Jerry and Renny Russell's *On the Loose* (Sierra Club); Lang's *Music in Western Civilization;*

Most frequently played recordings: Beethoven's Ninth, Bach's B Minor Mass; Berlioz' L'Enfance du Christ; Mahler's Second;

Most enjoyable outdoor sports: canoeing; riding; fishing; SkiDooing; skiing, skibobbing;

Most stimulating outdoor work: wood gathering and splitting logs; gardening; burning cartons and wood scraps in huge bonfires;

Most enjoyable indoor work: treating new wood in the studio; caring for the greenhouse and planters; experimenting with new cooking recipes;

Most enjoyable indoor activities: reading, knitting, hemstitching; listening to the stereo; playing shanghai;

Most exciting sensations: SkiDooing over fresh, clean snow; returning to the Valley after a brief absence; greeting the four burros, back from their winter pastures;

Most thrilling learning experiences: playing the piano and recorders; taking art lessons; studying intricacies of new lens for cameras and wonders of a movie sound camera;

Most interesting sights: an otters' slide; a bull moose with an enormous spread of antlers looking over the fence into the studio windows;

170

beavers at work on a dam;
Most joyful anticipation: another year just like this one.

January 15, 1969

MUCH of the holiday season brought storms, strong winds blowing day and night, deep snows, and drifting. Although we ventured out and managed to attend the usual holiday festivities and even hold a few ourselves, most of the time we spent at the windows, and from the warmth and comfort of the indoors watched the storms whipping about the cabin, rails of our fence gradually disappearing under drifts, the snow swirling in miniature whirlwinds over the sage flats.

After this recent storm the mercury fell to twenty-six below zero, the skies became clear, the peaks emerged slowly from white clouds in all their snowy splendor, the air sparkled in the sun, and millions of tiny jewels shone on the snow. The great expanses of white were marked by the winds like great sand beaches, carrying the mark of receding waves. Curious designs, curling and spinning, appeared in more sheltered places. The outdoor Christmas tree, ablaze with multi-colored lights, was laden with nature's own decorations, each branch and pine needle heavy with frost and snow. At night and in the morning our big picture windows had glorious shapes and figures on them, palm-like etchings in frost.

And then came the thaws, temperatures rising, eaves dripping, snow beginning to go down a little, rails of the fence starting to show once more, some of the taller sage bushes pointing their tips out of the expanse of white.

The garden was still in deep snow, but there, wonder of wonders, along the rocks which edge the walk, blown bare, we found—could it really be?—growing through the snow, a white and purple pansy. Breathlessly, we picked it, held it in our bare hands very gently, brought it in and put it in the vase of honor. True, its petals were a little bedraggled by the wind, its color was not so brilliant as a summer pansy's color, but there it was, fresh, cold, completely and perfectly formed. We rushed to the library window downstairs and looked close to the ground at our pansy patch there, and again we were amazed to see against a garden rock three more flowers, white, yellow, and deep red. They were nodding in the sun, their green leaves as fresh as in spring, and tight buds were in plain sight on each plant. After raging storms, sub-zero temperatures, a quick thaw—pansies in our garden on January 7th. We know we shall have hundreds of gay pansies which come up in the usual way at the usual time; we shall have them from early spring until late fall. They shall be dear to us, every one. But none will ever be so precious as this little bunch next to the library windows and the single one in the garden which proved that miracles are not impossible and can happen sometimes before one's very eyes.

February 1, 1969

WE NEVER KNOW exactly what to expect when we step out of the cabin to take the dogs for a walk over the snow-covered sage flats or along the bench overlooking the ponds and river. We never quite know what we shall see or what we shall meet when we uncover the SkiDoos and start over the snow, following our track through the gate, over the bridge, turning to cross the big meadows through the aspens and pines on our way to the parking lot. We never quite know. But we have learned to expect something of excitement, adventure, or pure wilderness beauty. We have never yet been disappointed.

The other day as we were walking with our dogs, we noticed that suddenly they began to raise their heads and sniff, pulling their leashes toward the top of the bench. We followed and saw in the fresh snow hundreds of little animal tracks, concentrated in one small area. We looked over the bench and saw something we had never seen before— an otter slide. No animals were in sight, but they had been there recently, we knew, probably the night before, and their slide was worn smooth where their furry bodies had raced down the steep incline toward the ponds.

Yesterday as we were taking the same path with the dogs, one of them stopped abruptly and looked all about her over the white expanse. By the quivering of her little body and the excitement in her sharp barks and whines, we knew something of interest was near. Sure enough, about fifty feet away was what looked like a white stick. But the snowy stick was a weasel, its brown coat now completely white except for a black tip on its tail. It rose on its hind legs—we could barely discern it against the snow—and we saw its head turn, its tail flick. Then off it scampered down the bench, leaving tiny, distinct tracks in the snow.

We had heard that several buffalo had broken loose from their reservation thirty or forty miles away and that one or two of them had been sighted on this side of the Valley. Again, on another walk with the dogs, we were startled to see enormous tracks, much larger than those of moose, trailing along the side of the road. We examined them closely and felt certain they must be those of one of the escaped buffalo.

We want to step quietly, to speak softly, and to look and listen

172

well for fear we shall frighten away or miss completely some of the fascinating and exciting sights which we look for and listen for and wait for each time we step from the cabin door.

"O may I join the choir invisible
Of those immortal dead who live again
In minds made better by their presence."

George Eliot

We remember years ago when we were in high school, how our mother once said to us, "You're missing the greatest novels ever written, and I'm going to give you one of them to start right now." She went to the book shelf and drew out a volume of George Eliot, the very fine limited, definitive Witley edition.

And now, years later, has come into our hands the superb biography of George Eliot by Gordon Haight. We have just regretfully finished it, having lingered over each page, fascinated by reading about Mary Ann Evans' early life, the care she gave her father after her mother's death, her devout Evangelicism in her youth, her eventual renunciation of organized religion, her numerous visits to Rosehill to see the Brays, her friendship with Herbert Spencer, her early studies, her passionate quest for knowledge, her work as silent editor of the *Westminster Review,* her translation of Strauss, her union with George Henry Lewes, her desire finally to write novels. Then the thrilling part when she began to write fiction and decided to use a man's name under which she would publish. And next the part where her stories are greeted with acclaim, all readers wondering, speculating, guessing who George Eliot was. Thackeray declared *Scenes from Clerical Life* could never have been written by a woman. Others said only a woman could have written them. Isaac Evans, Mary Ann's brother, said that he thought only his sister could have written *Adam Bede.* Impostors began to come forth, claiming to be George Eliot. Only Barbara Bodichen, an old friend, really guessed the secret before it was divulged, and her letter pleased George Eliot more than all the praise of all the critics. Barbara Bodichon, coming upon excerpts from *Adam Bede* in an Algerian newspaper, wrote, it "instantly made me internally explain, that is written by Marian Evans, there is her great big head and heart and her wise, wide views....It is an opinion which fire cannot melt out of me. I would die in it at the stake." Even John Blackwood, her publisher, did not know the secret until he had

173

dinner with Lewes and George Eliot one evening and Lewes was given permission by the author to reveal her identity. Finally the world came to know, as there was no keeping the secret any longer.

As we re-read her works, we shall recall what Emily Dickinson said upon being asked what she thought of *Middlemarch*. "What do I think of *Middlemarch?* What do I think of glory?" John Blackwood described her as a woman of "massive intellect." Herbert Spencer spoke of her as the most brilliant woman who ever lived. People from all over the world acclaimed her work and sent her signed letters or anonymous letters, full of praise, wonder, and adulation. She was sought after by the great names of Europe and America. While George Eliot was in Rome, the famous poet, Elizabeth Barrett Browning, wrote to a friend that it was being whispered abroad that the great British author was in town. When she attended concerts or the theater, the entire audience leaned forward to catch a glimpse of her and Lewes walking down the aisle to their seats. Artists, in spite of the glares of Lewes, would sketch her features during the performance. Strangers would drop to their knees to kiss the hem of her skirts.

A scholarly work, this recent biography by Gordon Haight. Written with such simplicity, such understanding, such exquisite taste, one can only wish George Eliot herself might have read it. But it is a comfort to know that in her own lifetime she received the recognition and appreciation which her works so richly deserved. And for those of us who read this biography, we shall be drawn back irresistibly to read and re-read her splendid books, to draw wisdom and strength and inspiration from her pages. And as we do so, we shall realize, as we can only hope she did, that she reached her highest goal—

> "That purest heaven, to be to other souls
> That cup of strength in some great agony,
> Enkindle generous ardor, feed pure love,
> Beget the smiles that have no cruelty—
> Be the sweet presence of a good diffused,
> And in diffusion ever more intense.
> So shall I join the choir invisible
> Whose music is the gladness of the world."

March 1, 1969

AND STILL it snows. All winter the chief topic of conversation in the Valley has been the weather, day after day of snow, cold night after cold night. Here at the cabin it has become a joke, and the first one up in the morning welcomes with a chuckle the others as they appear, saying, "Guess what—it's snowing!"

The snow accumulation around the cabin has grown to such tremendous heights that the problem now is where we can put it all. Great ten foot mounds of it lie at both entrances. Our sturdy Toro snow blower keeps the porches clear, but as we move it now, even its high spray of snow slides back from the heaps, and we had to level the miniature mountains at each door so they will be low enough for more snow to be blown over them. A few weeks ago we had two snow steps leading up from the porches; now there are seven. Our buck fence has vanished completely. Not a sprig of sage is visible on the flats, and the smaller pine trees there show only their tips. The tall poles which hold our clothes line in the summer time are short pegs rising above the deep drifts.

Often when we reach the parking lot, we see only a red fender, hood, or top of the Jeeps. Then we hold jolly snow blowing parties, brushing the light snow from the cars, searching for the electric cords leading to the engine heaters, using the snow blower to clear the few feet to the road. The road to the post office has become so narrow that it is only a one way track, with twelve foot banks of snow on either side which the plows have left.

The snow on the roofs has risen to over six feet in places, in spite of heavy winds which have blown much of it away. One of us loves nothing better than to climb up the ladder, wallow waist deep through the snow, cut it in blocks with a hand saw and push it over the edge with a shovel. Those below watch her legs disappear up the ladder onto the roof and soon we see great showers of snow falling, huge blocks of it tumbling avalanche fashion over the bench.

Sometimes the temperature drops sharply at night, the winds abate, and we say confidently, "Tomorrow *must* be clear. No snow could possibly fall when it is this cold." But the next morning we find the thermometer has risen in the night, and we wake up to another snow storm. Often at dusk the skies clear, the last rays of the sun gleam brightly on vast expanses of sparkling white. We then plan some out of door activity for the next day. We are reassured when we see the cold moon and stars shining brightly before we go to bed, and we are certain our plans will be realized. But the next morning, no sign of sun, only more snow.

Just now we have come in from taking a late afternoon walk. Our faces sting with the fine snow that has pecked our cheeks and foreheads. Our legs ache a little from having plodded through loose snow, as difficult to walk through as deep, fine sand. The cabins in the distance are huge mushrooms, the snow on their roofs meeting the snow level on the ground. Down the road the rotary plow is sending fountains of snow that swirl and rise in heavy white mists far into the air. Long trails from the top of the bench lead downward to the ponds, and we know that deer and moose have emerged from the forests to visit the open, spring-fed water. We peer through the fine snow and see perched on a cottonwood branch the huge form of a horned owl tearing and eating ravenously a fish held in its talons. We shall listen for its long hoo—hooooo-hoo after dark. As we come in and shake the snow from our parkas, we sniff the fragrance of dinner in the oven. A fire is laid. As we look toward the west, we see the peaks becoming enveloped in heavier clouds. We see thick white mists descending. We sense a muffled silence. On the first gusty, wintry blast of a rising wind, we recognize all too well what is approaching. We grin at each other as we set a match to the fire and turn on the lights.

April 1, 1969

We have a little tale to tell
About our darling Christobel.
She came about a month ago,
Pawing and sniffing through the snow.
And since, we see her every day,
And catch the scent of her sachet.
She lives beneath an old tree's root,
Above she hears the owls hoot,
And other birds fly close and near,
Her one defense they do not fear.
All birds her friends and allies are,
But we—we watch her from afar.

176

Her coat is thick and smooth and clean,
It shines with a seductive sheen.
Coal black it is, marked with white stripe;
She's elegant, but not our type.
Her face is small, her eyes are bright
And gleam with a flirtatious light.
Her paws are sweet, each in black mitten,
She looks quite like a playful kitten.
Her greatest glory is her tail
Which she wears proudly, like a sail.
We long to stroke our Christobel,
Such folly, though, we swiftly quell.
We dare not thus to tempt our fate,
For pets like her contaminate.
We throw her pieces of red meat,
Such feasts she wants us to repeat,
But we must learn our hearts to harden,
(Although we seek our darling's pardon.)
For after all, she's shy and wild,
By humans not to be beguiled.
So we must learn to keep our distance
And press her not with rash insistence.
We pity you and wish you well,
But tarry not, dear Christobel.
We hope you'll find another home,
Safe where no dogs or people roam.
But not near us, poor Christobel,
We frankly do not like your smell.
So build a home and find a mate,
We know how highly he will rate
Your beauties, charms, and winsome ways,
The fragrance of your perfumed sprays.
You'll raise your young, you'll find repose,
And never more offend our nose.
Your spouse and kits you'll not defame,
Their scent will be the very same.
So, on your way, fair demoiselle,
You darling, fragrant Christobel!

Silence, silence—
No mortal speech or rough, crude movement
To disturb the sunrise, mauve and rose, above the butte,
Reflected in still ponds below.
The great blue heron standing motionless there—
His stately reflection caught in black waters, too, in
Silence, silence.
First wild flowers bloom, unproclaimed,
Golden fritillarias, black and white salt-and-peppers, clear yellow
    buttercups.
A beaver loping clumsily over vanishing snows—
His plunge into ponds the only sound to break the
Silence, silence.
A jay's wild screaming, the one earthly noise to rise
To a hawk circling above, uttering its muffled calls.
A moose, leading her half-grown, awkward twins down the narrow road,
Only their mighty heads seen above the heaps of snow on either side,
As they move noiselessly in daybreak's
Silence, silence.
The morning melodies of bird symphonies,
Notes of robins, redwings, blue birds, flowing from the trees
In joyous cadences—
No human sound to startle or intrude.
Warm late afternoons, spring breezes carrying softly
Fragrances of cottonwood buds.
A brown and orange butterfly floating by.
Only the drowsy drone of a bumbling bee to interrupt the
Silence, silence.
The crescent moon, myriads of stars, sparkling overhead
And in the pools below.
The wilderness murmur of a full and rushing river.
A silent moth fluttering against the pane.
The eerie hoot of an owl,
Answered in the silent distance by another faint hoo-hooooo.
Music of the wilderness in the sweet darkness that
Protects all creatures of the wild,
All growing things of the wild, in deep
Silence, silence.

THERE ARE NOT many sights worth getting up at three-thirty in the morning to see. Not many, but some.

It's cold and dark at three-thirty in the morning, and a warm fire in the fireplace, laid the night before, brought comfort to our shivering bodies. Never was the aroma of hot coffee and bacon so appealing. Our voices were instinctively hushed, probably because of our excitement and the thrilling anticipation we felt. On that early morning recently when not a single streak of daybreak was visible, we noiselessly left the cabin, movie camera, slide camera, and binoculars in hand. The waning moon shone cold as it rose over the mountains, the stars were bright. Not a car was on the highway, all was still. Finally one of us whispered, "Do you suppose we may see just one? Even one would be worth this early morning trip."

On and on we drove near the sage, over bumps and bushes, all of us watching from the windows, careful to approach the designated spot with quiet and caution lest we frighten away the rare thing we had come to watch. Suddenly all of us drew in breath. There, directly in front of the car, picked up clearly by the bright headlights, was exactly what we had hoped to find. The strangest figure one could imagine—a small head, puffed out body, a strange thick white collar which hung low, tail feathers spread peacock-fashion in all their speckled beauty. We stopped, turned off the motor, and watched, fearful that we would frighten him away, but he was so carried away and absorbed by his queer strutting and dancing that he hardly noticed the presence of the car. As our eyes became more accustomed to the dark, we could see dozens, scores, hundreds of others just like him, walking near the sage, out into the open. Every one of them was hypnotically engaged in the same slow, pompous dance. They all uttered bubbly, liquid sounds, broken only by the loud slap-slapping of white collars against chests. Then the collars would fall into place for a moment, only to be blown out again, as the thumping continued. On and on they danced, shoulders and wings hunched forward, each bird oblivious of the others. They resembled weird, elfin monarchs, attired in royal robes with ermine collars, walking in pride and regal splendor. The tails were spread out, displaying to the full the beauty of the feathers which were held proudly and splendidly. The dance continued, forward and back, round and round, with the strange accompaniment of slaps and thumps, and soft cries. We glanced toward the east and saw the first rosy coloring in the sky. Soon, we hoped it would be light enough to take pictures, and just as the sun's first brilliance shone above the mountains, the camera began to click, the movie camera to whirr. And then, as if by sudden signal, the grouse began to move toward the sage, the dancing became slower and less frequent. All interest now seemed to be centered on pecking for food. Tail feathers were folded in the usual manner, white collars deflated. As we drove away and looked back, we saw nothing more than a few scattered birds moving in the sun's first rays, searching for food. The magic wand of daybreak with one stroke had transformed a flock of miniature monarchs dancing and strutting in the dark before dawn into a flock of ordinary, common sage grouse.

There are not many sights worth getting up at three-thirty in the morning to see. But we know one.

July 1, 1969

THERE ARE SOME possible disadvantages to wilderness living—some, but certainly not many. City dwellers, for example, might be appalled at the idea of having no trash collections. We, too, were a little dismayed at first, but we soon discovered that hauling the trash to the dump can be a most delightful task. We know we shall have some kind of adventure each time we set out, and if one picks carefully his time for going to the dump, he is certain to meet friendly people there who are enjoying the trip as much as he is.

As we ride down our rather bumpy dirt road, we hear cans and bottles rattling merrily in the rear of the Jeep, and we only hope that the broken glass doesn't spill out of its paper sack and scatter itself all over the floor. We turn onto the highway where we have to stop shortly to show our National Park season pass to the ranger stationed at the gate. Glancing into the car, he knows where we are going, and smilingly waves us on.

As we approach the dump turnout, we look for a hungry bear nearby or a coyote scavenging in the debris.

We drive close to the edge of the pit, to unload our cartons. It is tremendous fun to hurl the trash into the midst of the rest of the debris, hearing cans clash and bottles crash into splinters. Once inadvertently we threw away a new license plate for the canoe trailer, having picked it up with other things and without realizing it sent it flying along with the trash. As soon as we discovered our mistake, we hurried back with flash-lights as it was beginning to get dark, and with rakes uncovered cans and bottles and old magazines until we found it in its brown envelope, as good as new for our retrieving.

There are big containers along the highway here where we could

180

deposit our trash, but simply depositing a sack of debris into them is prosaic and uninteresting. We would miss the delicious and exciting chill which runs down our spine when with joy and careless abandon we give vent to all of our destructive instincts as we hurl a bottle through the air to hear it crash on an old set of bed springs or fling a worn and disreputable Western hat into the pit to see it land jauntily and rakishly over the handle of an abandoned snow shovel.

July 15, 1969

AS WE DROVE on we noticed a private plane flying low over the river. Then others appeared in the sky, their dull drone being the only sound to break the morning stillness. We drove through the small village, but as yet there was not much sign of life. Doors to houses were closed, and we knew that families were either still asleep or quietly eating breakfast.

We began to feel apprehensive, and our blood began to run a little cold. In spite of our planned day out of doors in such beautiful surroundings, it was a little like a visit to the dentist, knowing it must be done, but dreading the approach to his office. We drove on quickly and resolutely. The sun was bright, the sky was blue and cloudless, the peaks rose above us, utterly impervious to the fears and angers and anxieties of human beings.

Finally we reached the turn-off road taking us in a few seconds to our destination. We turned in at the pleasant, though now deserted home. We saw one other car there ahead of us. We got out silently, greeted our attorney friend who was in the parked car, and by this time heard other cars driving up the steep driveway, heard other voices, hushed and serious as ours were.

The first lap of the organized search was about to begin—through brambles, over fallen logs, through dense thickets. We were ready to receive instructions on where to go, what to look for, and what to do in case we should find the two bodies whose disappearance had led to the suspicion of foul and hideous murder.

August 1, 1969

IF YOU THINK it's exciting, you're right—up to a point. If you think it's fun, you're wrong—all the way. The excitement wears off after a while, and the work becomes grim and tedious. Like most people, we had never been members of a search party before, so had no idea what to expect. We soon learned.

All searchers assembled on the driveway of the house where strong evidence indicated the murders had been committed. We forced ourselves, while we were waiting, to look at the spot where the septic tank had recently been drained, and then quickly turned away. We dared to glance at the "stains" on the cement floor of the garage and shuddered at what they meant. Next we received instructions from the attorney in charge. First he briefed us quickly but carefully about the facts of the case, what was known about the suspect, his movements so far as could be determined, where he had been seen, who had seen him, where the possible area was for his disposal of the bodies. Then we were divided into groups of six or eight, each with a leader in charge. The leader carried a ball of string and used it to mark off a definite section, anchoring the string occasionally to the branch of a tree or a bush. About fifty feet on the other side another string had already been stretched. We were to walk between these two markers, keeping ten or twelve feet apart, glancing constantly on both sides of us so that we could be certain beyond a doubt that all the ground had been searched. When we reached the end of the previously strung marker, we were to turn and search another section of the same size in the same manner. It was imperative that we keep in straight lines so that no one would move ahead too fast or fall behind the party. It was equally important that we keep the same distance between each searcher so we would not inadvertently bunch together and leave wide tracts uncovered.

We were told to investigate every spot where the earth seemed to have been recently disturbed, where there were any freshly broken tree or shrub branches, any signs of footprints, or grasses bent low as if a person had passed through them. In case we should find the bodies, we were told to step back, under no circumstance to touch or move them, then to call the leader.

The lines formed, and we began to move very slowly—eyes riveted to the ground, heads moving first to the right, then to the left.

At some places we were waist or shoulder high in dense thickets, at others confronted by fallen trees, at still others faced with bogs and thick black mud. Occasionally a voice would break the silence by calling that someone was too far behind or too far ahead or that several of us were crowding together too closely. Sometimes one of us would find a suspicious looking mound of freshly dug earth or a place where the grasses had been bent low. But in no case did these fearful looking places prove anything more than a gopher's diggings or the bedding down place of some large animal. Our faces were scratched by brambles, our jeans were wet or dusty depending upon the land through which we searched, our shirts were torn by low hanging branches. But on we went, moving ever slowly, ever watchfully, hoping we would find something of significance, at the same time terrified lest we would.

The woods we passed through were quiet and peaceful. Once in a while someone spoke in a hushed voice about the mammoth Indian paintbrush glowing in red bouquets all around us, or the blue of the lupin, or the fragrant pink eglantine. We were diverted for a split second by an inch long baby frog who leapt to safety ahead of us. Someone discovered a bird's nest filled with new born young. A brood of fluffy ducklings swam on a boggy pond, guarded by their mother who flew up when she spied us, tried to divert our attention. We found numerous bones, too large for human bones and far too white and bleached to have been recently dropped, but inevitably they halted the party for a few seconds.

Three or four hours of searching, though the distance covered is not great, is about all that can be done effectively. Then one's mind becomes absorbed by the annoying insects, the heat, aching legs, so most of us stopped after lunch and headed for home. Lunches, however, were packed again that night. Alarm clocks were set. We were ready to start anew on the following day to continue the ghoulish search. Indefatigably we continued day after tiring day. How long will it be, we wonder, before we will be able to walk through a woods without glancing apprehensively to each side, without looking instinctively for recently disturbed earth, without stepping gingerly over mounds of dirt.

Just as *Cabin Comments* was ready to be issued, news came to us at seven o'clock on the morning of July 28th that the bodies had been found.

August 15, 1969

ONE SUNDAY AFTERNOON several years ago, friends of ours brought two newcomers to the Valley to meet us at our home. The man was an orthopedic surgeon, his wife became a newspaper reporter. During their residency in the Valley, they both were highly respected and valued citizens. We saw them occasionally after this visit, and when one of us needed knee surgery to correct a damaged cartilage, it was this man who performed the operation. When one of us broke her leg two years ago, it was he who brought the injured leg to quick recovery.

It was these two people who disappeared mysteriously from their home. Many clues led the law enforcement officers to suspect murder.

Earlier this spring the twenty-five year old son of the doctor and his wife moved here from Las Vegas and became a member of their household. Within two days after the disappearance of his parents, the son was arrested both for driving under the influence and for the illegal possession of firearms. Three former school friends who appeared from Las Vegas put up the $10,000 bond for him, and he was released from jail. Within minutes after his release, a murder charge was filed against him, but by this time he was on his way to Las Vegas.

Two fishermen discovered the bodies of the doctor and his wife. They were buried in a shallow grave no more than three miles from their home.

The extradition hearing has been held, and at the present time we are awaiting the return of the son and his trial which will follow.

(The son pleaded guilty at the trial, and was convicted of manslaughter on both charges. He was sentenced to serve two consecutive terms of 19 years each. Ed.)

October 1, 1969

ONE BY ONE the aspen trees on the bench above the cabin are turning golden. We aren't sorry, as we shall be glad to see this summer go. First, it was the gophers. They invaded the garden in hordes, chewing the cauliflower, brussel sprouts, broccoli. A live trap helped greatly, and we hauled off thirty chattering, furry animals to a grassy place across the creek, but our garden, because of their foraging, looked sad. Then the pocket gophers came, burrowing underground and cutting plant roots with their razor sharp teeth. We waged war against them, too, but still they continued their destruction. We marveled that anything at all came of the garden. The potato crop was successful, the carrots survived, and the peas were untouched, but the rest—oh dear! A fuse blew on our electric pump, and we were without water over Labor Day. Our stereo developed a disconcerting roar and rumble. But these were personal annoyances which soon were remedied. Other irremediable troubles appeared over the Valley and have continued all summer.

We don't regret that autumn is here and summer is on its way out. The Valley this year has had more than its share of accidents—people killed in drag races, in cars, in planes, on the battle front in Vietnam. Several of our older friends have died this summer, and that has contributed greatly to the unhappiness which has pervaded many of the days. The ghastly murder of two prominent Valley residents was one of the greatest tragedies, and it will be long before the scars of that evil are gone.

The grasses are dry and crunchy as one walks through them. Through the sage on the slopes, blonde colored undergrowth makes a striking contrast to the crimson of the huckleberry and Oregon grape. Along the road to the post office, the brilliant red of the choke cherry bushes hangs low, and in the river bottom the cottonwoods are yellow in the distance. The mornings are cold, and each evening we lay a fire and enjoy its warmth as night settles in and we hear the elk bugling in the forests above the cabin. A change of season will bring, we hope, a change of events.

The chipmunks are scurrying to and from the bird feeder for last nuts and crumbs before the cold winds and snow drive them into warm tree trunks for the winter. The humming birds and green-tailed towhees have vanished. We caught sight of the bright blue of a pair of Steller's jays and the gray and black of a camp robber. We are happy to welcome them back as they may bring better days with their return.

We see elk coming out of the forests at dusk, as many as fifteen or twenty at a time. Flocks of wild geese flying in perfect formation and honking as they go are visible almost every evening against the fall sunsets. We are glad of every sign of autumn we see this year, of every breath of autumn air we breathe, as we know that the summer has gone. That makes us happy.

Pleasant things have happened this summer, too—canoe trips, picnics, visits with friends from distant parts. Too many days, though, have held shock, disturbance, and sorrow. But golden days are here at last, having a way of making past days recede into the background. All of the out of doors, aflame with brilliance, lifts the heart and soul above the world's disasters to nature's splendor.

November 1, 1969

AFTER SIX MONTHS, it was decided that a piano was not enough. The beginner in piano was presented with her instrument on her birthday about a year ago and has since been following a self-instruction book which has enabled her to play the very simplest of tunes and read notes if they are not too complicated. Whether in self defense or in the desire to have fun with her own musical instrument, the other two members of our group have acquired an alto recorder and a violin respectively. The recordist, too, is beginning with a self instruction book, the violinist returning to an instrument she played years ago, taking a self taught refresher course and learning again the feel of a fiddle under her chin, a bow in her hand. So we are all more or less beginners, and if we are in

185

the class of ignorance at this time, we also are in the class of tremendous ambition to learn. We are at that stage when anything is possible. We take turns practicing in the library downstairs, all giving each other prompt praise and encouragement, whatever the sounds may be. Joy is unbounded as each new sharp and flat is learned, as each new simple tune is played haltingly from beginning to end. We became too ambitious at one time, however, and attempted to play La Paloma together as a trio. The result is better left unmentioned, but, undaunted, we continued to practice, and about a month ago decided we were sufficiently adept to try our trio once again.

This time we chose Mozart's Minuet from Don Juan as it has only one flat and the page of music is not too black with notes. At the beginning, however, we noticed the terrifying instructions, Andante ma non troppo. None of us had the faintest idea what that meant, but we refused to be intimidated and just played it without the Andante ma non troppo and we think it sounds very well. Each one of us has practiced this melody over and over again, alto recorder, violin, and piano. About two weeks ago we felt ready to play it together. The piano player explained that she had to play the first few notes alone, the other two coming in together after that. She had a difficult time restraining the other two before it was their turn, but at last they learned to curb their eagerness and be patient. Trembling with excitement and breathing heavily with the enormous responsibility of keeping up and playing the correct notes at the correct time, we were ready. The piano player found the beginning notes and placed her fingers nervously on them, saying to the others in a quaking voice, "Here we go!" The recordist moistened her dry lips and warmed her instrument between two shaking hands. The violinist rose, sedately but quaveringly, instrument tucked under her chin, bow poised. The pianist started timidly and fearfully. The other two joined in at exactly the proper note. Confidence was gained, and we continued through measure after measure, tooting, bowing, pounding the keys. It began to sound better and better, so we lost our timidity and fright and played more and more loudly. The rafters rang and the walls shook as we continued in our glory, far too thrilled to heed instructions for softer playing. We ended with a triumphant crashing crescendo and then fell into chairs, exhausted but exhilarated by our efforts, concentration, and first success.

We still play the same minuet over and over—that will always remain our pièce de résistance. Now we have markedly increased our sense of timing, to say nothing of having developed greater poise and stage

186

presence. When we finish, we all turn to an imaginary audience to acknowledge with condescending bows and patronizing smiles the roaring applause and shouts of "Bravo!" So insistent is our imaginary audience that we are searching for encores to satisfy the demands. We think maybe the first page of Paderewski's Minuet might be a good one. The first page only, as later on there is an instruction in big, bold, frightening letters—Brillante. None of us would presume to approach anything marked Brillante, so this encore will be a short one. The second encore we have chosen is Schubert's Serenade. Here the instructions say simply Moderato. We think we might be able to handle Moderato.

We shall continue to practice and play together in our trio. By Christmas, if we begin soon, we hope to have quite a repertoire of carols. We shall continue to rise and acknowledge the applause and appreciation of our imaginary audience. We shall continue to stop our playing often to break into peals of hilarious laughter and roll on the floor holding our sides at the funny mistakes we make and the queer sounds which come forth. But we shall persist, take our places again with usual dignity and over our shoulders bow our apologies to the members of our imaginary audience and continue. We are certain they will understand and smile indulgently as we proceed.

November 15, 1969

EVERY DAY we feel gratitude for sights, sounds, fragrances of the wilderness.

In the spring:
Delicate perfume of cottonwood buds; sweet scent of choke cherry blossoms; fragrance of cool earth, leaf mould, and mushrooms pushing through moist leaves; first trilled notes of a redwing; rushing of the river, deep and full; pink and white spring beauties, clear yellow fritillarias; flash of a blue bird against melting snows.

In the summer:
Fragrance of pine trees in hot sun; fresh aroma of sage bushes after a summer shower; eager chatter of burros as we approach them with carrots in our pockets; lilting song of the wrens, raising a family under the eaves; gentle splash of canoe paddles in quiet waters; roadsides gay with wild roses, lupin, Indian paint brush; jagged lightning, rolling thunder, black clouds, heralding a mountain storm.

In the autumn:
Pungent aroma of the first aspen log fire in the fireplace; smoky scent of

187

jackets and caps after a last chilly picnic around a camp fire; sound of the sledge hammer striking the wedge in a mighty log; bugling of elk on frosty nights; whispering of quaking aspens in a cool, fall wind; the Valley transformed over night into a land of scarlet and gold; white trumpeter swans against a blue sky.

In the winter:

Delicate smell of hot buttered popcorn and fresh apples; whiffs of snow in the still air foretelling an approaching blizzard; swish of SkiDoos skimming over crisp snow; the hard peck-peck of camp robbers, woodpeckers, Steller's jays at the bird feeder; dancing icicles forming a wintry decoration for edges of roofs; acres of snow sparkling clean and brilliant under a cold, full moon.

Every day we feel gratitude for sights, sounds, fragrances of the wilderness.

1970

AS YET, we haven't entirely made up our minds about 1970. True, the year is still in its infancy, and it would be unfair and unwise to make any pronouncements about it now, but so far we have had a few slight indications. There may be troubles in 1970, as there are in every year, but there is evidence that if troubles arise, they will be inconsequential and easily remedied.

First of all, the one of our group who planned a trip to Antarctica left our local airport amid shouts of "Good luck!" "Keep warm!" "Have fun!" "Bon voyage!" "Bring back a penguin!" We had word from her from New York where she was visiting for a few days. She reported that flights had been fine, that she was having a good time, and we were happy to catch a note of eagerness and excitement in her voice about the big trip which was to begin on Sunday. The phone rang here on Saturday morning. A telegram from her travel agency. Her trip had been canceled! We were appalled at the news, desperate with disappointment for her. We rushed to the phone to catch her if we could at the address she had given us. We reached her just as she was stepping out the door, and gave her the unwelcome news. She could not believe it. She said she would spend the rest of the day telephoning to see what could be done, what had gone wrong. She phoned us that same night saying there had been a fire in the ship's kitchen. The insurance company refused to grant protection unless every inch of the ship's electric wiring was inspected and pronounced safe. Never could all that be completed in time, which meant the news had been correct—no trip. After all the time spent in anticipation, in making reservations, in obtaining a passport, in buying necessary new clothes, in packing, in getting inoculation shots! She could have wept. We could have wept. True, another similar trip was scheduled in two weeks, but the passenger list was full and there could not be much hope of a cancellation now. At this end we began to prepare

189

for her immediate return, making room in her closet for new clothes not worn, in the studio for hundreds of films not used. Tuesday night she phoned again, and there was an unmistakable lilt in her voice. She was on the January 16 trip after all! Incredible, but a cancellation had come. She would go exactly where she had originally planned to go, she said, the ship would be in fine condition, and all was well. Trouble—but not serious and easily remedied.

Here at home we had our "sock-in" snow storm just before Christmas. Jeeps were taken to the parking lot, their engine heaters plugged in; motors of SkiDoos were started. Everything apparently was fine, but we had no sooner started one SkiDoo than wham! right into a snow drift we plowed and were stuck. That SkiDoo we left for the time being. We walked back through the deep snow to start the second one. That started like a charm, too, until crack! right into a hidden sage bush we rode, stuck on its gnarled trunk. We didn't dare to try the third machine, fearful that it might meet a similar fate and we would be left with none to take on a rescue mission for the others. By this time it was nearly dark, so we abandoned our job of digging out until morning. The next day, shovels in hand, out we went, chopped the sage from the treads and skis of the little machine, started the motor in a flash, and away we sped to get the other machine from its wintry drift. We made a track right next to it and, with only a little shoveling, moved it easily. Off we skimmed, over snow, through drifts, making a new track. No machine was in the least hurt, we were greatly relieved, and there were our three SkiDoos, each under its protective cover, right in front of the gate, ready for use at any time. Trouble—but not serious and easily remedied.

And then the temperature dropped—steadily, fast, until before ten o'clock at night it had reached 20 degrees below zero. Days were cold, too, and we waited to go for the mail until early afternoons when the thermometer rose to zero. Blue skies, bright sun, but bitterly cold. One morning, after several days and nights of this, we noticed the water pressure was low. Finally the water from the faucets was reduced to a trickle and a cough, and then all stopped in a last rusty gasp. Frozen pipes! Our reliable plumber lives miles away and was busy with innumerable other frozen pipes in the Valley, so we were thrown upon our own resources and ingenuity. We found the frozen pipe. We went to the attic and got down a fan, moved one of the greenhouse heaters as close to the pipe as it would reach, and then filled our hibachi with charcoal, lit it, and waited. In about three hours we heard a familiar and heartening sound, as beautiful to our ears as a favorite symphony. The pump was beginning to hum and bring in water—hooray! Pipes unfrozen, good pressure for water. Trouble—but not serious and easily remedied.

So we think that 1970 may have bounced off to a good start, after all. We know the trip to Antarctica will proceed with no mishap or disappointment and that it will be all and more than was expected. We know the SkiDoos are in splendid shape and will run with no difficulty over smooth, hard snow tracks. We know that when we turn on a faucet, we shall hear an unlimited supply of water gushing forth. The temperatures now have moderated considerably. We think we have learned a great deal in the past few days—to be patient when long anticipated trips are canceled, to be careful of drifts and hidden sage bushes when SkiDooing, in cold weather to keep the hibachi, filled with charcoal and ready to light, near temperamental water pipes. We sit by the fire on long winter evenings now, laughing over our past troubles, realizing that the uses of adversity can indeed be sweet, that this is our life, "exempt from public haunt," and finding good in everything.

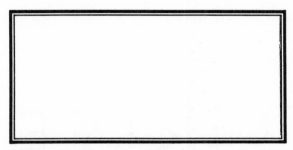

The frame contains a picture of the mountains and the cabin in a snow storm.

February 1, 1970

IT HAS CEASED to be funny. It has even ceased to be fun. We love snow, and when the winter skies grow gray, when the mountains disappear into whirling white mists, we settle back and look forward to two or three days by the fire with books, knitting, and music. We have long since learned to keep a plentiful supply of provisions on hand during winter months, so we are never troubled on that score. We love snow and snowy days—but this! Days and days and days of snow, high temperatures which mean more precipitation. We go to the Jeeps at the road in our SkiDoos and make a fine track; by the time we return in less than an hour, the track is completely obliterated. The rotary plow only three days ago cleared our snowy parking lot and left it clean and open. Now it is packed full of snow again. We used our Toro snowblower to clear the porches, but that no longer is possible as the little machine can not throw the snow high enough over the vast mountains that have accumulated around the porches. In the afternoons we shovel a narrow path to the breezeway where the wood pile is, and by evening there is no trace of the path. The snow on the level has risen, risen, risen until we see nothing of our five and a half foot buck and rail fence.

Yesterday between storms we put on snow shoes. Without them we sank thigh deep into the soft snow. Even the snow shoes sank a little and became clogged with heavy, wet snow. We glanced up occasionally and saw with joy in our hearts patches of blue sky. The sun ventured out once or twice. Soon we could see the peaks as the clouds lifted, the first time in days and days. When we went to bed, we could see the full moon shining brightly on the snow, illuminating the mountains, the sage flats, the bench above the cabin, the river below. We went to bed, happy and relieved.

Little did we know what was ahead. By the time we got up, the entire Valley was milky white, not a sign of a peak, not a sign of enormous dark pines standing at the top of the bench, not a sign of the black butte across the river. There was a deep silence everywhere which we have grown to recognize only too well. When we looked out the windows, snow again there was, wet snow, falling fast and giving no indication of abating. We groaned, sat down to breakfast without a word. We let the dogs out, and, with crest-fallen expressions, they stood motionless on the porch. They returned quickly, their coats white with huge wet snowflakes. And then before noon the winds came, demoniac gales which swept ferociously around the cabin, blew the snow in vast, twirling sweeps until the sage flats seemed to rise in white clouds and race away before our very eyes. One ski area was closed, ski meets were postponed, roads over mountain passes were shut down because of avalanches.

To keep up our morale, we tell ourselves that at least we don't *have* to go out, we have plenty of provisions, the mail at the post office can wait. And with all this winter moisture, we think how the Morel mushrooms will sprout by the million in the spring! Small comfort now. We smile feebly and try to remember what the sun looks like.

If we recall correctly, during our recent bitterly cold spell, when thermometers dropped to 30 degrees below zero at night, we longed for milder temperatures and snow. Well, we have it. We are sending this issue to Buenos Aires to greet our Antarctic traveler before she starts on the last lap of her journey home. We want to prepare her gradually and gently in advance for what she will find when she gets here. We may not have penguins and seals and whales, but.... Enough said.

OVER THE BENCH in back of the cabin and near the ponds lies an enormous tree trunk, obviously having lain there for a long, long time. This tree trunk is all that is left of a once powerful cottonwood. It is not particularly attractive, and it has been a positive nuisance at times when we were walking near the ponds and either had to climb over its rough trunk or crawl under it. But the old tree holds a secret which we soon discovered and for that reason has become very special to us, and we hope it will remain in its present form and condition for years to come. Hundreds of daffodils grow around it in the spring, but when they have gone, we almost lose sight of it because of the dense underbrush which grows around it each summer—nettles, choke cherry bushes, "sarvis" berry shrubs, and wild roses. In the winter we see a roof of deep snow covering the tree, and it is then that bright blue Steller's jays light on it briefly with pieces of food in their beaks and then disappear into the tree tops above to enjoy their meal. Dramatically marked black and white magpies also come to the old tree as do the singing chickadees. In the summer its rough bark is used as a bridge and a haven by innumerable chipmunks. Once we saw on its roots a hawk devouring a freshly caught fish; at another time we watched at one end of the old trunk the cat-like form of a great horned owl, his yellow eyes blinking sleepily in the blinding sun.

But the tree trunk is truly special to us because of the many small animals that make it their home. Far under the trunk, near the roots, there is a large protected space which summer storms and winter snows do not reach. This sheltered place has been discovered by wild creatures and has afforded them a temporary home. In the spring the first occupant of our tree trunk is Christobel, the skunk. We can see her foot prints all around in the melting snows, and when she comes to search for crumbs the birds have dropped under the feeder, she pounces upon each one, eats part of her meal there, and then promptly carries the remainder to her tree trunk home. Once when we startled her at a meal under the feeder, she became so alarmed that she took off at once, tumbling and turning somersaults in the snow until she reached the safety of the tree. Next the chipmunks arrive, and so small are they that the hollow space under the roots can accommodate any number of families. They scurry busily in and out all day long, eating their meals, held in tiny trembling paws, on the roof of their home, rushing with stuffed cheeks into the dark recesses below where they keep their cache of food. There are doubtless many tiny insects, spiders and beetles, who share the tree trunk home with the animals.

193

This winter one of us called the others to come quickly to the kitchen windows. By the frozen ponds we saw a ruffed grouse, looking, as she walked sedately about, like an elegant old-fashioned lady attired in hoop skirts. When she moved over the snow, one could almost imagine on her small feet a pair of ice skates, so smoothly and airily did she float along. There was a delicate tracery of her foot prints leading from the tree trunk home, so we know she must have paused there for a while during her search for seeds and berries still clinging to the snowy bushes.

We had not seen for some time our lovely marten Lucinda, and feared she had deserted us. But one evening there was the sound of a thud on the bird feeder, and when we went quickly to see what it was, there she was back again, tearing at the cloth mesh bag in which we keep suet for the birds. The soft orange fur on her chest shone in the light, and she looked at us through the window with the same old quizzical expression on her kitten-like face. She took a large piece of suet in her mouth, leapt gracefully from the window ledge down the log wall to the snowy ground. And, sure enough, she headed directly for the tree trunk home. Since then we have welcomed her back with bones and scraps of meat and have watched with pleasure the many tracks her paws have left in the snow and on the roof of her tree trunk hide-out.

After Lucinda, it will be Christobel's turn again. Then will come the hungry chipmunks. So the cycle will continue, bringing us at each season a different small animal or bird to watch. We offer the food, the old tree trunk provides safety and protection. The combination is a happy one for all.

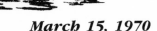

March 15, 1970

THE NEW red and white passenger ship sailed through the calm blue waters of the South Atlantic Ocean. The white wandering albatross and the dark giant fulmar or "stinker" followed behind, soaring in the air currents. We could see the radar arms on the mast revolving ceaselessly, and we knew that the ship was on the alert for icebergs. We had left the bleak but fascinating Falkland Islands behind us thirty-six hours before, and now we were on deck in the bright sun watching for our first sign of Antarctica.

We had been told, as we left the Falklands, that there might be rough weather ahead; we were surprised and relieved, therefore, at the calm seas. We had gone through the roaring forties and the furious fifties, and now were ready to cross the latitude line into the screaming sixties. Yet the sea remained still. But as we looked ahead, on the port side were two gleaming white specks to remind us that we were not in tropical seas. Two enormous icebergs gradually loomed larger as we approached. They were beautifully carved by the sea into intricate shapes, and the pristine whiteness of their sun-facing sides and tops was dazzling. Their caves and crevasses and gullies were turquoise and blue-green and azure. Some of the passengers on board were fascinated to find shapes of people, faces, animals in the carved ice. Many of us preferred to see nothing but the sheer splendor of their forms and colors. As our ship drew nearer and passed the great bergs, our cameras clicked and our minds imagined the huge mass of ice which must be submerged beneath the water, a mass large enough to support the bergs, huge as city blocks. To the starboard there were more. Large icebergs, small floating pans of ice, flat-topped bergs, sculptured mountains of ice, more and more of every size and shape. As darkness fell, there were many more than we could count, and we slept that night in wondering anticipation of what the next day would bring.

In the morning the ship was not moving, and we hurried on deck to see where we were. The winds slapped our faces with stinging snow; the gray clouds scuttled by and seemed to be within easy reach of our hands. The black and white indistinct shapes of mountains were all around us, enclosing us in a bay where the seas were rough and the winds loud and boisterous. Sheltered here in Admiralty Bay on King George Island in the South Shetland Islands, we had a taste of what the screaming sixties could be.

Soon we were told it was too rough for us to go ashore. Instead we would cruise around Admiralty Bay. Then we would head for the open sea toward the bay where the Russian and Chilean scientific stations are located. As we cruised, we saw high, sharp mountains rising out of the sea. Their volcanic blackness contrasted markedly with the many white glaciers. These contrasts were softened by the gray clouds which covered the tops of the mountains and created mysteries of unseen peaks. We did not stay long on deck but sought the warmth and protection of the lounge, thankful for the bright red parkas and balaclavas which had been issued to us.

Late that afternoon we went ashore to see the Chilean and Russian stations which are located within 500 yards of each other. We were enthusiastically welcomed at both stations and were shown the scientific equipment and facilities. Even the penguins along the shore seemed glad to see us. Later that evening we entertained the personnel of both stations aboard our ship, the "Lindblad Explorer." Our scheduled departure time was delayed somewhat by the hilarity of the gay party and the difficulty of persuading some of our visitors to leave us.

April 1, 1970

HOPE BAY is located on the very tip of the Antarctic Peninsula. We hoped that our desires to land at the permanent Argentinian Station there could be realized. Most of the time, even in the summer, this bay is choked by pack ice drifting north from the Atlantic side of the Peninsula, from the great ice shelves of the Weddell Sea. The next morning, there we were, anchored off the station, with blue and green icebergs all about us. The great glaciers of the region fall in ice cascades around the station. Going ashore in our life boats and rubber boats was a pleasure in the bright sun, but that evening we sailed a little earlier than expected because the pack ice was beginning to close in.

One of the most curious spots in the entire Antarctic region is Deception Island. We approached the island in the early morning and watched from deck as its dark bulk loomed ever larger on the horizon. The tops of the mountains composing the island are white with glaciers, but the shores are curiously dark. No glaciers reach the sea there. Our ship finally took us through a narrow passage called Neptune's Bellows, and we were inside a volcanic crater. There were no icebergs here, and the black sands of the beaches steamed in the cold air. When our biologist took the temperature of the water nearby, he found that it was 180 degrees Fahreheit, being warmed by the underwater heat of the volcano in whose crater we were anchored. This area was formerly a British Station, but all that was left of the station was the rusty, shattered remains of huge oil storage tanks. These had been shelled into uselessness by the British in World War II to prevent their being used by the Germans for refueling their South Atlantic and Pacific raiders. Eruptions of the volcano in 1967 and again in 1969 completed the destruction of the British

196

Station. We were told that the activity of the volcano made it too dangerous for persons to be left there unless they had a means of rapid evacuation. We were happy that our ship stayed just inside the entrance and did not penetrate deeply into the circular bay.

From Deception Island we again crossed the Bransfield Strait and sailed into the beautiful Gerlache Strait. Here the islands drew closer to the mainland; the glaciers were much thicker and more numerous; the sea passages were narrower and filled with ice. As we sailed into the bay which contained the Argentinian Admirante Brown Station, we thought we had never seen such rugged beauty. The sea was calm, studded with gleaming white ice. The mountains were rocky; the glaciers were brilliant blues and greens. It was here that we saw our second whale rise to the surface of the water and sink and disappear.

We thought we could touch the glaciers on either side of us as we made our way through the Neumeyer Strait to Port Lockroy on Anvers Island. The bright, sunny day kept us all on deck, and the penguins, acting like porpoises, vied with the scenery for our attention. At Port Lockroy, an abandoned whaling station, we went ashore to watch the thousands of gentoo penguins who entertained us with their human antics. One of us thought the vertebrae of the skeleton of a blue whale we found there would make perfect seats for the bar on our ship. The fact that the ship's ice-making machine had long since failed us was no problem. Here as elsewhere we collected ice for our cocktails from the bergs all around us.

April 15, 1970

AFTER ANCHORING for a night close to the British Base at Argentine Island, we proceeded south in an attempt to cross the Antarctic Circle and reach Adelaide Island. The outlook for this was not good, for we were told that a supply ship which preceded us on this route had taken sixteen days to push its way through pack ice to Adelaide Island. We made our first attempt in a blizzard which covered the ship with several inches of snow but which cleared as the day progressed. Pack ice was everywhere, and most of the time we could see very little open water.

197

We saw hundreds of Weddell seals, crabeater seals, and a few leopard seals, all resting on cakes of ice. They seemed indifferent as our ship passed close enough to them to nudge the bergs, but finally they humped their way off the ice into the sea. The ice became thicker and thicker, and at last our ship was stopped dead. We could make no further headway. We backed up, maneuvered our way out of the impasse, and turned around. When we reached relatively clear water again, we tried a new lead into the pack and again proceeded until we were stopped by the ice. Four times we did this and finally, because we did not have sixteen days to spend fighting the pack, we headed north, disappointed that we had not succeeded in penetrating the last twenty miles to cross the Antarctic Circle, but happy that we had not been "beset" in the pack as so many of the ships in earlier days had been.

The sight of the Palmer Station on Anvers Island brought a wave of patriotism to the Americans on board ship, for this was the first American flag we had seen since leaving New York weeks before. The approach to the station was one of the most beautiful sights of the trip. We maneuvered around huge icebergs, some of the most colorful we had seen. Seals and penguins were everywhere on the floes; some of the Adelie penguins were on the tops of the lofty bergs where they evidently were enjoying the scenery. Everywhere the birds—the skuas, the cape pigeons, the albatross, and the Wilson's petrels—flew and cried above us. The thick, massive glaciers on either side of the station emphasized the isolation of the buildings. When we went ashore, we found bulldozers being operated in typical American fashion over huge boulders, only inches away from precipitous drops. Two ships were tied up at the small dock, a Chilean supply ship and the motorized sailing ship "Hero," named after Nathaniel Palmer's ship in which he may have first discovered the mainland of Antarctica in 1820. The "Hero" is operated by the National Science Foundation and is entirely devoted to scientific work.

At Potter's Cove we went ashore to see the many sea elephants along the beaches there. These huge beasts, weighing many tons, hitched their bulk into the sea when we approached within inches of them, but otherwise seemed little disturbed by our presence.

That evening, at eleven o'clock, many of us were on deck taking pictures of the glorious sunset. The pink and yellow rays of the sun reflected on the glacier-covered mountains, and the blues and greens of the icebergs deepened in color as the sun sank lower in the sky. The black and white landscape made a startling contrast to the brilliant colors of the sunset. We lingered long, knowing that this was our last view of Antarctica.

ONE OF US went for the mail the other day. The two who were left at the cabin knew that something of interest had happened since the trip to the post office was taking longer than usual. When the third member finally returned, we knew from her excited expression and shining eyes that we had been right. "Well," she exclaimed, "what an adventure I've had! Come and hear."

On her way to the post office, she had noticed a strange looking bird by the side of the road and at the same time had seen a trace of blood on the snow near its feet. Several yards further, to her amazement, she had seen a similar but smaller bird and again there were drops of blood near the place it was standing. She stopped the car and went to the first bird who proved to be a Western grebe, rare in this area. Then she went to the second bird and found it was an eared grebe, also uncommon in these parts. Neither bird gave evidence of serious injury, though both seemed stunned. Fearing a coyote or hawk had hurt them more gravely than was apparent, she decided to visit our naturalist friend and inquire from him what could have happened. When she found him, they returned together to the spot, and he, too, looked at the grebes and thought from their appearance that it probably had been no predator who had hurt them. The two people soon left, having decided that it would be best to leave the birds where they were until they had recovered sufficiently from their bewildered condition and could resume their natural life. The surprising and mysterious thing was that they were so far from any water.

We were extremely interested in the story and spoke all day of the grebes, wondering what had injured them and what had become of them. Early that evening our phone rang and it was the naturalist. He said that he, too, had wondered further about the birds and no sooner had left them than he decided to return to investigate the mystery further. He found them exactly where they had been. When he picked them up to examine them more closely, he discovered at once where they had been injured. Their feet were bruised and one grebe was missing a toe. He was perplexed and could not understand what could have caused similar injuries to each. He looked around, found no answer to the problem, and suddenly his eyes fell upon the black topped road, glistening and wet from the early morning's brief spring storm. The solution to the question came to him quickly. The birds had been flying low in search of water, had seen the shining road in the snow storm, had mistaken it for a pond or stream, and had skimmed down to land on it. In so doing they had hurt their feet. The kind naturalist, eager to help them find water, had

199

carried them to his car, driven to nearby ponds, had slid down the steep embankment above the ponds, a grebe under each arm, and had deposited them into the water. He was glad to report to us that immediately they swam off, happy and safe. He had left them there, knowing they would certainly be able now to care for themselves. He scrambled back up the embankment and phoned us to tell the conclusion and solution to the mystery.

As we say, when we start on some simple, commonplace errand, we never can tell....

CABIN COMMENTS IS CELEBRATING A BIRTHDAY. SEVEN YEARS OF UNINTERRUPTED PUBLICATION. WE ARE GOING TO TAKE A "SABBATICAL LEAVE" AND RESUME THE PAPER IN THE FALL.

July 1, 1970

With the return of the Rufous humming bird, we know for certain that summer with warm, sun-filled days is here. A lush green is the Valley now after the June rains, and the tall bouquets of balsam root with their sunny, yellow flowers cover sage flats and gentle slopes. Meadows are humming with the lazy drone of bees over golden dandelions. The dirt road leading to the cabin, filled only a few days ago with puddles which we thought would never disappear, is now dry, and a cloud of dust follows the car as we drive in and out. The Morel mushrooms we picked last week are drying on strings at one of the kitchen windows, resembling dancing dolls as they bow and pirouette when a breeze catches them. The robin who built her nest on the rafters of our breezeway is feeding three hungry babies who stretch long, lusty necks when they hear her approach. Horses are in their summer pastures, and one day last week a big stock truck drove down our road and we saw with joy and excitement four pairs of long ears, eight bright eyes and knew our burros were back to be loved, petted, and pampered with carrots and oats. Butterflies of all colors hover over wild flowers in the yard, and moths appear silently from nowhere at night to spread their beautiful wings aginst the windows. Buds on the peonies are swelling, the lilac bushes show purple among the green leaves, some of the columbine is already in bloom, and yesterday we picked a tiny bouquet of lilies-of-the-valley. The delphiniums against the cabin are bushy and strong, and round, fuzzy buds cover the poppy plants. The kitchen garden already shows us we shall have an

200

abundance of fresh peas, carrots, onions, radishes, potatoes, lettuce, and cabbages.

Now is the time, when all spring chores have been finished, to turn our thoughts to mountain trails, canoe excursions, picnics and cook-outs, fishing along quiet mountain streams and lakes. Hot summer days, refreshingly cool summer nights. The whole Valley lies waiting.

October 15, 1970

Sing heigh nonny nonny and a nonny ho.
We're as mad as the wind when the gales do blow.
We're as mad as a hatter on a wild March day.
Sing heigh nonny nonny—we like it that way.
We saw two puppies—we couldn't say no.
We're mad and we're crazy, and this we know.
But they cuddled in our arms, they made little sighs,
They cocked little heads, they winked bright eyes.
Our hearts were trapped, and we were charmed;
We raised faint objections but were disarmed.
They're tiny as can be—only eight weeks old.
They're black and white, and their wiles manifold.
They play and they romp in the sun all day;
They have mock battles in the funniest way.
They chase their tails, they chew on ears.
Our words of scolding never cause fears.
They get their way, we take a back seat;
Their mastery over us is quite complete.
They really are dears. We think they're heaven sent.
(The mop is ready in case of accident!)
They look so sad if displeasure we show,
So at times like these, "Oh, just let it go!"
But we won't complain; we'll smile and forget
When they misbehave; we'll have our innings yet.
Our stocks, we know, will very soon soar.
Let the old bear die and the bull start to roar.
Our pups wax strong on good steak bones;
The one is named Dow, the other one Jones.
We know all is well with stock markets now,
Because of little Jones and his brother Dow.

201

So it's heigh willy winny and a willy wink.
We're not so mad as you might think.
The nation needs a lift, a touch of affluence,
So we got two mascots which makes good sense.

November 15, 1970

A FLAMING SUNSET flings its banners and ribbons across the entire sky. For this immensity, the wide and free expanses, the huge and mighty natural beauties around us we are grateful. We appreciate, too, the frequent exciting and thrilling experiences we have here such as the sight of a hundred sand-hill cranes in a hay meadow, twenty to fifty elk on the bench above the cabin, the mating dance of hundreds of sage grouse, an enormous harvest moon rising gloriously above the butte, or, over the limitless sweep of sky, the slow and ominous approach of a thundering, flashing mountain storm. We also like to pause occasionally and express appreciation and gratitude for the simpler and less spectacular things which fill our lives as well.

Yesterday we saw the last brave and sturdy dandelion growing near the path. Slender, blonde grasses wave gracefully beside the road, and through the dusting of early snow we can catch, if we are watchful, the ruddy color of the leaves of an Oregon grape plant. The low willow bushes shine red in the sun, and a few slender branches of a young cottonwood are outlined against the evening sky. A gray and pink striped pebble, wet with melting snow, shines on the dirt road, and from under a sage bush scampers a little mouse. The first snows have traced lace work patterns on all the wire gates, so delicate that the slightest breath of wind carries them away in a puff of powder. The heavy hoof prints of moose and elk are apparent everywhere, and near them in the wet snow are the tiny tracks of a weasel.

Not only in the early winter season, but all through the year, we find minute things to see, to smell, to hear—things which arouse in us feelings of wonder and admiration. A bright red jewel of a toadstool under an old log. The fragility of a dainty blue harebell. A shower of golden aspen leaves drifting to the ground. The miraculous symmetry of a spider's web against the clothes line.

For wondrous adventures, for mountain and forest and river splendor, for all of this we feel eternally grateful. But for the smaller, the less sensational things we feel a full measure of gratitude, too. Our hearts go out to a tiny chickadee with its subdued and quiet coloring quite as much as to a flamboyant jay or a flaming tanager.

BEFORE WE BROUGHT our two puppies, Dow and Jones, to their new home, we realized that there might be problems. We had no idea how our fifteen-year-old Bitters would receive them. We could not guess whether or not our pampered eight-year-old Tia would accept them. For a long time our older dogs have been masters of the cabin and the entire property. To share their home, to say nothing of our devoted attentions and affections, could, we understood after hearing the dangers of the generation gap, be baffling for them and might prove to be a damaging if not a positively traumatic experience. We felt concern, too, about how eight week old puppies would adjust to the staid ways of their elders.

When we first arrived at the cabin with the new puppies, we let them explore the yard alone, allowing Bitters and Tia to watch the new arrivals from the living room windows. Frightening barking and howling arose from the cabin as the two older dogs ran from window to window, voicing their outraged and insulted feeling about the two intruders. Then one of us went indoors, put Bitters and Tia on leashes and cautiously led them to investigate Dow and Jones at closer range. Bitters made a quick lunge in their direction and might have devoured both in one gulp had we not pulled back hard on his leash and taken him back into the cabin. It was not long, however, before he learned to tolerate the puppies not only in the yard but in the cabin as well, although doubtless he will always retain something of a disdainful attitude toward their immaturity and lack of judgment. Tia, more curious than resentful, looked the puppies over, even deigned to give their little black faces a welcoming lick or two, and it was not long before we watched her escorting Dow and Jones around the garden, to the porches, and back to the yard again. We were amused to see her small, blonde figure trotting from one end of the yard to the other, two black specks tumbling after her as they were taught their limitations and privileges. Tia has continued to supervise and watch them carefully. Bitters cares for them now in a slightly indifferent manner, calling them to their meals with a sharp bark, watching them devour their food, being certain they finish every crumb.

But the generation gap existing at the cabin was not solved so quickly or so painlessly as the above account might suggest. The learning process on the part of both the younger and older generation continues, and we find ourselves watching and learning a great deal. If the puppies overstep their boundaries and come too close to the older dogs when they prefer to rest, a low growl teaches them their place. The puppies have learned not to approach the older dogs when they are enjoying between-meal crackers; otherwise they know their ears may be nipped as a firm disciplinary measure. Dow and Jones are welcome to lie near the fire with Bitters and Tia close by, but it is the older generation which picks the choice spots first. Special privileges are accorded Bitters and Tia, such as sleeping on the sofas, curling up on armchairs to look out the windows, but the puppies soon were taught by their elders that their place is on the floor.

On the other hand, the puppies are given independence and freedom to play as much as they please. During their tumbling and cavorting together, Bitters and Tia sit by and watch with interest. They watch but never interrupt the puppy play or try to revert to puppyhood themselves. Only once did Tia try to emulate their fun. She had watched the puppies digging holes in the yard, and she went off by herself one morning to the library downstairs and dug a deep hole in the planter between two schizanthus plants, sending the dirt flying over chairs, sofas, carpet. She soon tired of this, however, and, looking a little chagrined, slunk up the stairs and back to the living room.

Dow and Jones have rawhide toys which amuse them and keep them quietly occupied during much of the time they are indoors. The older dogs have never once tried to take these toys from the puppies, but lie and watch them as they chew them, toss them into the air, struggle with each other for their possession. But when puppy jaws are tired of chewing, when Dow and Jones prefer another adventure, both Bitters and Tia approach the rawhide toys, sniff them, and then each takes one and settles down contentedly for a turn at enjoying them.

The generation gap exists, thank goodness, and we hope it always will. The puppies may play and romp as much as they like as far as their elders are concerned, provided they do not become too obstreperous and upset the family balance. They may have their toys unmolested, their dishes of food with no interference, their crackers with no envy on the part of Bitters and Tia. But for these privileges they must assume responsibilities. They must give consideration and respect to their elders. There are certain limits which the older dogs have wisely placed upon their behavior. Dow and Jones are learning these and are adhering to them. We see real progress being made because the younger generation is teaching the older great enthusiasms and new ways to approach old problems. And we admire our older dogs because, although they appreciate and do their best to understand the puppies' youthful and often ebullient behavior, they prefer to remain a little aloof with their more mature judgment, their wisdom, and their invaluable experience of life.

1971

January 1, 1971

WHEN IT ARRIVED, we were aghast. How in the world would we ever use it, this most expensive of Christmas presents? Where could we put it? Would it ruin the appearance of the entire cabin? When we saw it loaded on the back of an enormous truck coming down our road—what an oddity it was! The truck stopped on the other side of the gate, and through the rapidly falling snow, we could see the figures of two husky men carefully lifting it from the truck and hauling its two sections into place against the back porch. It was constructed, we noticed, of a lattice of two by fours, was about ten feet long and at least ten feet wide, and stood over five feet high. All three of us, the one who had given, the two who were receiving, knew its purpose, but we could not imagine ever being able to use it as we had planned—so high it was, so enormous! Perhaps, we thought, we can rent it out as a dance floor. Maybe it can be used to stage theatricals, even operas. Certainly the entire Nibelungenlied cycle could be presented here easily, with room to spare. We all were disappointed and disconsolate. The two of us to whom this structure had been given tried to keep up our spirits for the sake of its donor. An hour or so later, the truck appeared again, this time loaded with the last two parts of our gift. These parts resembled a jungle gym intended for a gargantuan child, but they proved to be two ramps for either side of the platform. These ramps, too, were unloaded, hauled into place, and firmly bolted to the platform. Our priceless Christmas gift stood complete in all its stark and naked splendor. It towered into the air to a frightening height; the ramps were steep, and we thought that never in the world would we muster the courage to use them. But wait.

Winter at the cabin and the reason for this lavish gift must now be explained. It is hard to imagine the vast amounts of snow which fall here; even people from town or from the other side of the river are amazed when they come to our area and see the heaps and drifts of snow which accumulate during the winter and early spring months. All of this we love and enjoy to the full with one exception. For years we have left our SkiDoos on the other side of the fence, a good hundred feet from the cabin door. We have lugged heavy boxes of groceries and packages through the deep snows. Sometimes in heavy blizzards the littlest SkiDoo would disappear from sight entirely and we had to dig for hours to find and recover it. Even after mild snows we always had to shovel away the drifted snows from the machines and also dig a short track for them to follow when we started them on their way. Certainly, we had thought, there must be an easier way. So the platform and ramps were planned and given as a splendid Christmas gift by their ingenious designer. We would drive the SkiDoos up the ramp and park them at the top where blowing snows could not drift around them. Down the other side of the ramp we would go to drive them out. A marvelous idea! Such hauling and digging it would save! How convenient to step out the back door and onto the SkiDoos without having to wade hip-deep through snow! How easy to unload boxes at the back door!

Shortly after the arrival of our gift, the heavy snows came. Snow and snow and snow and winds with drifting, swirling snows all about the cabin. Now is the time to try the platform, we thought. Fearfully, cautiously we drove the SkiDoos through the back gap in the fence, gained speed to get up the ramp, and suddenly there we were, on top of the world. How easy it had been! We were glad now for the ten by ten foot platform. The slopes of the ramps were gentle, not nearly so precipitous as it had looked at first. The SkiDoos now stand, high and dry, completely free of snow, and with no more danger of being submerged in drifts. Carrying in heavy packages is simple. And, wonder of wonders, the ungainly platform and ramps have become positively attractive as their sharp, bare outlines are softened with snow. We go to the windows many times each day to admire the new invention and the perky SkiDoos on top. And what a comfort to step out the back door and have them so near!

The puppies have discovered a new plaything and romp underneath and up, chasing each other in wild abandon around and around. Up the ramps they go, underneath where they have secret caves and tunnels. We stand and watch their play and laugh as we see two small black bodies appear and then in a flash disappear through tunnels and down snow slides they have made.

And what shall we do with it in the summer time when it again stands stark and bare? That problem was easily settled. We shall train fast-growing hop vines over its sides and shall decorate it with large redwood tubs of flowers on top. Perhaps we shall put redwood furniture on top, too, and in the early spring and late fall when the summer sun is not blazing, have picnics there every day. Thus it will add grace and charm to the entire cabin. We shall enjoy both levels, the one above, the one underneath the platform and shall call them quite proudly the lower and upper mezzanine. The monster has turned out to be a thing of beauty and use after all. The Christmas present which seemed impossible at first has already become an institution at the cabin. We can hardly wait to discover more uses for it, as yet undreamed of, because we know surely that its potential is unlimited as it stands there in all its glory to challenge our imaginations.

February 1, 1971

ON AUTUMN MORNINGS when the ground is covered with a powdering of light snow or in the spring when the ground is soft, we often see on the other side of our fence the hoof prints of deer, moose, and elk.

Usually there is nothing extraordinary for them to see—only the three of us sitting at the card table, or knitting or reading before the fire. It is much the same picture when we have company, only then there are more people to watch and perhaps more varied activities. Always there are, too, the dogs who amuse themselves by chewing on their big rawhide toys, or who play together with a discarded sock or mitten, or who simply lie before the fire and sleep. Such are the scenes which our visiting and curious wild animals will see on most evenings, but occasionally something different presents itself and must cause even greater wonder in their minds as they gaze in disbelief at what they see through our large windows.

For instance, last night we were listening to the Haffner Symphony, conducted by Bruno Walter. One of us, stirred by the music more than she could stand, seized a knitting needle for a baton, and leapt to her feet. She took her place in front of the fireplace at an imaginary podium and proceeded to conduct the entire symphony with fervor, grace, and understanding. The other two, sitting by, nodded in approval at her reading of it and remarked that she brought out very skillfully the strings in the last movement. At the conclusion, our fervent director gave a last flourish with the knitting needle, bowed graciously to her audience of six—the four amazed dogs were part of the group—and was gratified to hear the human voices shouting "Bravo!"

On occasions when we are planning to attend a formal affair of some kind, such as a wedding or christening, we feel we must dress in more appropriate fashion than our usual slacks. Several evenings before the event, we go to the attic, open suitcases and boxes, and bring down what finery we have saved from our more civilized days. We try on, model, and exchange various slips, dresses, hats, and gloves. On those nights the wild animals must smile to themselves at our show especially when they hear the gales of laughter which fill the cabin and when they see the dogs prancing around us and barking. If one keeps a piece of wearing apparel for seven years, we have heard, it comes back into style, and this we are finding true. Our long skirts no longer attract attention, and when we attended a wedding last summer, we even were complimented upon wearing precisely the most fashionable length skirt. During the mini skirt rage, one of us bought such a dress and kept it to burst forth upon the others as a great and daring surprise. She little realized what havoc and uproar it would cause when she entered our style show. One evening after the other two had decided what to wear at an approaching social event, had changed and exchanged garb several times until the best of our ancient wardrobe of dresses had been chosen, the third quietly went to her room, closed the door, and the others heard the faint rustling of tissue paper as she lifted her prize from the box. In a few minutes, she stepped forth in all her finery into the light of the living room. The other two looked up, faces set and attitudes ready for complete approval and cries of admiration. But what they saw caused their faces to drop, their hands to be clapped over their eyes to shut out the incredible sight. Then began shrieks of dismay. Here came our model, and, horrors, her skirt came no further than the middle of her thigh, showing a great gap between her stockings and the hem of the skirt. "You *can't* wear that!" the two shouted. "You simply can't. It's awful! If you do, we'll pretend we never saw you before. You'll have to drive to the party by yourself and stay away from us all afternoon. Wherever did you get it? It's shameful!" The model looked down and fortunately there were looks of dismay and consternation on her face, too. "Take it off this minute," the two cried. "We can't stand it any longer!" The dogs, seated in a circle, looked on but did not recognize the person wearing the mini dress. Finally they burst into furious barking and began to tear around the room like animals gone mad. Above the din and confusion, the model said sheepishly, "Well, it isn't exactly what I hoped it would be, but, you see, I was in a hurry when I got it and tried it on over the slacks I was wearing. That's probably why it looks so queer now." Then we all three broke into wild laughter. We became weak with hilarity. We rolled on the floor. From exhaustion we sank into nearby chairs. We looked at the strange figure before us and started in again, laughing until we ached and held our sides as we rocked back and forth. Without a word, the model returned to her room and came back, attired in one of her restored dresses. The mini dress was never mentioned again, neither of the other two knows what happened to it, but the suspicions are that it will appear with skirt or slacks some day and be worn quite stylishly as a tunic.

One can only imagine how shocked the wild animals on the other side of the fence must have been and how they cast down their eyes in embarrassment.

And then there was the spring evening when wild gymnastics were in full swing at the cabin. Faces set, in absolute silence, we flew over chairs, sofas, and tables. One of us suddenly ran to a corner, stooped down, only to spring up again and squeeze under a table. One stationed herself at a doorway, arms outspread, eyes glassy, as she watched the others continue their leaps and flights over the dining room chairs. One of us reached down in the midst of a jump and madly grabbed a small plastic bucket standing near the greenhouse. She whirled it over her head, lowered it swiftly, and over her head again it spun. The dogs entered the fray, thinking it some kind of new and exciting game. Over chairs and tables they, too, jumped, one of them grabbing on the fly a newspaper and delightedly tearing it to bits in his frenzy. All of us were breathless and hot by this time, but we continued our leaps and dashes until one of us stooped quickly near a closet door, swept the bucket over the floor, and spoke the first words since the tumult had started. "I've got it!" She flung open the door, stepped to the edge of the porch, and gently deposited a tiny and bewildered mouse onto the grass.

We could almost hear the faint and astonished applause of the wild animals at the successful conclusion of our apparent madness.

March 1, 1971

A SKIBOB resembles a low bicycle. It stands about eighteen inches high, has a long seat, and two handle bars. It stands on two short skis, one in front, one in back. Skibobbers wear short skis, each of which is equipped with a forklike piece of metal in the back which, when dug into the snow,

209

serves as a brake. Skibobs are ridden like a bicycle; it is possible to shoosh down a slope, or it is sometimes more fun to turn frequently in order to break speed and thus have a slower, easier trip down. If a skibobber chooses to shoosh down, his speed, we have understood, can be as great as one hundred miles an hour. In a completely unofficial race, a race just for fun, a skibobber at our ski area easily beat a fast skier down one of the longer, steeper slopes. The skibobber was waiting at the bottom for his skiing competitor, nonchalantly leaning against his skibob and feigning sleep.

The first patent on a skibob was issued in 1892, but it has not been until fairly recently that the sport has attracted wide attention, first in Europe where it has taken outdoor enthusiasts by storm, then in this country where it is becoming increasingly popular. Many ski areas provide special runs just for skibobs. At others, skibobbers are permitted their fun on the regular ski slopes. A paper entitled *Skibob Times,* published in Littleton, Colorado, tells of numerous contests for skibobbers; the fourth national championship was held in this Valley last month. The third world championship will be held at Mt. Rose near Reno, Nevada, later in March. Skibob enthusiasts hope that this sport will be entered as an Olympic event before the 1976 winter games.

None of the three of us aspires to be Olympic gold medal winners, but we are decided enthusiasts. Skibobbing can be learned very quickly, we have heard in as short a time as half an hour. The first and main tips are to sit far back on the seat, to grasp the front of the seat with your knees, to put your weight on the handle bars, and to keep your foot skis flat on the snow. This sport can be enjoyed by people of any age; we heard recently of a four-year-old skibobber, and the oldest known is a great-grandmother of eighty-seven. After a lesson or two and trial runs on gentle slopes, longer, difficult runs may be taken with ease. Accidents are practically unheard of—a year or two ago we understood that in Europe where people skibob by the thousands that only one accident had been reported—a broken leg. When we bought our skibobs, they were relatively expensive as at that time they were imported from Europe. Now the equipment may be had for as little as seventy dollars.

So much for the facts of skibobbing. Now for the fun. We have enjoyed runs at the ski area and found that our beginning runs, first on the easy slopes, then on the more difficult, were managed confidently and without difficulty or danger. On the day when we took our first runs, we were the only skibobbers on the slopes, and we were amused to see quite a few skiers waiting for us when we reached the bottom of the run, skiers who had questions and were so interested that some went immediately to rent a skibob and try it for themselves. As we skibobbed beneath the chair lifts, skiers riding up would call to us and inquire, "How do you get those things up on the lift?" We called over our shoulders, "Carry them on your lap, edge to one side of the chair near the top, then move them easily to one side, and ski down, holding them by one hand." One skier followed us up on the lift to see how it was done and was delighted to see us get off easily, turn the skibobs, and begin the wonderful ride down.

We enjoy skibobbing at the ski area, but just as much fun is packing our skibobs and skis onto the mushers' sled in back of one of the SkiDoos, and starting off on our own. As long ago as last summer, we picked out several hills not far from the cabin which looked good for skibobbing, and to these we often go. We take turns skibobbing as one of us has to drive the skibobbers up on the SkiDoo, turn around, and be waiting at the bottom for the next trip up the hill. There are several nearby hills which bear the tracks of our skibobs in the snow. Sometimes we leave long, straight marks, indicating we have shooshed straight down. At other times the marks curve and turn, indicating we have taken our time and enjoyed a slower run. Neither shooshing nor turning requires much skill, and, since there are four points of balance, the skibob skis and the two skis we wear, we experience thrills of speedy runs with no anxiety.

Recently a skibob enthusiast said to us with a grin, "Skibobbing is the greatest invention since beer!" We are inclined to agree.

March 15, 1971

OUR LIVING ROOM tables are always covered with books and magazines to which we look forward when it is time to turn on the lights and start the fire. Each of us has a night table by her bed where there are at least two or three books for reading before sleep. It seems there is never a time when we do not have an order placed at our favorite book store, not always for new books, because we find there are many old ones which we want to re-read; right now, for example, we are waiting for Trollope's books, *Barchester Towers* in particular.

In *Life* magazine we saw the pictures for a new British movie, the ballet of the characters from the Beatrix Potter books. Of course, we went right down to our library and hunted up the worn and battered little volumes, to leaf through them, to read a page here and there, to recite from memory whole sections from *The Tailor of Gloucester, The Tale of Tom Kitten, The Story of Benjamin Bunny.* While we were in the library, we went from shelf to shelf of books and came back upstairs with an

211

armful we wanted to re-read. We have had a wonderful time this winter re-reading old favorites and found ourselves captivated once more by many, the Joseph books of Thomas Mann, for instance. Though we knew the old Biblical tale of Joseph and Mann's expanded version of it, we read with as great a feeling of suspense as if we had never heard of it before, wondering if Joseph really would be released from the pit, if he would become Pharoah's chief assistant in Egypt, if he would ever meet his brothers and old Jacob again. We finished recently that delightful book of Arnold Bennett, *The Old Wives' Tale,* and though we well knew the stories of Constance and Sophia Baines, we found them as entertaining as ever; how we chuckled and were amused by the delicious Bennett humor! The poetry and plays of Yeats delight us as they did years ago, and we are now renewing our acquaintance with T. S. Eliot. One of the books we have re-read recently is an all time favorite of ours, Mary Webb's Precious Bane. We re-enjoyed completely all the loveliness and charm of that story, the tragedy, the joy, the delicacy and sensitivity of description, and the poetic language with which the characters speak. Not long ago we read for the third or fourth time Barrie's *The Little Minister* and wondered how we could have forgotten it for these past years. We know that soon we shall be deep in *Peter Pan, What Every Woman Knows,* and *Sentimental Tommy.*

But not all our pleasure in books is found in re-reading. There are scores of new books we enjoy, and many more which we hold in store for the future. At the moment we have on the coffee table in the living room two splendid biographies of one of our favorite authors, *Titania* and *The Life and Destiny of Isak Dinesen.* As we read them, we can hardly wait to begin again her utterly fascinating stories, *Seven Gothic Tales, Last Tales, Ehrengard,* and all the rest. We consider Isak Dinesen the greatest short story writer of them all. We read Hemingway's *Islands in the Stream* and liked especially the first part, "Bimini." We immediately began to re-read some of his others, *The Sun Also Rises, A Farewell to Arms,* and our favorite of them all, *The Old Man and the Sea.* On our coffee table the book to be read next is *Beyond the Aspen Grove* by Ann Zwinger, the exquisite account of her life and experiences at Constant Friendship, her family home in Colorado. Right next to this book is *The Tetons and the Yellowstone* with its superb photographs by Ansel Adams, its beautifully written text by Nancy Newhall. And so it goes—we can think of nothing more appalling or desolate than to be without many books, books close at hand, books within easy reach, books to which we can turn constantly and regularly.

We do not leave this Valley often; we think there is no reason

why we should. Here there is wilderness beauty we love and which surrounds us at all times. Never are two seasons or even two days alike. But
when the snows lie deep and the mountain winds sweep through the
trees, over the sage flats, and around the cabin, or on summer evenings
when outdoor activities of the day are over and all is silent about us, only
the rushing river or the lone hoot of an owl breaking the stillness—it is
then that we begin our travels, far and wide. To Nanny's mud cottage
near Thrums, to St. Luke's Square in Bursley, to the peace and quiet amid
the daffydillies and primmyroses at Sarn Mere, to a dark and forbidding
castle in medieval Denmark, to the pomp and glory and splendor of
ancient Egypt under the Pharoahs. That, we think, is the finest way of
all to travel and to see the world and meet its people.

April 15, 1971

IT WAS ONE of those days.

First, as we were eating a quiet breakfast, one of our dogs set up a
frightful barking. She ran from one back window to the next, leapt on
beds, over chairs, all the while putting back her head and uttering the
most terrifying howls. Immediately the other dogs joined the chorus, and
all four began racing from one end of the cabin to the other, stopping
long enough only to jump on their hind legs and look from the windows.
One of us went to grab a camera, certain that there was something in
the river bottom worth photographing. The other two, tumbling and
stumbling over racing dogs, rushed to the windows to see what in the
world could be the cause of such wild and ungovernable behavior. Our
eyes opened wide as we saw first one stately coyote, then a second, a
third, a fourth, and finally a fifth wandering through the trees near the
ponds. They glanced disdainfully at the cabin, indifferent to the tumult
they certainly must have heard. Finally the coyotes disappeared, after a
while the turmoil at the cabin subsided, and we returned to our breakfasts. Minutes later the furor started all over again, only this time from
the front windows where the dogs had spied the five coyotes coming
up the back bench and walking leisurely over the crusty snow on the
sage flats. Finally they disappeared toward the timber and once again the
cabin became quiet. But not for long. The barking and chasing began all
over again as the dogs rushed again to the back windows, again sending
tables and chairs flying. We, too, went to look and saw an otter moving
in its awkward, humpy fashion over the snow toward the river. The
barking continued until the otter had disappeared from sight over the
bank. By this time we were cross and irritated as once again we straight-
ened rugs and furniture and overturned pots of flowers.

For some time we had noticed at the cabin that our water pressure was low; while water was being run in one part of the house, it was difficult to get even a drop anywhere else. Our faithful plumber had promised to come and raise the pressure and start things moving again. About nine o'clock on that fateful morning, one of us rode out on a Ski-Doo to get him at the gate. As the SkiDoo chauffeur came in with the plumber, she said disgustedly, "Guess what *now!* We've got a flat tire on the Jeep Wagoneer!" It is almost impossible to fit our small jack under this car, particularly when the car is standing on ice, so we knew that we would have to get someone from town to do the job. There might be several days of waiting. We forgot the tire, however, in our eagerness to have the water pressure raised, so we went to the basement with the plumber to watch him do the job. The pressure was raised, the water turned on. Still only a trickle. We had expected the job to take an hour at the very most, but from nine o'clock until late afternoon all of us were working and watching and trying to help correct the trouble. And what trouble it was! Some of the pipes were disconnected, and, horror and tragedy! there were quantities and masses of thick brown clay which had collected at the pipe joints, particularly around the filter. We scooped, scraped, ladled, brushed, sopped, and mopped until finally, after hours, the pipes were freed of the dreadful clogging. The hot water tank was drained and cleaned. The ice cubes in the ice-making machine were a dull brown. The water from the faucets was a molasses color and had to be run at full force for a long, long time. Finally, finally the water came crystal clear again with a beautiful gushing sound in an unimpeded flow. Everything near the hot water heater, however, near the filter, near all the faucets was splashed with the spattered brown clay and had to be scrubbed and scoured. We ourselves were covered with it from head to foot. In the midst of all this, the puppies, who were making nuisances of themselves by grabbing and running off with plumbing tools, were collared and put into the studio. They jumped against the door as we closed it and by chance threw the latch and locked themselves in. One of us spent considerable time rummaging through everything, looking for the key. When at last it was found, the naughty ones were released and sent out of doors to play. All of us were wet, dirty, tired, but triumphant. We took our plumber back to his car at the gate and he said, "Why, with my big jack, I can change that tire for you in a minute!" Bless him, he did.

About dinner time one of us was carrying a bag of trash up the stairs from the basement, and whoops! the flimsy bag burst, scattering tin cans all over the library floor and the steps. By this time all of us moved in silence, saying nothing. Quietly, with clenched teeth and forced patience, we picked up the mess, found a stronger bag, and removed the trash to one of the SkiDoos for its journey to the dump in the morning.

Enough for one day, we thought. But not quite enough yet. We had not reached the end of that day's trials. As it grew dark, again the dogs raised a wild furor. Through an open window came a familiar scent, and a flashlight trained on the snowy bench picked up in its beams the scurrying, black and white figure of our fragrant Christobel. Oh dear! we sighed. Now we shall have to watch every step we take in the dark. We must keep the dogs at our heels constantly or all of us will be contaminated by the deadly aroma and will have to be isolated until it wears off.

That evening before the fire, when the house was again clean, when the trash had been disposed of, when we knew the Jeep was wearing four good tires, when we heard the music of gushing water from the faucets, when we looked at the four dogs lying peacefully and angelically on the hearth, we remembered the irritations of the day. We listened to the distant lone cry of a coyote. We saw from the front windows the snowy peaks, clear and sharp in the moonlight, the stars shining brightly and incredibly close. We took deep breaths of the pure, fresh, mountain air as we went out for another log for the fire. The stupid little irritating events of the day fell back into their proper place. Each of us knew what the others were thinking. First one of us started to laugh, then the others joined in, now seeing only funny incidents instead of tragic ones. And haven't we been the sillies, we said, to permit such things to spoil for one minute the wonder and splendor of the world about us!

June 15, 1971

OUR THOUGHTS have been turning to animals. Maybe it was the perky little chipmunk we saw chewing and tugging assiduously on an old rope we had left on the front porch railing. She came back time after time, and we discovered she was pulling out bits of the frayed rope and carrying it away for her nest. Perhaps it was the new-born moose we saw in the willows near the river bottom. The baby and its mother both stopped their amble through the trees and glanced up at us where we stood on the bench above, flicked their ears, and then continued their journey. This baby, about a foot and a half high, fuzzy and brown, was the first we had seen this season. A week ago the big stock truck turned into our road and we saw four pairs of burro ears sticking over the top. Fidelity, TNT, Esso, and Loli—all back for the summer. After they had been unloaded into the corral, had their hooves neatly trimmed by our favorite wrangler, they were turned into the big meadow where they began their investigation of old and familiar haunts. We visited them later that afternoon. No sign of them anywhere. We called each by name, but no response. Aha, we thought, this is their usual game, and we must fall in with it and play along. We tramped over the meadow, peered under trees, searched near the creek. Still no burros. We pretended we were going to leave, but stopped to glance over our shoulder as we reached the corral. Four gray figures were emerging silently and slowly from the woods, coming as always in single file. They had played their game long enough and now wanted to have the reunion. We walked toward them in feigned surprise, stopped, put our hands on our hips, and exclaimed, "Well!" They walked toward us, then stopped in their tracks, looked at us mischievously, and in burro fashion answered, "Well!" Then they came to us and stood patiently as we curried them, all the while discussing with them the kind of winter each had experienced and what the exciting events of the past months had been.

All of this camaraderie between the burro family and those of us who live a short distance away at the cabin, made us think of an animal story we heard recounted in our living room. A young man, his wife, and two children, so the story went, lived at a nearby ranch, the man being employed as general caretaker. His position was entirely satisfactory to him, he was well-liked by his employers, they were well-liked by him, and he enjoyed his work. Everything seemed happy and pleasant for all concerned. Suddenly, we were told, the young man decided to leave. No one knew why, and all were puzzled that he would give up such a good and satisfying job. The secret finally came out. The young man had a very fine horse, a show horse, whom he had taught to perform several unusual tricks. As a young horse, only a colt, he had been promised by the man that if he behaved well and followed instructions carefully, in three years he would have a reward. The man would then take him on the road. "Now," said the young man, "the three years are up, the horse has behaved well and has done just what I told him. I'm not about to break my promise to him." When we heard this story, we were dumb-founded. Our first reaction was one of incredulity; then we began to see the humor of it and broke into gales of laughter. The funniest part, however, was yet to come. After our laughter had subsided and we were quietly thinking over the amazing tale, the man who told it to us looked up with an understanding smile on his face and said to us in dead earnestness, "And, do you know, by that time the horse had probably forgotten all about the promise!"

Yesterday morning it was raining hard and the wind was blowing fiercely around the cabin. One of us went to the kitchen, opened the refrigerator, and put a handful of carrots in each of her blue jean pockets. Then she went to the coat closet and put on rubber boots, a raincoat, and a rain hat. As she started out the door, the other two called and asked where she was going in such a downpour. She answered that she was going to the burros. "In this weather!" they exclaimed. "Why do you go out in all this rain and wind? You can go tomorrow just as well."

The raincoat clad figure turned to the other two, and as she put her hand on the door knob, just ready to leave, she said firmly, "Why am I going to the burros today? I'll tell you why. Yesterday I promised them I would."

The other two nodded earnestly and silently in approval.

July 1, 1971

WHEN WE WERE city dwellers and were striving constantly to maintain a fine, attractive lawn, we scorned dandelions. We would attack them with all kinds of pronged instruments and poisons, but try as we might, we never were entirely successful in eradicating them from the grass. Just as we thought we had conquered them, another sunny, yellow head would pop out to taunt us.

In this Valley there are vast meadows where dandelions can be completely beautiful. To us spring has never really arrived until one of us returns one day from the post office and shouts jubilantly, "The dandelions are out along the road!"

We will travel miles out of our way to see an especially lovely mountain meadow golden with them. We know an old deserted log cabin, surrounded by dilapidated sheds and barns whose forlorn appearance is made glorious by the surrounding meadows of dandelions.

Earlier this season we picked one of the brilliant blossoms to examine it closely. The long, slender petals growing on the outside, the soft rounded tuft of them in the center are not coarse at all, as we had always thought, but delicate and feathery. As we used to do when children, we held it under our chins to see if the yellow glow would shine there indicating that we liked butter. We picked an unusually stout, strong stem and blew through it to remember the toot-toot we used to think amazing and wonderful. We made the same wry faces when we tasted the bitterness on our lips.

And the perfection of a dandelion when it has gone to seed! We picked one of these this morning and looked at it carefully, noting its perfect, round symmetry, not one seed out of place, not one break in the pattern of the fragile white dome on the long, hollow stem. And then, as each seed breaks loose from the flower, the air is filled with myriads of tiny white parachutes, floating gently with the breeze, first sailing upward, then drifting down to settle on a blade of grass, to be caught in a spider's web, or to decorate with white down the coal black coats of our puppies. Many of them land in the bird bath, and there they resemble long, thin water craft, each with a round white rudder, looking as if it would at any moment begin swirling to set the boat in motion. Fragile, exquisite things they are, and we wonder now that we ever failed to see their beauty or appreciate their airy delicacy.

We have learned over the years spent in this Valley that often the common things, the wild things are the loveliest of all. One of them, dear to our hearts, is the golden beauty of the dandelion, in a few days transformed magically into its ball of exquisite white stars.

July 15, 1971

THE WORLD belongs to the young. We realize this increasingly during these sunny summer days. We know it will not be long before the older generation, now reigning supreme, will give way to its children. We watch with interest this cycle continuing on and on.

In the morning when we go to the meadow to visit the burros, we are amused by the loud squawking of a family of young woodpeckers in their nest in a hollow aspen tree. We stop for a moment under the round hole, which serves as the entrance to the home of the brood, and listen to the furious clamoring within. One morning the bright red head of one of the parents popped out at the entrance. After a second, the entire adult bird appeared, paused, then flew off in search of nourishment for the children. No sooner had it left than the shouts from within rose high and insistent again. On the way across the meadow where the burros were happily rolling on one of their favorite dust spots, we saw a mother gopher dart out of her hole, soon to be followed by a sharp little nose, two bright eyes, then the entire furry head. A second baby gopher joined the first one, and the pair remained motionless as it looked out upon its new world of grass and trees and creeks. As we approached, the mother gave a warning call, and in the flash of an eye the babies disappeared into the safety of their underground abode. On the island below the cabin, a cow moose warily led out her small brown calf. She began introducing it to its new surroundings, first going to the pond, then to the shade of an old cottonwood, and last to a group of willow bushes. Then the cow stepped through the underbrush on the way to the river, the baby trotting behind, following its mother's lead and instructions faithfully. Under the eaves on one of the rafters of the breezeway, a mother robin

218

raised a family of four. All day long she flew back and forth, her bill carrying worms and caterpillars which she stuffed down the hungry throats of the fledglings. A pair of Western bluebirds took over the little house we had hung for them near the saddle shed; the lusty young are now perching saucily on the power lines or coming to exhibit their charms on the front fence. We have stopped the car several times and walked noiselessly down the path to a nearby pond to see a pair of trumpeter swans and their three cygnets swimming placidly on the still water. The cygnets stay close to their parents and try to imitate them, bobbing under the water and, in a comical fashion, fairly turning somersaults to right themselves. Already, young as they are, they have adopted the stately manner of the two adults and have learned early their ways of grace and dignity while swimming. As we were riding to the post office the other day, we saw ahead of us two fawns, so young that they still wore light spots on their coats and wobbled unsteadily on their long, spindly legs. They were having a fine time playing in a sunny spot on the road, caring not at all for dangers which might threaten. Their mother, however, apparently standing with watchful eyes in the brush nearby, called them to her and away they darted into the trees. One, however, unable to endure its insatiable curiosity, came running back, stretched its neck to look once more at the car, and then bounded off to join its mother and twin.

An old cement block standing on end in back of the cabin attracted our attention because of a nervous chipmunk who came to inspect it. We had seen a weasel in the vicinity of the cabin, and undoubtedly the chipmunk had spied it, too. It was not long before we saw the chipmunk scampering through the tall grasses, carrying something gently in its mouth. This was deposited in one of the holes of the block. The chipmunk made several such trips up the back bench, each time with something which it hid in the same manner. We discovered that it was bringing, one by one, its litter of young to be left in the block. Finally the whole family of children was safely tucked from sight, and the mother seemed to breathe more easily. We watched the babies for several days and saw first one diminutive head appearing at the top of the block, then another, then another. Eventually the weasel disappeared, and only then would the mother permit her little ones to grow more adventuresome, to climb out of the block, to run around the edge of it, and to play in the grasses near it. All danger being passed, finally the babies were allowed to roam where they chose.

We watch with admiration the patient determination of the parents of the wild as they train and teach their young. With approval we observe

219

the children of the wild learning their lessons eagerly and obediently. We marvel that any educational system can be so simple, so natural, so uncomplicated, and at the same time so effective.

August 1, 1971

KEEPING OUR fast-growing pansies properly picked is becoming a full time job. The fifty or sixty plants in the garden are covered with blooms of all kinds—white ones, white ones with purple faces, pure yellow ones, yellow ones with brown faces, light blue ones with darker blue faces, deep red ones, bronze-colored ones, pale apricot-colored ones, and one plant of black ones. We spent a long time recently picking hundreds of blooms, but we did it leisurely and with no feeling of hurry. We had the whole morning to spend at this happy task, first picking the pansies edging the kitchen garden, then those growing under the library windows.

It was a clear, sunny morning, and as yet the sun was not hot. We looked around us as we moved from one plant to another, filling our basket slowly and peacefully. It had rained the night before, and the faces of the pansies still held silver drops of moisture. We put down our basket of pansies a moment to look up into the leafy branches; seeing a flash of black and orange, we knew the black-headed grosbeak was there. We picked up our basket and moved on to the next pansy plants, stopping to see the silver trail a snail had made on the cobblestone path, saw it disappear into the bed of lettuce. We continued with our pansy picking until our basket was full, then went in to arrange the little flowers, one by one, in vases filled with cool water.

That evening after dinner we looked at our pansy-filled living room, at the bouquet of them on the dining room table, another on the buffet. All were there, just as we had picked them that morning, the apricot-colored ones, the black ones, the blue, the white, the yellow, the red. We touched them lightly as we passed, stopped to straighten a blossom here, put a stem farther into the water there. We knew they were really far more than bouquets of pansies. They held the blue of the morning sky in their petals, the song of a grosbeak, the brilliance of red on a black wing, the silvery track of a snail, the wing whir of a humming bird, a teasing chipmunk, the hopping of a baby toad, and the exquisite beauty of a spider web, studded with pearly drops of rain.

September 1, 1971

AFTER DARK about a week ago, we heard over the bench a strange singing, similar to that of a drowsy bird who had been roused from sleep. We went to the windows and listened. The chirping continued, and then another chirping, fainter yet the same, answered a few feet away. The singing continued too long to be the song of a bird, and, mystified, we returned to the living room. We took the dogs out for a last run. We forgot the singing, turned off the lights and went to bed. The cabin became silent.

At three o'clock, Tia began an angry barking which the other dogs answered in low growls. The one of us whose bedroom opens to the breezeway got up, and the other two could see from their bedrooms her flashlight playing over the bench and on the stack of kindling near the studio. Tia's fury continued and by this time all four dogs were at the windows, sniffing and barking too. Suddenly the one of us with the flashlight shouted, "Porky!" The other two were out of bed in a flash, each rushing from her bedroom, followed by wildly excited dogs. Each one of us knew precisely what to do. The one out first turned on the breezeway lights, saw against the studio log wall the big form of a porky ready to move from the light into the safety of the darkness. She grabbed a long piece of kindling and guided it back onto the breezeway and up against the stack of wood. The porky tried to climb up and over, but failed and was cornered. Another one of us snatched the trash can and threw it over the porky. One ran for the trash can cover and as she passed the bed of geraniums in the corner cried in terror, "Here's *another* one!" We turned and, sure enough, its head and back just visible among the pink and red blossoms, moved another, this one smaller and obviously baby following its mother. The baby scuttled down the breezeway to its mother, and as we lifted the can a little, docilely squeezed under to join her. There were grunts and mutterings of protest from under the can, but we had them captured and their anger was to no avail. Now—if only we could slip the cover under, turn the can right side up, and secure the can slightly, and at last, inch by inch, we slipped the cover underneath. All three of us helped to turn the can over, hearing the heavy bodies tumbling down as we did so. One of us ran for a rope, and through the two handles it went to tie the cover firmly. One of us ran for the Jeep, another opened the gate, and when the car stood ready with its tail gate down, we all lifted the can and moved it in. Again angry sounds from within. We went back to the cabin briefly to be sure the dogs were all right, to get jackets and gloves as the night was frosty, then hurried back and started our journey across the river. With every bump we hit on our little dirt road, furious protests rose from within the can, but when we came to the paved road, all became quiet except for cooings of reassurance and comfort from the mother to the little one stuffed in beside her. Then we heard faint answered cooings and knew the mother and baby, if not comfortable, at least were resigned.

221

One member of our group was so jubilant at our success that she shouted and waved at every dark house we passed, "We did it! We got not only one, but *two*!" and then she would break into uncontrolled laughter of joy. On we drove, not a car or light in sight, the porcupines continuing their soft cooing to each other. Our excited one in the front seat continued her shoutings of joy and wild laughter. We crossed the river, turned sharply on the highway, drove to a deserted ranch where we slowed down and turned off the road. We saw a wide expanse of sage, just right to receive our two prisoners. We went to the back of the car and out came the big trash can, lifted slowly and then put down on the ground in the beams of the lights. Breathless with excitement we gingerly untied the rope and one of us, holding firm to the cover, turned the can on its side. "Watch out for their tails!" she shouted as she removed the cover. "Stand back and let them run ahead of us!" We all stood back and waited. Nothing happened for a second or two, and we could imagine the two furious beasts within, waiting to pounce out and take cruel vengeance for the indignities they had suffered. We waited, eyes fixed on the open trash can, not daring to breathe. Slowly one furry head emerged, then the rest of the clumsy body. Quills rose, tail lashed, and the ugly animal humped off toward the sage. Then we gave the can a gentle shake, and the baby appeared, its quills raised murderously, too. The mother turned, the baby saw her, and together they rustled off in the dry grasses and vanished into the dark out of the rays of the car lights. Shaking with nervousness and excitement, we threw the can back into the car, got in ourselves, and drove back. Mission accomplished.

As we drove down our road, we saw the cabin blazing with lights we had forgotten to turn off. We put the trash can back, ready for the next emergency, and, shivering and shaking with the cold and the thrills, went in to make hot cocoa before we returned to bed. We glanced at the clock. It was four-fifteen A.M. We hugged each other and danced about in delight and joy, knowing our four dogs were safe from *two* porkies at least. Never again shall we mistake the singing and cooing of a porcupine for that of a bird. It will alert us no matter when we hear it. And when we do, we and our trusty trash can will be ready to make the next capture. The more occupants of the can, tumbling about and angrily protesting, the more gleeful we and our family of dogs will be.

September 15, 1971

THE AIR in the morning and after the sun has dipped behind the mountains in the evening is chilly; no more do we go out without jackets and gloves. The first snow has come to the peaks. The days are sunny and bright, the nights clear and sparkling with stars and a waning yellow moon. A stillness fills the Valley, and again as always at the change of season, nature seems to be holding its breath, in preparation this time for the burst and glory of color which soon will brush every shrub, every bush, every leaf. These are the best days of all for walks through the woods, by the river, through the sage. These are the best days of all for canoeing on a silent, glassy mountain lake. These are the best days of all for picnics, often with a small fire built to keep fingers and toes warm. We might be inclined to say that these are the best days of all and end it at that. We might. Until we remember, with each change of season in the wilderness, we always feel that the best days of all are here, be it the first soft spring days, the first days of hot summer, these golden days of early fall, or the days when the first snows powder everything with glistening white. All days are the best here. All days are filled with their own particular beauty of a very special kind. But at the moment, we can imagine nothing lovelier or more welcome than the days we are experiencing now, the days of brilliant autumn.

October 1, 1971

ONE FROSTY MORNING last week, we decided that this was the day. We waited until the sun had melted the frost from the bushes and twigs, until the air was warm, and we knew we could pick rose hips in comfort with no fear of suffering from icy fingers. We packed our lunch and started off, each with a deep bucket ready to receive the beautiful fruit. We drove to our favorite picking patch, exclaiming as we got out of the Jeep about the abundance and size of the hips shining in the sun. We picked silently, the only sound being the rattling of the hips on the bottom of our tin cans. Soon, however, as we picked more and more, even that sound ceased, and we knew our buckets were filling. Bush after bush we saw ahead, hips on the next ones beckoning us on when we had finished one bush. We were careful always to leave great numbers of the scarlet berries for the grouse which we know love them as well as we do. The sun grew warmer, we shed our jackets and gloves, and picked barehanded, in spite of the thorns which painfully penetrated our fingers.

It was not long before our buckets were full, and as each of us peeped into the buckets of the other two, we realized that we had plenty for this year's supply of jelly and syrup. We all were hungry so we headed back to the car for our knapsack, deciding to climb a short hill from the top of which we knew we would have a splendid view of the mountains in the distance. We moved slowly up the steep incline, stepping between sage bushes, over big stones and old logs. Finally we reached the top, saw a few feet away an abandoned, rusty hay rake, and knew that our luncheon table and chairs were ready. We settled ourselves, took out our lunch, and looked around us—snow-capped peaks on one side, gently rolling hills and valleys on the other. The aspens showed a distinct golden touch, and we knew in a very few days the leaves of all of them would be a mass of yellow, shaking softly and whispering to each other in the wind. Near our feet we noticed a large hole, freshly dug, and knew a badger had chosen this scenic spot for his winter home. On the old fence near us we saw a flash of blue as a Western bluebird alighted to investigate the strange performance taking place on his hay rake.

We ate our lunch slowly, watching the masses of white clouds move swiftly across the blue sky, saw them cast dark shadows on the sunny slopes of the peaks. We looked beyond the fence at six or eight placid cows watching us with unblinking stares. Knowing our afternoon's work was cut out for us, we finally and regretfully packed our picnic things and returned to the Jeep. As the hot sun in the car shone on our buckets of hips, we sniffed their sweet fragrance.

The sun on the breezeway was warm when we returned to the cabin, there was no wind, and we sat there, each with her bucket, cleaning the hips of stems and blossoms. That evening we knew we had picked many more than ever before; there in the kitchen they stood in three large china bowls. The next morning we added water and cooked them slowly, enjoying through the entire cabin the unsurpassed fragrance of the little hips, rolling and tumbling in the simmering water. That night they were left to stand, and the next morning put into jelly bags and hung over deep bowls to receive the rosy juices. Next day we had the happy task of adding sugar, apple and lemon juices, and boiling down the mixture. The glass jars were sterilized and set ready to receive first the boiling apricot-colored syrup, then after a little more cooking, the heavier juices which make delectable rose hip jelly.

Slowly and carefully the filled glasses were sealed and taken to the basement shelves where all the sweet smells, the cool, pure mountain air, the warm sun, our happy picnic on the old hay rake, the curious cows, the dry grasses rustling in the wind were preserved along with the fruit for snowy winter days when we bring out the syrup for hot cakes at breakfast, the jelly for hot muffins at dinner. We are very certain that the greatest joy of all in making syrups and jellies lies in harvesting the fruit ourselves, garnering at the same time memories of woods and hills and mountain meadows and a bluebird flashing through yellow leaves to perch on an old hay rake.

224

October 15, 1971

THE SURPRISES and exciting discoveries of this Valley are unlimited. A few days ago two friends called us and said they had something wonderful to show us. They had discovered it near one of the mountain lakes and wanted to share its magnificence. They told us to bring a canoe and to wear hiking boots as we would be walking a short distance over rough ground. We would plan to eat our picnic lunches near the spot where the object of grandeur was. They hinted it had something to do with a most unusual tree. We would want cameras with plenty of film.

The cottonwoods and aspens were golden that morning when we started on our pilgrimage. The hawthorne and underbrush along the road were crimson, and the willows in low, swampy places pure yellow. The sky was blue, and the mountains, standing out sharply, were brushed with traces of snow. We turned off the highway onto a rough dirt road over which we bumped through muddy ruts and puddles. We drove around the last bend, and through the trees we could see the smooth, glassy lake ahead, the mountains in the distance casting clear reflections on the still water. As we drove closer, we could see two white trumpeter swans swimming near shore, could hear the quacking protests of numerous ducks who had been disturbed by our intrusion. We unloaded the canoe and began paddling quietly to the designated point near a small grove of pine trees. Two of our party preferred to take the foot path through the woods, and we in the canoe could see them in the distance, appearing in an open space, only to disappear where the willow bushes grew thick. There was not a sound. Suddenly we heard a loud crack, like the report of a gun, and saw a tree near shore topple and sway for a second and then crash to the ground. We were relieved to know our walking companions were safe as we caught a glimpse of them through the trees. We were mystified by the fallen tree, but paddled on and stopped at the appointed place which the other two on foot had reached just before. "A beaver!" they said in answer to our inquiries about the tree. "A beaver felled the tree just as we passed. He heard us coming and scuttled away through the brush ahead of us."

We slung our knapsacks on our backs and started up a short hill ahead. We trudged over dead logs, through twisting sage bushes, noticing scarlet kinnikinnik covering the ground, admiring the golden aspen leaves above. We stopped frequently to look back at the clear, blue lake with the wondrous mountain reflections. We then continued forward and up, expecting to see at any moment the wonderful sight which we knew lay ahead. "There it is!" one of our friends shouted, and we all stopped to look ahead at the clearing just beyond. What a sight met our eyes! On the side of the hill lay the tremendous remains of an ancient tree, having been toppled over, perhaps seventy or eighty years ago, by slides and wind. There was little left of the once mighty trunk, nothing at all of the branches, only the massive upturned roots. We exclaimed in wonder, then moved on to examine it more closely. What a mighty and awesome thing it was! The gnarled and twisted roots rose higher than we. Soft browns and grays colored them. A small cave had been formed under the roots and fantastic shapes had been carved by winds and rains and snows. We came close to it, felt its strength and sturdiness, climbed on the gigantic roots, and marveled at the strange figures and forms which nature had fashioned. We walked around and around to see its powerful form from every angle. We were silent as we examined it, feeling the softness of its wood, noticing a tiny aspen tree beginning to grow at its base. New life, we thought, taking the place of old.

We spread our picnic lunch at the spot from which we could view the old tree best. A solitary and perfectly formed young pine tree grew a few feet from it, offering us shade from the sun. We felt the velvety softness of thick green moss growing on an old log nearby. During our entire lunch, we kept looking at the old tree, finding new shapes as we looked, subtle colors we had failed to notice at first. As we walked slowly down the hill, we stopped every few feet to look back at the ancient tree once more. We paddled back to the Jeep, enjoying the hot sun on our backs, the sparkling mountain lake, the distant snowy mountains, the complete silence, but most of all the memory of the venerable tree, more beautiful now, perhaps, than when living in a forest with others of its kind.

_1972_

**January 1, 1972**

ONE OF THE WORST mountain storms we have ever experienced struck early last week. Soon after breakfast, the snow began to fall so fast that in minutes we could watch it pile up on both porches. The wind began to roar in blasts around the cabin, sending clouds of powdery snow from the roofs, hurling it in sheets against the windows. The hanging bird feeders banged against the dining room windows, the SkiDoo covers billowed out from the little machines, a pair of snowshoes clattered down from their nails on the log wall. A tall, dead pine tree on the island below fell crashing to the ground, another soon following it. The branches of the enormous cottonwoods in back of the cabin twisted and writhed in the wind. One of us went to the dining room windows and between gusts looked out at the SkiDoos. What she saw made her cry out in alarm, "The little SkiDoo has lost its cover!" We all rushed to look, and, sure enough, our little Élan, stood bare and exposed to the storm its cover having been ruthlessly snatched by the wind and carried goodness knows where or how far. We ran to the windows and tried to look for it, in the river bottom below, in the tops of the trees, along the sage flats. It was impossible to see far, and we tried to reassure ourselves that when the storm had subsided, certainly we would find it. We continued to peer out the windows all morning. No bright yellow cover in sight. We thought it might be wise to phone our friends along the way to the village asking them when they saw a yellow, billowing SkiDoo cover flying by their front windows to reach out quickly and grab it. We had visions of its being draped around the flag pole at the post office or caught in a tall pine tree near the butte.

Shortly after noon the storm abated considerably. The wind died to a whisper almost as suddenly as it had begun, and the snow now fell more softly and quietly. In mid-afternoon two of us saw the third member of our group strapping on her snowshoes, and we called to ask where

227

she was going. "I'm going to look for something," she answered as she disappeared around the side of the studio. The two of us left in the cabin knew well for what she was searching. We could see her figure moving through the snow at the top of the bench, her head turned first down, then up as she examined every drift, every snowy branch of the trees. At last we saw her return. After she had taken off her snowshoes, she came in, elation and victory in her voice as she cried, "I found it!" Thinking she had indeed accomplished the impossible, the two of us cried, "Where?" "It's over the bench," she told us, "way down at the bottom, caught between two tree trunks." All of us immediately began to think of ways to retrieve it. Our plans were well laid, and we went to bed that night, happy to think that the next morning the little Élan would again have its comforting cover to protect it.

The next morning we started on the rescue mission, two of us on snowshoes, one on skis. We moved the few yards from the studio to the designated place on the bench from which point we caught sight of the bright yellow cover. We had with us 100 feet of new clothes line which we knew would be indispensable in dragging the cover back, in pulling back the brave one who was going to descend the hundred steep feet to retrieve it. She took off her skis, tied one end of the rope around her waist, grasped one ski pole in her right hand, sat down on the edge of the bench, and gave herself a slight push. Down she bumped, a-whoopin' and a-hollerin' in glee as she went, controlling her speed with her feet dug into the snow. From above we saw her come to a stop just above the yellow cover. "Grab it with your pole!" came shouts from above, and she moved over cautiously, reached out with her pole, and after an attempt or two, caught the cover and waved it triumphantly at the two waiting above. Shouts and cheers rose from the top of the bench, and after the cover was secured to one end of the rope, up it was pulled to the top. None the worse for its flight, not a single tear or rip. Then we turned our attention to the one below and discussed the best method to drag her back. We fastened her second pole to one end of the rope and hurled it down to her. She grasped one pole in each hand, turned, and, waist deep in snow, began the precipitous ascent. She moved by inches, calling, "Pull!" Then we'd give a hard tug on the rope until we heard her call back, "Enough! Now slacken." She'd rest for a minute, test the strength of the snow ahead of her, and if she found it hollow in places around shrubs and bushes, she'd pat it down hard with her mittened hands, thrust her pole into it, and then, finding it more solid, move on another inch. "Pull!" we'd hear, then "Enough. Slacken." From above we followed directions carefully, ready to tighten the rope sharply if we saw her take a misstep. Slowly, slowly, moving with difficulty through the deep snow, she inched her way up. Finally she got up high enough so we could speak in ordinary tones. Giving one more strong tug, we drew her to the top where she found it easier to throw herself onto the snow and swim through it until she was safely over the cornice. We were all breathing heavily with excitement and exertion. We stood for a minute and looked down at the slide she had made through the snow on her swift descent, the cavernous holes in the snow her legs had made as they worked their way up. Then, breathing easily again, we strapped on snowshoes, slipped into skis, grabbed the rope and the yellow cover, and trudged back to the cabin. We shook out the cover and with great ceremony and pomp slipped it over the Élan, this time securing it with double strength against any future storm.

We went into the cabin, took off our snowy parkas and hoods and boots and mittens. Not even Hillary on his conquest of Everest could have felt more satisfied or proud than we.

January 15, 1972

We thought we'd had plenty; we all cried, "Enough!"
And welcome were sun's brilliant rays.
It stopped; it had ended—the white, fluffy stuff.
Ahead lay blue skies and clear days.
But you've heard the old adage
About counting your chicks
Long, long before ever they've hatched.
And nature's surprises just never grow dull;
She still has a bag of good tricks.
And what's that appearing right over the peaks
A-whirling and howling with snow?
"Have mercy, take heed!" we cry in alarm.
"Show pity on mortals below!"

The wind has grown fiercer than ever before,
The sun quite vanished from sight.
The snows pile high at windows and door,
The drifts reach a frightening height.
A neighbor just phoned to give us the news,
We swooned when we heard her soon say,
"A weather forecast we thought you could use,
There's *more* wind and snow on the way!"

229

So here we three sit, with shovels in hand,
There's just nothing more we can say,
And unless all these blizzards we bravely withstand,
We'll be waving adieu until May.

There are three gals of Wyo.
Whose friends just never will know
    Why they *choose* snow and ice
When the South's paradise.
The truth is—they're part Eskimo!

February 15, 1972

ONE OF US has a sister living in the east of France, near the Swiss border. This sister is famous for her superb garden, all kinds of brilliant flowers, delicious, sweet fruits, wondrous vegetables. Last year we sent her a package of flowering cabbage seeds, hoping she would find them as spectacular as we had found them the year before.

In France the growing season is much longer than it is here. We read with interest, then with hilarity, the letter written on November 5, describing the wonder and amazement the flowering cabbages had created.

The cabbages in France grew and grew and grew, taller and taller and taller, until they must have resembled Jack's bean stalk. And then they headed, gloriously, splendidly, until the heads were as large as big, round platters. They were kept in the garden especially for friends and neighbors to see. They were the usual green and yellow, green and red, and their size was spectacular—giant cabbages on tall, slender stilts.

A cousin from Switzerland saw the cabbages and exclaimed in wonder. One was gently dug up and presented to her. This particular cabbage, having blossomed out on a remarkably tall stem, was cone-like and resembled an evergreen tree in shape. Wonder of wonders, along the long stem blossomed tiny red cabbages, giving promise that they, too, might become as large as the top cabbage. When the cousin went to the train to return to Switzerland, a crowd gathered around to see the magnificent plant she was carrying. In the train, people came to her seat to view the unusual sight. They stood before it in surprise and disbelief, they asked questions, they told other passengers about it. By the time the cousin had reached her destination, everyone on the train had come to look at the cabbage. When she arrived in Switzerland, the customs officials were overcome by the sight, and so interested were they to examine the cabbage more closely, that it is quite possible a few unscrupulous people skipped by them without their notice. The cousin thought at first she would try to pot her plant, but another and better idea came to her. The day after she arrived home, she carried it carefully and gently to the cemetery where she set it between the graves of her mother and father. There it stood in all its regal splendor. Word soon passed among the people in her Swiss village that there was a most unusual sight at the cemetery. Many of them visited the two graves, marched sedately by, and saw the miracle there, the enormous cabbage nodding on its tall stem, the little red cabbage children bobbing up and down below. The people were silent in admiration and amazement.

So—at the top of our seed list this year appears flowering cabbage. If frosts come too early, we shall transplant a few of the plants into the warm, sunny greenhouse. We have already chosen the spot in the roof where we can cut out a hole in case our cabbages try to emulate the grand heights attained by their tall and stately French sisters.

April, 1972

ABOUT THE NEW arrivals we had learned much. We knew their age, their appearance, their ancestry. Both parents, both sets of grandparents, many, many great-grandparents for generations past had been born in Scotland. We knew, therefore, that the arrivals themselves would be as Scotch as heather.

Day by day the time for their arrival drew closer. We stayed near the telephone waiting for the call which would tell us they were on their way to us by plane. One morning early our phone rang, and a distressed voice at the other end said, "We had hoped it would be today, but it can't be. A terrific blizzard struck last night, and all airports for miles around are closed. We'll try for tomorrow." There was no alternative but to wait. The next morning our phone rang again, and the same voice, this time cheerful and gay, said, "They are on their way. They might arrive later today, but surely within the next twenty-four hours. Don't worry—all will be fine, and we wish you much happiness with them!" We were a-tremble with excitement, checked the plane connections, packed the little yellow plastic bag, and waited impatiently for the time to come when we could meet the late afternoon plane. Many friends called us inquiring about the arrival, and two said they would meet us at the airport to be on hand for the glad reception.

Soon after we had reached the terminal, our friends arrived and joined us. We all saw the big plane approaching in the sky, watched it dip to the airstrip, and come roaring to the landing point. The door was opened, the stairs lowered, and a few passengers walked casually along the walk and into the terminal, their luggage following on carts shortly after. But nothing for us! Nothing at all! We became more distressed by the minute. "Is that all, absolutely all?" we asked the baggage attendant. "That's all for today, ma'am," he told us. Disconsolate and disappointed, we turned to the parking lot, found the Jeep, and started home. "What can have happened?" we asked each other. "Where are they? Do you think they're all right?" None of us knew, and there was nothing to do but wait until the next day.

One of our group said she thought it would be foolish to meet the 7:46 plane in the morning. She suggested we meet the noon plane. Then if they did not come on that one, we would meet the last one of the day which comes in just before five. But one of the members of our group said firmly, "I'm meeting *all* planes tomorrow, beginning with the early one. I'm not going to miss a single one." So it was agreed that we'd all meet the early plane, futile though it might be. That night at the cabin was a worried one. We tried not to imagine what might have happened, we talked very little about it, but all knew what each was thinking.

It was surprising how our hopes revived and our spirits rose the next morning. We got up before daybreak, had an early breakfast, fed Dow and Jones, and played out of doors with them for a few minutes. Then we dressed in warm jackets and caps, took the little yellow plastic bag, and each started a SkiDoo and headed for the cars at the road.

As we turned into the airport, we saw in the far distance the plane arriving. We rushed into the terminal. It was empty except for a few sleepy-eyed people waiting to take the plane out. When they overheard our excited conversation, our inquiries at the desk, they immediately sat up, awake and interested. They asked us questions, crowded around the door with us to watch for the possible arrival. No passengers got off. Therefore no luggage would be removed, we thought. But we had failed to see one of the airport attendants go to the plane and remove something from the back luggage compartment. We did see him return, however, and cried out in delight. In each hand he was carrying an identical large box which looked like a tiny house. He took them into the baggage department, then brought them to us. Something moved inside each one. There were exclamations of excitement from the people standing around to see. We took the boxes carefully and gently outside to the big luggage platform, the eager people following us. First we opened the little yellow plastic bag. We took out a small dish for water, a handful of newspapers, a few puppy biscuits, and two small harnesses and leashes. Then, with the greatest of care, we opened each box. From their dark interiors, we lifted out two soft little balls of black and white fuzz and held each close in our arms. Each little animal looked up at us and was apparently reassured by our comforting words. Each then cuddled into our arms, making soft, contented puppy sounds. Our border collie puppies, flown over two thousand miles to us, had finally arrived.

Dow and Jones at the cabin greeted them with a warm and boisterous welcome. The bewildered little puppies, only seven weeks old, tottered unsteadily on their short legs through the snow. Ever since their arrival they have proved their fine breeding by behaving with mature judgment, good taste, and high intelligence. They are now almost three months old and have doubled in size. Dow and Jones act as their nannies, we supervise their feeding and training, and the tedious plane trip has long since become a thing of the forgotten past.

And their names? Our burros are named TNT, short for AT&T, Fidelity, short for Fidelity Fund, Esso for Standard Oil, and Loli for Long Island Lighting. Our black boys are Dow and Jones. We could not desert the idea of the stock market for the new twin girls. So one is called Capi, short for Capital Gains; the other is Tiki, short for Ticker Tape. Our stock farm is complete, and our average in love and amusement and fun is soaring.

May, 1972

THIS IS THE season of cottonwood catkins. Little, squiggly things they are, about three inches long, each tipped by a sticky bud shell. They are an annoyance as they drop from the trees in back of the cabin and are carried by the slightest breeze all over the porches, the breezeway, the porch furniture. When a strong wind blows, they come down by the hundred and persist in sticking tenaciously to everything they touch. We sweep them up several times a day, but in spite of that, we humans continue to bring them into the house on our shoes and the dogs on their paws. We think we have cleared them all away, but another puff of wind brings down more, and we start all over again to brush and sweep. We look often toward the massive trees, and are relieved when we see the fresh new leaves beginning to appear and know the catkins will be gone for another season.

So, much as we may dread the irritations which catkins cause, much as we may grumble as we sweep them from the porches, vacuum clean them from the carpets, extract them with careful fingers from the backs, paws, ears, tails of the dogs, there are many wondrous things at this season which reduce the bother of catkins to something trivial. Even catkins have their charms. If you take one of the sticky bud shells in

233

your fingers and smell it ever so gently, the most delicate, subtle perfume is sensed, the most enchanting, we think, in the whole, wide world. And if the puppies manage to collect enough of the sticky shells on their backs and ears, no matter in what part of the cabin they are tumbling and playing or sleeping quietly, they carry the delicious fragrance with them wherever they are.

> So we will stop our fretting,
>> And no resentment feel,
> For even messy catkins
>> Have enchantments to reveal.

August, 1972

THERE IS A wild delicacy which we have not harvested in great quantities before and for which we searched with success about a week ago. We planned the excursion a few days in advance and on a clear, sunny morning were ready to go, two big plastic bags, hip boots, and rakes in hand. Our search, we hoped, would result in our finding large beds of watercress which grow plentifully in the Valley but are sometimes elusive and difficult to find. We had found a fine bed of it several years ago and thought we knew exactly where to find it again. We drove slowly down the narrow, winding road, noticing the profusion of wild flowers growing on either side. Soon we reached the vicinity where we thought the springs were running clear and cold and where we hoped to find the cress. We parked the car and walked a short distance over fallen logs and rocks and through dense brambly bushes, only to find that our precious bed of cress was now surrounded by fences. We slipped under, walked a little further into the woods, and suddenly came upon an old log cabin, immaculate and attractive, with gay geraniums growing in pots in the windows. An elderly gentleman came out and we told him of our mission. He smiled and said we were welcome to help ourselves. He motioned to a place up the creek where he said we would find plenty of cress. We stopped to visit with him for a few minutes and then started off. It was not long before we found a vast growth of the cress, and, excited and eager to begin picking, we put on our boots and stepped into the cold water. Soon we had raked in enough to fill both our bags. On our way back through the creek, one of us stumbled on a slippery rock, lurched sideways, and fell in. It was not a serious fall, but we heard her gasp as the freezing water began to fill her boots and soak her blue jeans. She was up in a second, laughing heartily, and still clinging tenaciously to a prize piece of cress which she had not relinquished even during a sudden

234

dip into the icy mountain creek. As soon as she was on dry land, she lay on the ground, lifted her legs and let the water from her boots gush out. Her only comment was, "Now I feel lighter." All of us were wet and muddy, the one who had fallen resembled an authentic water nymph, but we had our cress and were delighted. We walked back to the Jeep, deposited our bags in the back, and headed for home.

Now we know there is no romance in buying watercress in a store. It does not mean driving through meadows of wild flowers, it does not bring a walk in the sun over rough terrain and the adventure of crawling under fences. When one buys watercress, there is no charming log cabin in the woods, geraniums at the windows, or a visit with a friendly old gentleman. There is no fun of raking in the watercress or the sudden splash as one of us slips by accident into the creek, gets wet, and thus furnishes her companions with a touch of humor on the expedition. Hereafter we shall greatly admire all watercress tied in neat bunches in the store, but we shall pass it by and know that the time is at hand when we must go in search of our own cress and, with it, our own adventure.

November, 1972

Great Mother!
Changeless—impervious—eternal—
Hear and receive our thanks.
Gratitude from the wilderness
For all living things,
Both great and small.
All, in your eyes,
Significant and blessed,
However hidden or unobserved.
Gratitude
For all wild beauty.
For young things
Seeing and traveling
Your world
For the first time.
Keep them safe and nourished
During snows and winds to come.
Gratitude
For mighty trees,
Now stark and leafless,

235

Resting until your gentle ways
Appear again.
Gratitude
For wild flowers
Now withered into dust.
Protect their roots
Until your earth is warm
And life begins to stir anew.
Gratitude
For high, fierce winds that sweep
Through forests dark.
For clouds of gray
And smell of snow.
For sprigs of sage in garb
Of fragile white.
For high, white peaks against
A clear blue sky.
For fragrance of wet tree trunks,
Branches bare.
Gratitude
For tracks of tiny creatures
Etched on covering
Of early snow.
For cries of coyotes, bugling of elk,
For hoot of owls
On still winter nights.
For pure, cold air,
For pristine flakes of frost.
For these
Our gratitude .accept,
Great Mother!

1973

January, 1973

THE RAMSHACKLE thing sounded like an old-fashioned coffee grinder. The letters *a, k,* and *s* stuck exasperatingly. Unless we remembered to pause a second after striking each of these, and unless we waited until the keys fell back into place, all following letters piled on top of them. One had to train himself to count to three after he struck those dreadful letters—*k* (1, 2, 3); *a* (1, 2, 3); *s* (1, 2, 3). It was most annoying, particularly when *a* and *s* occur in words so frequently. One would think the letter *k* appears seldom, but, oh no—it comes often, so it was *s* (1, 2, 3) *k* (1, 2, 3) *y* or *k* (1, 2, 3) ic*k* (1, 2, 3). We rattled and counted on, and if our copies of *Cabin Comments* for the last few issues have looked untidy, if the letters have been sadly awry, now we can tell the whole sad story.

Over three months ago our comparatively new and fine Smith Corona electric typewriter began to misbehave. The letter *n* became wobbly, and once, in a frenzy of typing, we were astonished to hear a strange sound and see the head of the letter *n* fly from its long shaft and go hurtling through the air. Without the letter which had departed in such a sudden manner, the line of typing looked like this: "At oo the su became warmer a d the wi dows bega to clear of frost. Whe the mercury rose a little higher, we thought we'd spi out o the s ow machi es a d go for the mail a d a doze ora ges." Such foreign appearing language meant beyond question that the typewriter needed speedy repairs. We called long distance to see when the repair man from the nearest large city would be coming to the Valley. There are no typewriter repair shops here. We were told that he would come at the end of the week. We explained our troubles and asked that he bring with him a new letter *n* so that possibly the machine could be fixed that same day. We also emphasized the fact that we were in need of a new ribbon. The week came and went, no service man called. The next week came and went—same story. At the end of the next week, we phoned again and were told that he would surely be there the following Monday. We repeated carefully, distinctly, and slowly what was wrong with our typewriter and again asked that a letter *n* be ready to put on. We stayed close to the phone all day the following Monday, but no call came from the service man. We waited till Thursday and phoned a third time. We were told he would be in the Valley without fail the following Wednesday and again we told of our woes concerning the letter *n* and the new ribbon. On Wednesday the rain was coming down in torrents. Our little dirt road leading to the main road was filled with swift-flowing rivers. The rain poured from the roof, and the depressions in the yard were miniature lakes. And then the phone call came. We grabbed raincoat, cap, boots, and the sick little typewriter, and down the road in the Jeep we splashed, fearful that the man would disappear before we could get to the post office where we were to meet him. But he and his bright yellow service truck were waiting. He put the typewriter into the back compartment and we explained again about the letter *n* and the new ribbon. We had brought the head of the letter *n* with us; the man looked at it and thought he might be able to fix it that night at his motel and return the machine the next morning. Oh joy! All waiting ended, a repair job done over night! That certainly exceeded our greatest hopes. But the next day came and went and no typewriter waited for us at the post office. We supposed the trouble had been more serious than had been apparent at first glance. It was then we turned to the old typewriter which we use in emergencies. It was *k* (1, 2, 3); *a* (1, 2, 3); *s* (1, 2, 3). A week passed, two weeks, three weeks, and finally a whole month. Another phone call to the shop, and we were told a new part was necessary, had been ordered, and would be in any day. Back to the *k* (1, 2, 3); *a* (1, 2, 3); *s* (1, 2, 3). We were sure the machine would have been returned in ample time to complete the next issue of *Cabin Comments,* but our certainties were built on false premises. After we had struggled with that issue of *Cabin Comments,* we waited another week, a second, a third. Another long distance phone call, and we were told this time a tracer had been sent out for the missing part which apparently had long since been sent from the main office. In our desperation we thought of buying a new machine, but decided in a more sober moment that that would be foolish, so back to the wheezy old machine with a *k* (1, 2, 3); *a* (1, 2, 3); *s* (1, 2, 3). Another week, another, still another, and we phoned again, ready to ask for the return of the typewriter, repaired or not. Already it had had time to go around the world several times in search of its own missing part. But this time, *this* time we could hardly believe our ears. We were told the machine had been fixed and would be returned very soon. We weakly asked,

238

"When?" and were told that the truck was just waiting for a load of furniture to bring to the Valley. What, we wondered, does a load of furniture have to do with a repair service for typewriters, but we did not dare ask. The following Monday, over three months since that fateful rainy day, we received a call telling us our typewriter was in the Valley and would be delivered to the post office. Oh, the dreams and the plans for typing the next day, oh, the relief of getting letters written, starting the next issue of *Cabin Comments* on a typewriter which hummed along beautifully, the new ribbon printing clear and black, the poor little letter *n* with its head in place once more! The next morning as we entered the post office, a general cry went up, "Your typewriter is here!" How dear the little machine looked to us as we held it close in our arms! We peeked under the top, and there, bright and shining and new, was the precious letter *n*. We glanced further, and, horrors and grief, no ribbon, *no* ribbon at all, not even the spare spool! Our disappointment and shattered plans were beyond belief and description. We burst into the cabin where the others were waiting eagerly to see the recovered typewriter with all its missing parts in place again. "No ribbon! A letter *n* but no ribbon, not even the spare spool to wind it on!" The others moaned in sympathy and dismay. One finally said in outrage, "Write the president of the company, write the Secretary of Commerce, write Ralph Nader, write *somebody!* Over three months and here it comes back with no ribbon!"

But in cooler moments it was decided to call the company *again*. This we did the very next morning and the cheerful voice which answered said, "Yes, we know all about it. The repair man came in this morning and told of the boo-boo he had made, so a new ribbon, *plus* an empty spool is in an envelope addressed to you and will be mailed immediately. No charge, and we're sorry for your inconvenience." We faintly gasped, "That's all right and thank you." Two days later the wonderful little package was in our post office box and we took it out tenderly and gently. *Now, now* we'd be able to write *Cabin Comments* without any more frustrations or troubles or counting. We opened the little package when we got home, and there was a fine new ribbon just waiting to be slipped into place on the machine. We took out the empty spool and discovered— you won't believe—that some big fat man had sat on it or some heavy package had been dumped on it, and it was squashed past recognition. By this time all of us were too exhausted with frustrations to say a word, but we got out screw drivers, hair pins, pliers, forks, tooth picks, nail files, drills to see if we could straighten the poor misshapen thing, but to no avail. It just bumped wobbledy wobbledy when we tried it. We decided not to phone the company again, and one of us said, "I'm going

239

to phone the store in town where we got this typewriter. True, they don't repair machines, but certainly they must have spools and ribbons." She promptly went to the phone, dialed the number, and got our good friend to whom, we all agreed, we should have gone for a ribbon in the first place. "I have a ribbon right here, a spare spool with it, and I'll mail it at once. You won't get it today, but surely tomorrow," she said. The next day the package arrived, spare spool in fine shape, and a beautiful new ribbon. It was put on the patient typewriter in a matter of seconds and now you will have *Cabin Comments,* it is hoped, in a neater, more professional-appearing copy. And look, behold, and wonder: *k* no counting, *a* no counting; *s* no counting. And how our fingers fly with no need to pause. Joy, oh joy—kkkkkkkk, aaaaaaaaa, sssssssss, and the dear little decapitated *n* has its head once more and is performing perfectly—nnnnnn. Annoyance forgotten, typewriter in excellent shape, neat *Cabin Comments* for you. Our joyful delirium knows no bounds.

May, 1973

Our housework's neglected,
Our laundry just waits.
Intention is proper,
But soon dissipates.
Our breakfasts are hurried,
Lunch grabbed on the run,
Our dinners are finished
When scarcely begun.
The newspapers tell of
High prices for meat.
It doesn't concern us—
We've no time to eat.
Our sewing and knitting?
Untouched now for days.
Because we are lost in
A brain-stretching maze.
We get so bewildered,
And sometimes quite tense.

We fear we are losing
All good common sense.
We utter sad cries,
We shriek frightened wails.
We even have taken
To biting our nails!
What's happened? It's dreadful!
We've found a new game
That absorbs us completely;
We'll ne'er be the same.
All thoughts turn to check mates,
Not games that are drawn.
Oh dear, now you've captured
My knight with your pawn!
The bishop swoops in
With purpose so keen;
His wicked design is
To whisk off the queen.
Be careful of kings
And staunchly defend;
If one of them falls,
Game's come to an end.
From morning to night
We indulge our new hobby.
Our model right now
Is that Fischer named Bobby.
A thought-tickling game
Which we play to excess;

We really weren't living
Until we found chess!

August, 1973

FOR US, some days in the Valley are "big" days, and we are awed by
the splendor and the immensity around us. Towering peaks, rushing
river, wide expanse of sky, enormous white clouds, a sky-wide, flaming
sunset. "Big" days are those in which we see powerful bull moose, a herd
of thirty or forty elk, a buck deer with a tremendous spread of antlers. A
huge bald eagle soars overhead, a great blue heron rises from the bank of

241

the river, a hawk with fearful beak and claws perches on the top of a massive pine tree below the cabin. We notice large yellow sun flowers by the roadside, we stand by the back windows and exclaim about the profusion of mammoth, white water hemlock growing near the ponds. The yellow pond lilies are so big that, even from a long distance, we can see them clearly on the lily pads. These are the "big" days, the ones that make us realize the magnitude of the land in which we live, the great size of living things which surround us.

But there are days, too, when we are equally impressed by the small things which lie around us. Such a day was yesterday, a "little" day, when the things we noticed most were infinitesimal compared with the big and the mighty. A tiny humming bird, wings a-whirr, hovered over the red petunias in the garden. A baby toad, no larger than the tip of a little finger, hopped ahead of us as we went to pick fresh lettuce. A quick chipmunk scampered under the delphiniums as he heard our steps approaching. A black beetle with a bright red back clung to one of the columbines, and we paused for a second to admire its coloring and graceful flight.

That evening as we were having dinner on the breezeway, we were amused to see a light, airy parachute drifting down to the bouquet of flowers on the table. It was the seed of an oyster plant, as dainty and perfect in its way as a snowflake. Later that night as we put out the chipmunks' breakfast of bread crumbs and peanuts, a little gray mouse scampered along the bird feeder. We looked beyond and saw in the moonlight the profusion of small white everlasting blossoms growing under the window. Next to them, the bright coral bells in the shape of elfin caps. As we turned out the living room lights, we saw against the window pane the last contribution to our lovely, "little" day—a tiny moth, fluttering its small, lacy, white wings in utter elegance and beauty.

October, 1973

THE ANNUAL line storm, the fall storm which follows the line of the mountains, came early this year, during the first few days of September. No peaks in sight, just heavy gray clouds, and at the cabin the rain dripped all day and all night from the eaves. The porches were wet, the ground was wet, and our entry hall bore witness to the rain outside by dozens of small black flowers in the shape of dogs' paws. When the clouds over the peaks disappeared, still clinging, however to their bases, the sun shone on clean, fresh snow on the summits. The air is crisp and cool; no more lunches on the breezeway; fires every night and morning in the fireplace.

We look up at the fresh snow on the peaks, at the aspens and cottonwoods turning color, at an occasional leaf which the wind carries down, and we listen at night for the familiar bugling of elk from the bench above the cabin. We say to each other, "Autumn will be coming soon." And then suddenly we see the red underbrush, we spy two or three elk emerging from the forest above, the first to head for the river and cross it on their way to the refuge near town. We see the tawny-colored grasses growing among the sage bushes. We look at each other in surprise and astonishment. Autumn will not be coming soon, we know now, autumn is already here in a burst of blue skies, white peaks, brilliant fall colors, and the arrival on the bird feeder of the first tiny, hungry chickadee.

November, 1973

AT&T, THE FATHER burro, is the sensible one of the group. He always practices wisdom and common sense and carefully thinks out a course before adopting it. He knows exactly where he wants to go and when. He knows which parts of the pasture yield the finest sweet grasses. If his two daughters, Esso and Loli, behave in an unseemly way in their adolescent enthusiasms, he simply moves aside, pretends not to notice, and leaves any disciplinary action to their mother. Fidelity, the mother, is a worrier. She insists that the two children behave properly and act in a lady-like manner. She will tolerate no rudeness in the meadow; a good nip on the hind quarters brings the girls into line when they disregard what she has taught them. Esso is stately and dignified. She would never dream of resorting to rough behavior. She walks with grace, she eats with delicacy, and if ever she is guilty of an unmannerly act, she is greatly ashamed and is cross with Loli who has been the one to involve her. We suspect that, when alone with her family, Esso is very vain. Loli, the baby of the family, is the most boisterous and fun-loving. She enjoys taking a soft nip at our sleeves, she grabs bandanas from our back pockets, she pulls hats and caps from our heads. Needless to say, she is the one upon whom her mother's eyes are generally fixed. These are our burros.

Sometimes when we visit the pasture in the summer time, the burros play hide and seek with us, and we must then play the game with them. We call and call and search and search, but not a single burro is in sight. We look apprehensively at the gate and wonder if by any dreadful chance they could have escaped and at the moment are wandering in mischievous glee over the sage flats, no fences or cattle guards to hold them. We walk on, continuing to call, but not a sign of our friends.

Suddenly one of them, usually AT&T, thinks the game has gone far enough, and he steps on a twig or pokes out a long gray ear from behind a tree to let us know their hiding place. We look closer and see eight big brown eyes watching our every movement, eight long ears alert to hear us as we approach. We throw our arms around each gray neck, in relief that they are there and safe. They seem to wink at us as we give them their carrots. Once when we walked into the pasture, we were terrified at the loud screams and unearthly shrieks we heard. We feared some child was in terrible trouble and hurried on to find out. We found the burros in the shade of the trees, resting from their play, two lying down, one rolling in the dust, the fourth standing by. All seemed well and unconcerned, but the cries continued. As we came nearer, we saw three coyote puppies playing in and out among the burros, howling and yelling as they tumbled and ran about. The inquisitive coyotes stopped their play and watched us coming closer; then they darted off into the underbrush.

1974

DEDICATED TO
MARGARET BURNETT SIMPSON

January, 1974

You were a bonnie lass, Margaret Burnett. There are those we know who say they still call you Maggie darlin', and Maggie darlin' it will always be. Bonnie you were, and smart as a whip, too, with a sense of humor from the day you were born which never once failed you. And courage—such courage! Perhaps it all came to you a short while before you were born when the Bannock Indians went on the war path and threatened the Shoshone Indians. Your mother at that time was probably quite desperate for fear the child she was carrying would be injured. But the Commandant at Fort Washakie in Wyoming ordered all women, children, and old people to be evacuated. The old Ninth Cavalry escorted your group to Salt Lake City where you were born. When the Bannock uprising was over, you returned to Wyoming, a state where you belong, a state which has had good reason to be proud of you ever since. Your father was a scout and an Indian fighter in the Western Territory. He became Indian agent at Fort Washakie and was a good friend of the great Chief Washakie. Years and years later—do you remember?—the Chief baptized your little grandson. When he picked up the baby, he caught a faint fragrance of bath powder, and from that moment on, your grandson, Harry Barker—later to become a member of the House of Representatives in Wyoming, then a state senator, president of the state's Fish and Game Commission, to mention only a few of his honors—that child was baptized Piaquana which means in Indian "sweet smelling."

Yours was a large family, Nanny—five brothers, two sisters. The only ones left now are the three girls, you, Eva, and Ida, the long-lived ones of the family. The West gave all of you its strength, its fortitude, its unsurpassed freshness and beauty. Do you remember attending school in Lander when you were a little girl?—Lander, at that time a small frontier town with few if any of the marks of sophistication or urban living. You

245

and Bertie Martel, who still lives there, must have memories galore that the two of you recall when you visit together. Then came a glamorous period in your young life when you went to stay with your grandparents on their plantation in Texas and you attended school there. Later you went to St. Stephens near Riverton, Wyoming, to teach school. Hardly more than a child you were, Nanny, but it was there that the most significant thing of your life occurred. A fine young man who was studying Latin from the priests there caught your eye, and, of course, you had long since caught his. Bill Simpson was studying law under Douglas Preston in Lander, and on October 18, 1893, you and he were married in the Episcopal church at Fort Collins, Colorado. Your first home with Bill was the Fremont Hotel Apartment in Lander, and in 1895 you moved to Jackson, Wyoming. Wyoming was really your home, and no matter how often you left or for how long, you would return to the state which has always claimed you as its own.

And Jackson at that time—do you remember? A little shanty town of 150 or 200 people. Your Bill and Charles Deloney, father of Legislator Bill Deloney, built and operated the first store in Jackson. Nanny, you who have been back to Jackson many, many times since those early days, you more than anyone else must have been pleased, appalled, repelled, charmed by all the changes that have come since. But it is still Jackson, Nanny, and your friends here are legion. Do you remember the primitive Crabtree cabin where you and Bill lived? How you must chuckle to yourself when you hear of the frustrations and helplessness of those of us in the Valley now when our electric power goes off for a few hours! You managed so beautifully without any of the modern conveniences upon which we find ourselves so dependent. Do you recall that the only eggs to be had in the Valley were those garnered from the nests of geese and ducks along Flat Creek? Your grandson Harry, the one Chief Washakie baptized Piaquana, says to this day you dislike game meat as you had so much of it in those early days in Jackson. And do you remember Ma Reed and her cafe, the only one in Jackson? And your winter trips "up country" to visit your friend, Mrs. Lucas, who lived in the vicinity of Jenny Lake. What gala times you had as a number of you made the long, long trek from Jackson. With our cars at the road and our sturdy snow machines at the gate, ready to take us flying over the snow, we wonder how you made the trip from Jackson to the cabin of Mrs. Lucas. By sleigh, by snowshoes, probably. But the trip was well worth it with the gaiety, the laughter, and the knowledge that when you arrived, Mrs. Lucas would have fresh baked goods to serve you. She made trips to Idaho Falls, then called Market Lake, and bought supplies of bread, cakes,

246

cookies. When she returned home, she would toss them all into the nearest snow drift, perhaps the world's first deep freeze.

And then in the years to come there were your three children, Virginia the first, the mother of little Piaquana; there was Glenn; there was Milward, all of whom plus the grandchildren and great grandchildren—all of whom consider you the greatest person they have ever known. The years passed, Nanny, some of them gay, some of them not so gay, but, we are sure, you would agree with the old French saying that there really is no such thing as a happy life, only happy days. Certainly you had a share of those. And, what is infinitely more important, think of all the happy hours and happy days you gave to so many, many people, and still are giving them. You lived for a little while in Meeteetse, Wyoming, where your Bill entered a law partnership with Atwood C. Thomas. You lived also with your grandson, William Simpson Brady, at Coronado. Billy—such a fine, straightforward-looking young man, a graduate of Annapolis—was to be killed off Guadacanal while leader of a squadron of Navy air fighters. Then you returned to Jackson and later went to Fort Duchesne, Utah, where you lived with your gay and lively sisters, Ida and Eva. You lived for a while in Denver, went to Arizona in the winters, but now at last you have returned, as all your friends knew you would, to your beloved Wyoming.

There have been moments, many moments, of pride for you, Nanny. You are the oldest living member of the Order of Eastern Star in Wyoming. You are a charter member of Olivet Lodge in Lander as well as Ruth Chapter in Meeteetse. St. Margaret's Guild in the Episcopal church in Cody was named in honor of you. You were state president of the American War Mothers, and you were on the original Board of Directors of the Buffalo Bill Museum at Cody. And your son Milward, Nanny! How you must have glowed with pride when he went off to the Harvard Law School. But little did you realize then—did you?—how distinguished his career as a lawyer would be. Did you ever dream that one day he would be Governor of Wyoming and then United States Senator? Goose bumps, Nanny, you must have felt, just as we are feeling them now as we write these words.

But none of these things, Nanny, is so important as you. Doubtless they all were the result of you and all you always were and are. Such a sense of humor, Nanny! Do you remember, oh, do you remember when Milward and Lorna and you moved to the Governor's mansion in Cheyenne, and Milward was inaugurated as Governor? A press photographer took your picture and interviewed you. In reply to his question, you said that indeed you were the mother of the Governor. You were asked where you lived, and you answered, "Presently in Denver," but, thank goodness, you hastened to add proudly, "but all of my life in Wyoming." And then the reporter, shameless fellow, asked your age. And your answer: "Young man, the photo will reveal the age." Delicious! And when your son Milward said to you one day, "Mother, you are a great inspiration. When the Lord made you, He broke the mold." Your answer: "He probably had to." Never have people heard you speak ill of anyone. When your youngsters used to bring you tales of others who displeased them, always you spoke of the person they were discussing and skillfully, oh so skillfully, mentioned his good characteristics, his fine points. No matter what sorrow or disappointment or hardship you had to bear, Nanny, always it was done with charitableness, with tremendous courage, with incredible serenity.

Has the Lord really broken your mold, Nanny? All of us hope not; we can only believe that there are lives, young and old, whom you have touched, lives following your splendid example of courage, of calmness, your ways of love and charity, and always your sparkling sense of humor. Now more than ever such as you are needed to give the rest of us assurance, confidence, and hope. You are a hundred years old on the 24th of this month, Nanny—a venerable age especially when measured day by day, year by year in all the abundance of great qualities you have brought to the lives of those around you. The world has need of your kind, Nanny, and so with our hearty congratulations, with our love, and with our gratitude, we are hoping that you may go on and on for at least another century, bringing to all who know you your wisdom, your strength, your grace.

February, 1974

ICE-BLUE SKIES above snowy peaks. Cabin logs that crack sharply. In the sun, blinding white snow that, on the porches, squeaks and crunches under heavily booted feet. Under racing dogs' paws in the yard, deep snow that sounds iron-hard and hollow. Windows covered on the inside with frost in the design of palms, ferns, tropical plants and fish. One tiny hole in the window frost made with the warm palm of a hand to enable an eye from indoors to look at the outdoor thermometer.

Then came a blizzard which blew and raged for three days.

Nearly everything in the Valley stopped during the blizzard. The radio station carried messages of meetings canceled, telephones were busy as people called off social engagements. There was muffled silence everywhere until we saw on the road in the distance the blinking lights and heard the roar of the plow as it came to clear the highways and side roads.

248

People turned to indoor jobs, to relaxation in front of big fires in the fireplaces, to watching the drama and excitement of the furious storm.

And then the cold came. The thermometer dropped to minus 38 at the cabin, to minus 44 at the little village nearby, to minus 52 down a canyon leading out of town. Again appointments and meetings and social engagements were postponed. The highways were deserted. Cars would not start, jump cables were in great demand, plumbers were called by dozens of helpless people whose pipes had frozen. When our four dogs went out, they rushed back at once, holding up first one cold paw, then another. We ventured out only to bring in huge armloads of wood to keep the fires crackling from morning till night. Mail was forgotten, shopping was forgotten, and we were grateful for the stock of provisions we had in the freezers and on the shelves.

We and the dogs alike amused ourselves by watching the flurry of activity on the bird feeder. The chickadees, ordinarily sleek, small birds, now were puffed up to twice their normal size. By the dozen they came for suet, seeds, and pieces of bread. The camp robbers, too, arrived in hordes, as did the woodpeckers whose noisy hammering could be heard at the bag of suet from dawn till dark. The Steller's jays, too timid to come to the feeder, waited on the snowy ground below for any crumbs of bread or seeds or pieces of suet that would be spilled over. Rebecca, our wild little pine squirrel, appeared during our breakfast, a dark streak of fluffy fur racing along the logs, leaping onto the feeder. She ate abundantly of the food she always found and then, with a piece of bread or a peanut in her mouth, would race back along the logs, leap to the half-buried clothes line post, hurry through the snow to the first big cottonwood, then off to a branch of a choke cherry bush, then down the bench where she seemed to fly through the air to another bush, and from there up a cottonwood to a hole in the trunk. Into it she would disappear, deposit her food, race back up the bench, grab another morsel, then repeat the journey down. Occasionally magpies or camp robbers, who had discovered her cache, would try to slip into Rebecca's hole in the tree and steal her food, but, quick as a flash, the dark, furry body would appear. With cries of anger and with quick darts at the birds, she would be successful in driving them away. Then Rebecca, her morning tasks completed, would go to a strong branch, curl herself up in the sun, and go to sleep, a round, warm ball of fur. Once while she was napping on a branch in back of her tree, a sly chickadee sneaked up to her cache and stole some of her hidden supplies. Rebecca must have heard the flutter of tiny wings or the intrusion of little claws. She darted around and drove the chickadee off.

249

Timothy, our snowy white weasel, appeared often during the cold spell. He was difficult to see against the snow, but we learned to watch for him and could spy him as he sped over the snow, then darted into a drift, his black-tipped tail disappearing last. Suddenly he re-appeared some feet away through another hole in the snow. His agility amazed us as he jumped up the log wall, fell back, tried again and again until he managed to get up to the feeder. Between Rebecca and Timothy, our supply of suet for the birds was diminishing so fast that we hung the suet, tied in a cloth mesh bag, from the rafters where we thought they could not reach it. Rebecca eyed it hungrily, sat and tried to devise a way to get it, but her attempts proved unsuccessful. Timothy, however, had better luck. He crawled up the eaves, moved out above the bag of suet, then dropped down to it, holding on with his teeth only until he could pull himself up with his tiny claws. We hated to see Rebecca disturbed because she could not reach her favorite food, and we were distressed to see Timony's antics to reach it, so we threw small pieces onto the snow. The little animals seemed most appreciative as they seized their treats and disappeared with them held firmly in their mouths. Timothy introduced his wife Cordelia to the feasting area one day, and ever since she, too, has been a frequent visitor.

Finally the blizzard stopped, as it always does. Warmer days and nights returned, as they always do. It was an exciting time, a dramatic time, the weather in the Valley at its most violent, and merciless. We, knowing it would end before long, sat back before fires in the fireplace, read, listened to records on the stereo, worked on knitting and quilting and needlepoint, experimented with new recipes. Timothy, Cordelia, Rebecca, and the birds entertained us as no TV program ever has. We were privileged to witness nature at her wildest and most savage, and, at times, her most splendid. Life seemed a little dull and commonplace after it was all over.

March, 1974

A DAY CAME not long ago when there really were no morning tasks. The house had been freshly cleaned, the greenhouse was in fine shape and the snapdragons, calendulas, yellow oxalis, geraniums were reaching gratefully toward the early sun. The refrigerator was well stocked with our recent cooking. Laundry had been finished and put away. A whole morning, *morning,* we thought, to do as we pleased. Musical instruments to play, recordings to listen to on the stereo, handwork to do. What leisure, what luxury! We promised ourselves that not one bit of work would we do, even if we had forgotten something. The nagging voice within seemed to murmur in assent.

We stood in front of the fire for a few minutes after breakfast and watched the sun striking the snowy peaks. Then our attention was turned to a big black moose making its way toward the willows in the distance. We glanced at the clock and saw that it was not yet nine o'clock, and once more we reveled in the thought of a whole morning to do with as we pleased. We got a book and were ready to open it when we thought perhaps we'd rather finish the sleeve of a sweater we were knitting. So out came the knitting bag, but we laid it aside for a while and decided in favor of the book. After reading a few pages, we stretched and yawned, glanced at the clock again and saw it was barely nine-thirty. It wasn't possibly time to think of getting lunch, so we looked around, stretched our legs as we sat on the sofa, got up, pulled a lamp shade straight here, adjusted the angle of a pillow there, picked off a withered snapdragon flower from a bouquet on the table, and sat down again. Maybe the dogs needed fresh water, so we got up again and refilled the dish in the kitchen. We thought the silver might need polishing. But, no, we had promised ourselves a morning free from work, so we stood in front of the fire for several minutes and watched Timothy, the weasel, as he scampered up the outer logs of the cabin. We wandered out to the dining room and stopped at the bird feeder to watch the activity there. Perhaps a few more peanuts should be put out for Rebecca, the hungry pine squirrel, so we got out the tin can and scattered a few nuts on the snowy ledge. We remembered a button that had come off a shirt in a recent laundering and were strangely exhilarated at the thought of sewing it on. But again we remembered no work this morning, just fun. "Well, here's your morning," said the nagging voice within. "Go ahead, have fun. Do some of those things which seem so appealing when you're busy vacuuming, dusting, ironing, polishing the furniture, baking a cake. Go ahead," the wicked little voice continued. "The minutes are ticking away fast. Another such morning may not come again soon." We began to feel nervous and frustrated. Disturbing pressures to hurry and have fun were building up around us. We tapped the barometer—that's fun, isn't it?—and looked at the outdoor thermometer. We glanced at the clock and saw that it was only ten o'clock, a whole hour before we had to give the dogs their lunch of dog biscuits. Maybe they need another bowl of fresh water, so we took care of that, making the job last as long as we could. Idly and with an unaccustomed fatigue that seemed to be coming over us, we wiped a few crumbs from the kitchen sink, removed a smudge from the door of the refrigerator, wandered back into the living room, picked up our knitting, and half-heartedly began to knit a row, purl a row, then put the sleeve down, and looked out the window.

The dogs were at the door, so we got up and let them in, yawned, sat down again, and wondered where we usually got the energy to perform our usual morning tasks. We wondered if something physical was wrong. A touch of anemia perhaps. We have heard that hepatitis makes one languid and listless. We went to the mirror to see if we could detect a yellowish cast to our skin, but not a sign. The dogs were banging around the kitchen, eyeing the cupboard where we keep their biscuits. A little early to feed them, but they've been playing hard, so it might be nice to surprise them with an early lunch. We re-filled their water dish. We, too, will have an early lunch, we thought, and take a nap. What an exhausting morning!

The afternoon seemed more normal. We felt rested and knit on the sweater sleeve with genuine enjoyment. We read a little and practiced our musical instruments in the library. We looked at the clock and noticed that it was late afternoon—where had the time gone? We gave the dogs their evening meal, started the preparation of ours, and looked forward to an evening of shanghai, chess, and recordings on the stereo. And tomorrow, we thought, what a day tomorrow will be! Usual, pleasant little chores, a custard to make, an Irish stew to start early. What a fine day coming up!

Could it be, we wondered, as we got ready for bed, that a morning of pure leisure with nothing to do can be the most exhausting morning of all? Could it be that our fatigue in the morning came from simple boredom? We heard the nagging voice within chuckle and whisper a message in our ear as we dropped off to sleep:

> The mornings that do pall and lag,
> That make your spirits feebly sag,
> The ones that make you dull and bored,
> The only ones that are abhorred,
> Are those when for your fun you try
> Too hard, and then it slips you by.
> The mornings are, you'll find, real fun
> When there is work that must be done.

April, 1974

SPRING in the Valley is a restless child who can't make up its mind. Spring in the Valley is a teen-age boy who wants to assert himself and be a man at one moment, but the next one prefers to retreat into the comfort of irresponsible childhood. Spring in the Valley is an adolescent girl,

252

smiles and laughter one day, sulks and tears and sighs the next. We are reminded of the poem by Edna St. Vincent Millay of an irritated mother who tells her little girl she must settle down and not run in and out all day long. Either she must go out of doors or stay inside. "But, mother," the child remonstrates, "I can't decide. I can't decide."

November, 1974

ALL THROUGH OCTOBER we began to notice how short the days were growing, although they continued to be sunny and glorious. We worked out of doors in our shirt sleeves and became uncomfortably hot in the warm Indian summer sun. "Like summer afternoons," we said to each other. "Surely this can't last much longer." But it did last, on and on—bright blue, cloudless skies, sunny days, clear, starry nights with Northern lights pulsating above the peaks. There was no wind, and, although some trees stood bare, many were still full and carried the last autumn colors on their leaves until late in the month. Then came a sudden wind and the air was filled with shining gold pieces which danced and twirled to the ground. We lifted our heads and said with a sniff into the air, "Snow is on the way."

We feel safe and secure, thankful for all that we have, thankful for all that we have done, and our thoughts turn with understanding to the familiar words of the old Thanksgiving hymn—

All is safely gathered in,
Ere the winter's storms begin.

1975

THERE IS NO single word to describe the feeling. "Happiness," "contentment," "satisfaction," "peace"—no one of them is quite what we feel. The German word "Gemütlichkeit" comes closest, but we want a word in English so we thought we would coin one of our own. So coin a new word we did and that word is "featherly" which carries the meaning of lightness and warmth. Featherly, featherly, featherly. We feel featherly, we like situations which induce featherliness. There, we have it.

It is at this time of year that we most strongly have feelings of featherliness. In summer, spring, and fall when we can get out of doors easily and quickly, when roads and trails are open, when access to the cabin is simple and unhampered by snow and winds—then we feel happiness and contentment and peace. It is the cold, the snow, the icy winds, the drifts through which we drive our snow machines, the comfort of a blazing fire in the fireplace that make us feel featherly.

When we see dark clouds sweeping down from the peaks, when the birds fly low, when a strong gale blows about the corners of the cabin, that is the setting for our feelings of featherliness. If the cars are both safely at the end of the road with their engine heaters attached to the electric outlet, if our snow machines are on the platform, headed out, if there is plenty of fresh food in the refrigerator and freezers for us and the dogs—that's featherliness. A mountain storm may be raging through the Valley, we may look out and decide that we'll forget the mail today. We give up any thought of venturing out and instead stay indoors by the warm fire—that's featherliness. Sometimes after a heavy snowfall during the night, we hurry with our indoor chores, eager to get out of doors for jobs there. We run our new Toro Sno-Pup over the porches, blowing the snow away, until both porches stand clear and bare. We bring in armloads of kindling and logs to keep the fires blazing. We stop to watch the four dogs tumbling and rolling in the snow or to see a flock of Bohemian wax wings alight in a cottonwood tree in back of the cabin. When all has been finished, we stamp our boots free of snow and go in. A kettle of turkey or tomato or water cress soup may be bubbling on the stove and the fragrance reaches us in the entry as we take off our cold parkas, mittens, and boots. That's featherliness. Occasionally on bitter cold days, the SkiDoos are difficult to start. We try and try to turn over their motors and are just about ready to give up and go indoors until the temperature rises a little. We try once more and suddenly and surely comes the roar of the little motor as it turns over and chugs away—that's featherliness. Once in a while on wintry, blustery days the electric power goes off when a tree is blown on the lines or the lines become heavily encrusted with ice and break. We bring in more wood for the fireplaces, have meals prepared over the coals, look disconsolately at the stacks of dirty dishes that are waiting to be put into the dishwasher. Then, all of a sudden, we hear the motor of the pump, the hum of the refrigerator, the click of the electric baseboard heaters. That's featherliness. When we see the chickadees, the woodpeckers, the camp robbers, the jays hungrily pecking at the food we have put out for them—that's featherliness. If Timothy, the weasel, should peek from the snow on the outside cooler of the greenhouse, turning his tiny white head toward the bird feeder to see if we have left scraps of meat for him—that's special featherliness. We see our stacks of books growing smaller as we take one after the other of those we have finished to the library shelves downstairs. We worry for fear our supply of reading material is running low. Then we go to the post office and see a package notice in our box and find that it is another stack of books recently ordered. That's featherliness. We have a few distasteful winter tasks like hauling on the SkiDoo the week's trash to the trash can at the end of the road, or reading the electric meter at the far end of the garden now deep in snow, or taking out ashes from the fireplace. When these jobs are well finished, that's featherliness. When we slip our booted feet into the bindings of our skis, take the poles firmly in our hands, and begin a trip over the snow-covered sage flats to a grove of aspens in the distance, that's featherliness. And how featherly we feel as we sit on our bright red space blanket spread on the snow and sip our sherry as a prelude to a lunch of hot soup and sandwiches. When we turn on the flood lights in the greenhouse and sit down to dinner, we look at bright red carnations, golden calendulas, pink snapdragons, huge blossoms of red and pink and white geraniums, cascading red and blue petunias—then we feel completely featherly. When we sit down in the evening before the fire to play games of shanghai and chess, hearing the wind howling outside, feeling the comfort and peace inside—that's featherliness. And then when we put our games away, stoke up the fire, settle down with our handwork or knitting, first having turned on a fine concert on the stereo— that's featherliness. Especially when we have plump, shiny chestnuts to roast later on.

One of the greatest feelings of featherliness comes just before bedtime, after games and handwork have been put away, the stereo turned off, the greenhouse heat checked. We take the dogs out for the last time till morning and laugh as we see them plunge through drifts and race over snowy paths. Then we bring them in, close the door, shake snow from our hoods and parkas. We turn up our electric blankets, open wide the windows of the bedrooms for a minute to let the cold, fresh air pour in. Reading lights over beds are turned on, dogs curl up in their wicker baskets. We reach for a book on our night stand. After an hour or so, lights are turned off, the cabin is dark except for the last glow from the fire in the fireplace. Everything has been checked, all is well, dogs and humans are at rest. Each of us settles down to watch for a minute the snow whirling from the roofs outside, to listen to the deep voice of the mountain wind through the bare trees. With pleasure we anticipate the next day. We give the dogs a last pat for the day and know that this, above all, is featherliness.

February, 1975

The wind blows harsh from the mountains
Turning snow into wraiths of smoke.
The wind blows cold from the mountains,
And it's not for timid folk.
Oh, you who sit by the fire,
'Tis you who will never know
The wind that comes with the force of a brute,
On your face the sting of the snow.
All of us can't be nurtured
By winter's icy blast,
But, oh, my lad, and ah, my lass,
It's with this *our* lot is cast.

March, 1975

IT DOESN'T MATTER what season of the year it is, each of us always has at least one book going, more likely two or three. We are sometimes fearful that we may exhaust the new books we have, but that thought does not alarm us to excess as our library is full of books we have already read and are waiting for a chance to re-read. Just as we are ready to get a copy of Hardy or George Eliot or Dostoevski or Conrad or Isak Dinesen, we hear of a new book we simply must read, so our re-reading of the old favorites is postponed at least for a time.

For instance, there were the two delightful books by James Herriott, the first of which we read a year or so ago, *All Creatures Great and Small,* and the equally entertaining sequel, *All Things Bright and Beautiful,* which we have just, regretfully, finished. We hope there will be a third, there must be a third. We had never realized that the experiences of a veterinary in a small Yorkshire village could be so entertaining, so funny, so charming as these true stories about Jim and his animals.

That Quail, Robert by Margaret Stanger was a lovely story. Soon after that, we traveled to Newfoundland, Labrador, Greenland, to the Shetland Islands, to Scandinavia, to Russia, to Paris with the Lindbergs in *Locked Rooms and Open Doors,* Anne Morrow Lindbergh's most recent volume of diaries and letters, describing her life from 1933-35. Then came *Wandering through Winter* by Edwin Way Teale, a delightful account of the author's 20,000 mile journey through North America, visiting and contrasting winter months in various parts of the country. This book is not new, having first appeared in 1957, but a new one by the same author has just been published, *A Naturalist Buys an Old Farm.* That we ordered and with excitement and high anticipation unwrapped the package when it arrived the other day. On our coffee table to be read very soon is a copy of Rutherford Platt's *The Great American Forest* in which the author tells the story of trees for the past 100 million years. We are re-reading the poetry of W. B. Yeats, interested always in his poems of great Irish heroes, of love, of thoughts on life and death. All of us were pleased when we read that Norman Cousins, editor of *The Saturday Review,* had published a new book, *The Celebration of Life.* We sent for it immediately, had to wait some time for its arrival as the demand probably was tremendous, but now have the slender volume ready to read. It is Cousin's answer to general feelings of despair and futility at the present time and his answer, in the form of Socratic dialogue, that there is still much cause for hope. The book makes us think of the December 14 issue of *The Saturday Review* in which well-known world figures presented their reasons for feeling hopeful about the future of mankind and gave concrete reasons for their optimism. The article which we thought the best was one by René Dubos entitled "The Humanizing of Humans" which is an extract from his book *Beast or Angel?* We are eager to read the entire book and have it on order.

257

One of the finest books we have read in a long time is Lewis Thomas' *The Lives of a Cell* with the subtitle, Notes of a Biology Watcher. If you read this book, do not become discouraged by the first few pages. Such words as prokaryocytes, eukaryotes, amebocytes, apocrine, bombykol may not be common household words to the average person, but somehow this doesn't matter. Keep on reading, and suddenly the whole thing will become clear. If anyone is so ignorant or so arrogant as to consider mankind superior and above the rest of life around him, let him read *Lives of a Cell*. He can only conclude, perhaps with a strangely unaccustomed feeling that a death blow has been dealt to his vanity, that all life is ineluctably interrelated and that man is an important part but by no means the most important part of the earth. And then the final chapter, the great final chapter. One reads the facts, enjoys a touch of humor, but when he has finished, he has the sensation that he has missed something. He goes back and re-reads this final chapter and, suddenly, its tremendous significance is apparent. Quietly, simply, Lewis Thomas closes his book with a powerful crescendo, and the reader begins to understand the mighty thoughts of which he now is becoming aware. And such writing! Simple, forceful, intelligent, with many a touch of exquisite humor. When one has finished this book by one of the country's leading scientists, his desire is to start straight from the beginning and re-read it, knowing that it will be re-read many times so that not one bit of its wisdom and truth will escape.

A friend of ours kindly sent us a copy of Annie Dillard's *Pilgrim at Tinker Creek,* hoping that we would find the same enjoyment in it that she had. We read it in turn, each one impressed by the fascinating accounts of insects, muskrats, and all growing things as observed by the author in the course of one year in Virginia. We were horrified and occasionally repelled by some of the accounts, but always intrigued. We shall remember the praying mantis laying her eggs, the field of grasshoppers, the tree with lights, the things of wonder and mystery which Annie Dillard saw through her microscope. Inspired by this reading, our microscope will be put to good use this summer, and we think that never again shall we walk carelessly or unobservantly through forests, meadows, or by streams and rivers.

Edwin Newman's *Strictly Speaking* came as a shock to us when we read what people in every profession and business, from outstanding figures in government to the lowliest sports announcer, are doing to destroy the English language. In their desire to seem erudite and authoritative, they are coining ridiculous, meaningless words, taking two pages of confused and confusing writing to say what would better be said in two meaningful sentences. Although written with marvelous humor, there is an apparent underlying fear on the part of the author that the distortion of the language may well mean the eventual distortion of society.

And always on our coffee table, kept within easy reach is the incomparable book, *In Wildness...,* containing superb photographs by Eliot Porter which accompany a text by Thoreau. This we pick up often, reading a paragraph here, another there, finding something new on each reading.

And so our reading has gone this winter. Thank goodness, we think, there are still plenty of books to be read, there will be mountain storms which will keep us indoors for at least parts of blustering days and nights. How many more people we shall meet and enjoy how many more places we shall visit, how much more we shall learn!

April, 1975

SPRING SONG AT MOOSE

We thought we knew this climate,
We thought we knew it well.
The weather's strange caprices
We'd often dare foretell.

The days of spring seemed closer,
With redwings by the pond.
Two juncos and four finches
With suet did abscond.

The air grew mild and balmy,
The snow began to melt,
A southern breeze blew gently,
Like days in May it felt.

The sun shone warm and brightly,
So all our winter gear
Went up into the attic
To wait there till next year.

We brought down lighter clothing;
Now we would never need
Those heavy woolen sweaters,
Those slacks of woolen tweed.

Our thoughts turned very quickly
To picnics by canoe,
To gardening, to fishing,
With spring—a rendezvous!

We'll eat our lunches out of doors
Oh, very, very soon.
Why, in the twinkling of an eye
We'll say "Hello!" to June.

We were so very shrewd and smart
We knew the answers—all.
We quite forgot what cometh
Before a mighty fall.

The skies grew black and cloudy,
The winds began to blow,
And what is that we see outside?
It surely can't be *snow!*

But snow it was and howling winds
That raged and roared for days.
We brought our winter things back down
And kept our fires ablaze.

The barometer was playing tricks,
It hit an all time low.
Wherever do they all come from,
These heaps and drifts of snow?

We thought the snow was melting,
We heard the juncos sing.
How were we so completely wrong
About an early spring?

"I fooled you," laughed old Winter,
'It's spring!' you just now swore.
But with a mighty blizzard
I'm back again once more.

"Don't try to push me off so fast,
My ice and cold don't spurn,
You foolish, stupid people,
Will you never, ever learn?

"You thought you were all ready
Sweet spring to warmly greet.
There's fury in my muscles.
Your words I'll make you eat."

So we might as well be happy,
Since in the north we live,
We might as well hail winter.
There's no alternative!

July, 1975

WHEN ALL the birds had returned and the air was filled with their songs, when the ponds were completely open and ducks were swimming in and out among the tall grasses, when the pond lilies were ready to bloom, we put our magnifying glasses into the pockets of our jeans and made our first trip to one of our areas of exploration and observation. On the way down the precipitous bench, we clung to shrubs and young trees to steady our footing over the rough ground, being careful always to avoid grasping the prickly red stems of the wild roses which grow there in abundance. We saw at our feet yellow johnny-jump-ups which were blossoming everywhere in tiny nosegays. We noticed above us, in the crotch of a big cottonwood, the deserted nest of a pine squirrel. Near it was last year's nest of a robin, tucked in firmly on a higher branch. When we reached the bottom of the bench, we saw the old log which is used in turn by the martens, the weasels, the chipmunks. We noticed several holes which disappeared darkly into the log and probably led to winding tunnels where the animals store their winter's supply of food and have their nurseries. A little farther on, as we made our way over swampy earth between rotting logs, we noticed a spider's web on the lower branches of one of the aspen trees. This we stopped to examine with our magnifying glass. We had just read about the miracle of a spider's web in Karl von Frisch's *Animal Architecture,* and, sure enough, there was the delicate frame which he described and all the geometrically perfect strands which formed the rest of the web. So fragile but at the same time so strong is the web, that we do not wonder that humming birds use threads of it to bind together their tiny nests. We stooped down to look into the shallow water at the edge of the pond and saw a pale moth struggling to get out. We took a twig and gently lifted it to safety and freedom and left it sunning itself on a leaf. At the bottom of the pond we saw strange water creatures, only a fraction of an inch long, which could either walk in the mud at the bottom or swim effortlessly through

261

the water. We sat down on a huge fallen log and looked closely at the reddish lichens growing along the trunk. We broke off a small piece to examine later under our microscope. We glanced up the steep bench and saw how the undergrowth had sprung up almost over night. We saw the shiny, sticky leaves on the cottonwoods and reached to bend a branch to our noses to catch the delightful fragrance. We saw under a fallen aspen a short distance away clean, white chips and on the ends of three chewed branches the unmistakable marks of beaver teeth. We got up and looked again into the shallow water at our feet. This time we saw a sluggish snail moving slowly in the mud. We reached over and carefully picked it up. Immediately it withdrew into its small spiral shell, only the wet, slimy foot showing. We put it back and soon it emerged again and continued on its way over the mud. We looked into the water farther on and discovered at the bottom the lacy skeleton of a leaf, only the delicate veins remaining. This, too, we saved to take back to the cabin to examine through our microscope. We stooped to pick up for further microscopic examination some feathery moss with thin green threads growing above the softer green carpet at the base.

We have discovered that in back of the cabin there is an abundance of wild life—snails, spiders, and other insects—to study, and from whose life styles and behavior there is much to learn.

August, 1975

WHEN ONE HAS a piano and lives far from a city, keeping the piano in tune is often a problem. We either have had to call someone 125 miles away to make a trip to our cabin or have had to wait until we heard on the radio that a piano tuner had come to the Valley for a few days. But not long ago, a young woman phoned and asked if our piano needed tuning. Indeed, we replied, it did. She asked if her brother could tune it for us. We told her to have him call and tell us when he could come. We were relieved to know that at last a piano tuner had come to town. A day or two later the brother called and said that he had a full time job and would have to come before or after work. We told him we would prefer that he come during the day if possible rather than at night, and he agreed to come the following day in the early afternoon. The next morning he called and said that he could not come after all, but that his younger brother would tune our piano for us and would come the following morning at nine. The next morning at eight-thirty the younger brother called and said that he had to be out of town that morning but would come the next day at nine. That evening it was the older brother who called and said that his younger brother had gone to summer school, but that he himself would come the next day at two in the afternoon. We sighed and agreed. At noon of that day he called again and said that his work shift had been changed and suggested, since we did not want him to come at night, that he come at five in the morning before work. We gasped and told him that would be a little early for us, so he said that he would come the next day directly from work. He said that if we did not mind his coming dirty, he could make it by five-thirty, or if we preferred him to be clean, he would be here at six. We, eager to have him come and tune the piano and be on his way, said to come at five-thirty, even though dirty.

By this time we were becoming suspicious. He had never given his name. He had put us off many times. How did we really know he was a piano tuner? Where, we wondered, did he get our name? How did he know we had a piano? We are three women who live alone, our nearest neighbor being a mile away. In our minds we began to conjure up all manner of things which might happen if our piano tuner proved to be a phony or one of the none too honest vagrants who sometimes wander through the Valley during the summer. Recently we had heard on the radio the grisly tale of a distinguished looking man who called on people, represented himself as a doctor, and offered a free medical examination. Then he took the person's blood pressure and gave him a capsule. When the victim had slept off the effects of the capsule, he looked around to find that his home had been stripped and robbed of everything in it. We phoned a friend of ours who also has a piano to see if he knew anything about the piano tuner. Our friend had not heard a word. Becoming more and more concerned, we called the sheriff's office to see if any such person had been reported there. We told our tale and the officer agreed that it did indeed sound suspicious.

In the meantime, five-thirty was approaching. We glanced around the room to see what we could use as a weapon in case the piano tuner proved to be other than a piano tuner and wanted to gain access to our home for foul play. We spotted a large and heavy fireplace tool which we use to poke and arouse a lazy fire. One of us agreed to stand near that and have her hand on it just in case. The owner of the piano was the one appointed to meet the tuner at the gate, lead him around the house, through the garden, down the slope in back of the cabin, to the library and the piano. She gave careful instructions to the other two to watch her all the way, first from the dining room, then the greenhouse, finally the kitchen until she and the piano tuner were in the library downstairs. And as a last instruction, she said, "And, for heaven's sake, don't take any capsules!"

263

She had no sooner uttered her last admonishment, than a car drove up, stopped, and a young man jumped out and called, "I'm the piano tuner." Our dangerous moment had arrived. He lifted from the trunk of his car a large chest which we only hoped contained no lethal weapons, time bombs, or capsules. The owner of the piano went to the gate to meet him. One of the two left on guard in the cabin said in surprise, "Why, she's got a hammer in her hand. I hope she doesn't kill him!" The young man looked to be about eighteen, had a round, child-like face, innocent blue eyes, blonde hair, neatly cut and combed. We began to feel braver. He was taken to the library where he set down his big chest, opened the piano, took out his tools, sat down, and was ready to begin. We left him alone, but kept the door to the library open, moved our table and chairs close to it, and sat down for a game of shanghai and chess. So far, so good.

From the library came sounds that were extremely professional. The young man was working with care and thoroughness, and in a manner which indicated he knew what he was doing. He seemed to have a feeling of rapport with the piano and worked with greater understanding and sensitivity than any piano tuner we had had previously. Plink, plunk, plink, plink went the keys. We tried to imagine what it would have sounded like at five o'clock in the morning. On he worked, meticulous in his desire to leave each note clear and in tune. We relaxed at our games and began to think we had been foolish scared cats to have had any fears. Nevertheless, three women alone...

When he had finished we went to the library, check book in hand to pay him. We complimented him on his work and said we would be happy to recommend him to friends who had pianos. He looked up, grinned, and said, "But don't recommend me until you see if I've done a good job." An honest thing to say, we thought. We began to like our piano tuner. And then he paused a minute as he was putting his tools away, and asked rather timidly, but eagerly, "Would you mind if I stayed for five minutes or so and played?" We told him to go right ahead, bracing ourselves for what we feared might be a wild blast of discordant rock music. We went back upstairs and settled down with our handwork, expecting the worst, only hoping it would not continue long.

September, 1975

THE PIANO TUNER ran his fingers over the keys and began to play— could we believe our ears?—began to play Chopin. A Chopin prelude, a nocturne, a waltz, as we have seldom heard them played by an amateur.

264

Lovely, fluid music, trills executed beautifully, sensitive, exquisite interpretations. We put down our handwork to give all our attention to listening. One of us coming in from the garden stopped in her tracks, mouth open, eyes wide. She dropped into the nearest chair, and she, too, forgot her handwork. We peeked through the door to the library below. There sat our piano tuner, fingers nimble, strong, sure, bringing forth such delightful music that we hoped he would go on and on. After another Chopin prelude he stopped, obviously ready to leave. We went down again, check book in hand. We complimented him on his playing and said that it had been a splendid recital, but all too short. We sat down on the step to write his check. As he was closing his tool chest, we said, "We're going to make this check for a little more than your price of twenty dollars." Naively, curiously, he looked over our shoulder as we wrote in the amount and then he stood back in amazement. "Thirty dollars! I just hope it's worth the twenty I charge. Nobody has ever given me a ten dollar tip before." And then he stopped and thought a moment. "In fact," he continued, "no one has ever given me a tip at all."

We asked him if he had ever heard a famous pianist, and he said he had heard only Rubinstein and Van Cliburn. "In person?" we asked. He answered, "Oh, no, just on tapes. Have you ever heard them in person?" We told him we had and also the greatest of them all, Horowitz. He looked at us incredulously and said, "But how much does it cost to hear great pianists like that in person?" We told him that we had many recordings of great pianists and asked if he would like to hear some. His eyes danced as he said under his breath, "Imagine me hearing a man like Horowitz!" We took him upstairs and got out our recording of Horowitz playing Chopin. We handed him the album, which he hesitated to take because of his dirty hands, but as he settled down in a chair, he forgot his dirty hands, and began reading on the back of the album, the information about the composer and the artist. He listened to the music like one in a dream, one foot on top of the other, head bent, hands in his lap. Every once in a while he would whisper to himself, "He's changed it there" and "There again he's changed it." Then he would raise his head, and his fingers would fly through the air over imaginary keys as if in imitation. When one side of the record was finished, we asked him if he would like to hear the other side. He said, "Oh, yes! But I don't want to butt in here. You mustn't let me butt in. I have all the time in the world. All I would do if I returned to my trailer in town would be to read the Scriptures. I have plenty of time, but you just tell me when you want me to go." We said we'd play the other side and then he could come again to hear more records another evening.

265

When the record was over, he rose and said, "I've been studying the piano since I was eight. My teacher, I know now, has been wrong in some ways. *This*," he nodded toward the stereo, "is the way it should be played. I could learn more by listening to recordings like this than by taking any more lessons." When he returned to the library to pick up his tool chest, he stopped to run his fingers over the piano keys. They held a magic fascination which he could not resist. It was with great difficulty that he finally tore himself away.

As we walked to the gate with him, we again complimented him on his playing. He said quietly that he owed it all to his parents who had made piano lessons possible for him. He told us he lived in a little village just over the mountains from this Valley, that he was one of thirteen children, that an older brother was now away for two years on a Mormon mission. At the present time our piano tuner was doing hard manual labor—welding huge storage tanks—to earn money so that he, too, could go on a mission in the fall. He told us simply and with no trace of conceit or boasting, that in high school his basketball team had gone to a tournament at the University of Wyoming. He stopped a second to be certain we understood fully and said, "Have you ever heard of the University of Wyoming?" We smiled to ourselves and said that we had heard of it. While he was there, he had discovered where the Fine Arts Building was and had wandered in, found a piano in one of the practice rooms, had sat down, and started to play. As he was playing, a man came and asked if he were a student at the University. The sixteen year old boy had said that he was not, just a ball player in the tournament, and as proof he showed in his coat lapel his identification label. The man told him to continue his playing and he listened thoughtfully as the boy did so. "That man" as our piano tuner called him, asked him to come to his office the following morning. Right on the dot he appeared, played further for "that man" and several others who were there. Then, after a brief consultation of the professors, it was announced to the boy that he could have a full four year scholarship in music which would pay for his room, board, and tuition. But the boy answered that his heart and mind were set on going on a mission so he could not accept. But "that man" told him to return after his mission was completed and the same scholarship might still be available. "The only thing I want now," the piano tuner said, "is a piano I can use while I'm here this summer. I've asked around but can't locate one. I go home on week ends, but I want a piano here—week ends are too far apart."

As he left, we reminded him to come to play our piano and to listen to more recordings. He called the very next day and asked to come that

266

evening, but, unfortunately, we were not going to be home. Then he called two days later, after his week end at home. He has been coming twice a week ever since. Never have we had such an appreciative listener to our records. The music he plays delights us.

He asked one evening if we had anything by Beethoven. Again we smiled to ourselves and replied that indeed we did have much of Beethoven's music and asked him what he would like to hear. He said, "I'd like to hear his Fifth Symphony." He listened to the entire symphony with rapt attention. Then we asked him if he had ever heard any of Beethoven's other symphonies, the Ninth, for instance. He had never known there was a Ninth. When he heard it, his whole being expressed admiration and wonder. He said, "Now I know where the Ode to Joy comes from! I used to play it when I was eight years old—in a simplified version, of course," he added.

We have learned that at fourteen our piano tuner won a Youth Music Festival prize when he played one of Chopin's waltzes. We played that same waltz on recording and at the conclusion, he chuckled to himself and said, "But I never played it *that* way. I just played the notes. This is how it was meant to be played." He was transported into another world when he heard Beethoven's Moonlight Sonata which he himself plays. He spoke of the Presto agitato movement and said, "Most people play that too fast. They probably want to show how good they are. But that's not how Beethoven intended it to be played, I'm sure." When he heard a recording of Rubinstein playing the Chopin Scherzos, he said at the end of one, "He struck two bad notes there." At the conclusion of another, "His hands weren't together at the end." Often when our piano tuner comes to listen to records, he brings his music with him and follows the scores, making notes during the recordings. We said to him after he had made his comments on Rubinstein, "When you follow the score, can you tell when the musician changes something or when he strikes a bad note?" Very simply he said, "Well, I think I can tell it without the score, just by listening."

Early in our friendship with our piano tuner and without his knowledge, we got in touch with the kind Mormon bishop here and told him about this talented boy. The bishop immediately arranged to have him use one of the pianos in the Sunday School whenever he wanted to. Now he can practice daily after or before work, for as long as he wants to. In return, he plays a selection or two for the Sacrament Service on Sunday nights.

Incidentally, we phoned the sheriff's office to report that our piano tuner was entirely all right.

267

He will be leaving on his mission in the fall and we shall miss him. He assured us he would keep in touch with us and then he added shyly, "And when I have completed my mission, this will be the first place I'll head for. I am so excited each night when I leave after hearing music that I can hardly talk and can think of nothing else. I have received my Patriarchal Blessing. The Lord wants me to advance in my music." And then he added, "You know, music more than anything else can change a person's life."

And that is the story of our piano tuner. Who knows how the story will continue? Maybe, written in his stars, there is the life of a concert pianist, maybe of a composer, of a fine teacher. And if not fame perhaps a life wherein music will play a tremendous part and always bring him joy and satisfaction and strength.

1976

IN THIS VALLEY there are many unique features which even the most casual visitor will notice and admire—the towering peaks, the wide expanses of sage flats, the winding and rushing river, the massive pines. In this Valley there are also other unique features which are less obvious, but those of us who live here know they exist. One of these features is the people who live here—in town, in outlying villages, in more isolated areas on ranches. To one who does not live here or who visits the Valley only occasionally for short periods of time, the people may seem like any others who live in small towns or country areas. But these people have a special measure of thoughtfulness, of kindness, of strength, of courage, and endurance which we have found unequalled. The women as well as the men display qualities which characterized their pioneer ancestors. We know women who can swing a bale of hay as deftly and strongly as any man. We have seen many a woman mending heavy buck and rail fences in the spring. They can maneuver a big stock truck with as much skill as their husbands. We had a load of gravel delivered to the cabin not long ago, and it was a woman who brought it and spread it. We know a young woman whose husband shoes horses. In the spring when he is especially busy, she helps him and is as adept at shoeing even the most uncooperative horses as he is. When someone from the East remonstrated with her about doing such heavy, difficult work, she simply looked up, smiled sweetly, and said, "Oh, hell!"

We think back over the years we have spent here as permanent residents, and among our happiest memories are those which include the kindness and thoughtfulness of the people among whom we live. We remember, for instance, the first Christmas we spent here. The day before Christmas was cold and gray. There had been a storm a few days before, and the ground was covered with soft, fluffy snow. Late that afternoon we heard a small plane buzz the cabin. We went to the door and recognized the plane of a friend. He waved and smiled and then dropped a large package attached to a home made burlap parachute. Our friend waved again and called "Merry Christmas!" We put on our snow shoes and went out to retrieve the package. When we returned to the cabin and opened it, there was a big Christmas ham and a box of Christmas candy.

More recently our hearts were cheered to hear the experience of a neighbor of ours who was having trouble with a painful back. He was concerned about his pile of fire logs and how he would split and stack them for winter use. About this time he had to leave the Valley for three or four days. When he returned, he found that friends had gone to his cabin, had split every one of his logs, and had left them neatly stacked on his porch. A young couple who lives near us often lends us a hand with house work chores or with yard work. They have told us to call on them at any time we may need help with anything. When we pay them for their help, they protest and say they would prefer to help us with no pay at all.

The man who services our SkiDoos came to get them late this fall. When he returned with them, he said, "I'll come to service your machines any time you need me, in any kind of weather, so if you get into a tight place with them, don't fail to call." Our jolly Culligan man came to deliver salt for our water softener. He called over his shoulder as he left, "Any time you need a good pair of strong arms to help you with anything, I can be here at a minute's notice." Our dentist knew we were having trouble setting our flag pole in the yard. He offered to drop by with his four husky sons and do the job for us. But that same day another friend came by and the job was done in the twinkling of an eye. One of us had knee surgery a few years ago, and after several days in the hospital, her surgeon wanted her to try crutches. He wanted to be there to see how well she could handle them. Crutches were needed within half an hour, there was no way we at home could get them to her, so in our desperation we phoned a good friend in town, asked him if he would go to the drug store, pick up a pair of crutches, and deliver them to the hospital. His answer was, "I'm delighted you called on me. Of course I can do it right away. I'm on my way." We deeply appreciated his help in an emergency, but even more appreciated the pleasure he seemed to take in doing it.

Snow came early this year, and getting our four burros to their winter pasture presented a real problem. The kind lady who keeps them for us during the winter, phoned and said she would call for them in her truck. After much pushing and pulling and coaxing and cajoling, the four burros were finally loaded. The road was bumpy with deep ruts and heavy snow, and we feared that the little animals might have a rough time of it, jiggling and joggling and possibly falling down. Our fears were quieted, however, when the phone rang that afternoon, and the lady reported that the burros had stood the trip well and at that moment were quietly grazing in their pasture. As a special treat she sent us a picture of the burros with her Christmas card to give us a greeting from them, too. After a summer picnic when all of us had been away from the cabin, a friend phoned and asked if we had looked into our refrigerator recently. We rushed immediately to see what was there and found a big plateful of delicious Rocky Mountain trout which he had caught and left for us on his way home. That same friend and his kind wife appear each year to help us put our canoe trailer on end so the heavy snows will not break the floor boards. They come to see if our roof needs shoveling after heavy snow storms. If they think our snowmobiles have been buried under drifts of snow, they appear to help us dig them out. During heavy blizzards our kind postmistress always phones to see if we are all right or need anything.

We could go on and on with more tales of the kindness, the thoughtfulness, the fortitude, the perseverance of the people in this Valley. And there isn't a person who lives here who couldn't equal or surpass our tales with similar ones of his own. We think of the people here as matching the peaks, as matching the wide expanses of sage flats, as matching the powerfully flowing river and the mighty trees.

February, 1976

WINTER MUSIC

First rosy rays of a rising sun on
Silence, deep silence, white velvet silence.
Broken only by
Songs of chickadees in cottonwoods,
Then ferocious pecking of woodpeckers as bills attack
Chunks of suet, or insects in logs of the cabin.
The scratch, scratch of the snowy weasel's claws as
He creeps stealthily and softly across the feeder
Toward a choice bit of food.
Muted melodies of the river, winding quietly through
High banks of snow.
Silence shattered by gusty, fierce winds
Sweeping mercilessly over

Sage flats, tearing back through tops of trees.
Ravens, black against gray skies, flying low,
Crying discordantly, announcing a storm.
Roar and rumble of an avalanche
Pouring its burden of snow and ice
Down a distant canyon.
Startling cracks, like gun-shot reports, of
Cabin logs in sub-zero temperatures.
Then
Human sounds, less wild,
But offering, too, their own peculiar music—
Ponderous snow plows in the distance
Pushing slowly through drifts
Crazily sculptured by winds.
Early morning blasts dislodging mighty avalanches
To insure safety for skiers.
Approach of a snow machine,
Skimming effortlessly over hard, snowy tracks.
Planes flying low, circling the airport,
Hoping to land.
The hush-hush music of skis gliding over powdery snow.
The crackling conversation of logs
Burning in an evening fire in the fireplace.
Rising from the river bottom
The mystic howl of a lone coyote.
And then—
A cold, silver moon,
Ice-splintered starlight on
Silence, deep silence, black velvet silence.

March, 1976

ALL OF US, having been city-born and city-bred, had never realized how
many different kinds of snow there are. A fine, dry snow that pecks at the
windows often forecasts a wild storm. Then the snow blows in every
direction, off the tops of roofs, swirling by the windows at an insane
pace. The fine snow cuts the face with its sharp needle pricks, the high
winds can cut the breath for a second, so we, humans and dogs alike, have
learned to turn our backs to the raging of the storm. Each log on the

272

cabin is outlined with snow, as are the rafters under the eaves where the diabolic winds have hurled snow up and under. The greenhouse windows are completely shaded with white. As we walk over the porches, the snow creaks and crunches beneath our boots.

Then there is the soft kind of snow, the kind that falls in enormous flakes, noiselessly, lazily, steadily, covering trees and fences and forming lacy designs on the metal gates. This kind of snow makes visibility poor, but is the most beautiful of all. When one is in the yard after dark and looks back through the white falling snow upon the lighted windows of the cabin and sees the flames of burning logs in the fireplace, he thinks that never in the world was there anything so quiet and peaceful and enchanting.

And then there are the ground blizzards that swirl and sweep close to the ground, although there are bright skies and sun overhead. This is the kind of snow through which it is difficult to drive as the roads are whirls of snow which rise and fall and twirl about the car. One can become dizzy in such a storm and feel totally helpless in seeing the road ahead or where he is going.

In the spring the texture of the snow is still different. Then it becomes heavier as the moisture content is greater. The air becomes warm, and gentle chinook winds take the place of icy winter blasts. This snow melts rapidly and through the snow first appear small dark spots, lacy and ice-covered. Then appears the top sprig of a sage or bitter bush. Once the snow begins to melt, it disappears amazingly fast, and before we know it, we can again see sage and bitterbush in every direction we look.

And the whiteness of the snow! It sparkles and gleams, as bright and clean on the day it melts as on the day it fell. Skiing over it on a sunny day is like traveling through fields of diamonds. When the day is cold and the river begins to steam in the late afternoons, we know that on the following morning every twig and branch on the trees will be covered with delicate frost feathers. These are so light that the slightest breeze will send them spinning through the air. Then diamonds are not only on the ground but miraculously falling through the air in every direction. On very cold days, each indentation in the snow, left by a human foot-print or an animal paw or hoof holds deep blue shadows, breaking with their color the world of white. We have to be careful when we come onto the porches not to bump our heads on the snowy edge of a roof. The cabin itself settles in for the winter and seems to grow lower and lower as the white snows become deeper.

On many evenings, the sky is ablaze with color. Part of it may be dark rose, deep blue, or flaming gold, and the rest is aflame with ribbons and banners and streamers of red, lavender, pink. The entire Valley is alight with the sunset colors, the snow reflecting all of them. It is then that chores wait, dinners wait as we watch the heavens above, the rainbow-tinted snow below until the splendor grows even more intense and then finally fades into the soft grays and mauves of evening.

April, 1976

ONE OF US has just had a birthday, and another will have hers within a few days. Our thoughts, therefore, have been concentrated recently on birthday gifts and celebrations. Each one of us knows exactly what she wants for her birthday dinner: one always chooses beef tenderloin, twice baked potatoes, and for dessert a spice cake with chocolate mocha icing. Another consistently chooses turkey and all that goes with it and insists that her cake with candles be a white one with orange icing. The third, less conservative, prefers a big shrimp salad with strawberry sundaes taking the place of the conventional cake. All of us, too, are equally certain and emphatic about the gifts we want. There are the usual articles of wearing apparel–shirts, parkas, gloves, slacks, boots. But always, too, there is something special and most unusual which comes either because it was asked for or because the donor knew it would prove useful and preferred to present it as a surprise.

When we first came to the Valley to live permanently, we realized that three women alone in a wilderness area must be as self-sufficient as possible. We did not want to burden friends with requests for help, but wanted to learn to do necessary, if unaccustomed, jobs for ourselves. In emergencies, of course, we must call upon professional help from town, when our hot water faucet in the kitchen misbehaved and sprang a leak, or when an electric switch was not acting properly, or a window pane cracked. But for the relatively insignificant things that need repair, we are resolved to administer the necessary aid ourselves.

Our will and eagerness to learn were there, but we found that frequently our tools, simple screw drivers, hammers, etc., were totally inadequate. So, on each birthday, new tools were given as gifts, strange gifts, perhaps, when compared to the gifts we used to present to each other when we lived in the city, but highly prized here in our do-it-your-self-when-possible living. For example, one of us was overjoyed one year to find among her other birthday gifts a fine electric saw. What a vast improvement over the small hand saws we had been using! The saw proved so successful that its new owner hinted that it would be fine to have a gasoline saw, too, which she could take into the woods with her and do much of the trimming and sawing on the spot. On her next birthday she was thrilled to find a light but strong chain saw which has proved invaluable on wood gathering expeditions.

If something around the cabin needed sanding, we used to spend hours and hours and a great deal of energy by taking a piece of sandpaper and rubbing, rubbing, rubbing until the job was finished. One of us soon found among her birthday gifts a fine electric sander which does the job in a tenth of the time. Often we needed an instrument to bore a hole, so on another birthday one of us received an electric drill with all the necessary bits.

Snow machines are built for hard, often rough use; they are sturdy and strong, but things do go wrong with them on occasion, and their motors need careful attention. Not long ago, two of us availed ourselves of the opportunity to take a snow machine mechanics course, and since then not once have we had to call upon the professional mechanics to help us out during the winter months. In the fall they give a good check and tune-up to our machines, but after that we oil and grease them ourselves, change spark plugs when necessary, and even change driving belts. All manner of new tools were needed for these jobs, long nosed pliers, for instance, special kinds of wrenches, all of which were provided, wrapped in flowery birthday paper, and tied with bright ribbons.

One year a brand new roto-tiller for garden use in the spring was presented as a birthday gift, its handle decorated with ribbon streamers of pastel colors. The owner of this looks forward each spring to plowing the garden, bobbling along, both hands held firmly on the handles of the tiller. The other two of us laugh when we see her shaking and bouncing as the rough, noisy little machine makes its way through the moist earth. There is a wire boundary fence bordering a small part of our property. Winter snows and winds can bend and twist it so that a repair job is necessary each spring. A bright, shiny yellow wire stretcher was given as one thoughtful birthday gift which made this work simple and easy.

And so our birthday gifts are presented, appreciated, and used. At Christmas and at birthdays, of course, there are other gifts, too—new recordings for our stereo, books, new camera equipment, objects of art which adorn the cabin, new knapsacks for picnic lunches, new skis. But always there are the other gifts, the tools which have proved and will continue to prove useful. They have made the difference between our being self-sufficient and independent or reliant upon others for their tools and their help. The most popular adult education course in the Valley is called Powder Puff Mechanics. We all hope to enroll before long and increase our knowledge of mechanics further. Who knows? We may even learn how to take our cars apart and put them together properly or repair a clogged drain or a leak in the roof. And *then* what new tools we will need! And how our lists of desired birthday gifts will grow!

July, 1976

THE VILLAGE of Moose is really nothing more than a small settlement, but probably one of the most famous in the world. It is in the center of a renowned and extremely popular tourist area which attracts people from all over the world for its skiing and winter sports, as well as for its multitude of summer activities. The village itself consists of a cluster of homes occupied by the Park employees, The Grand Teton National Park Headquarters and Visitors' Center, a post office, and a small grocery store, bar, and gas pump. In the summer time a filling station and a tackle shop are open for the convenience of tourists. Also in the summer time, under the name of Moose Enterprises, there is a chuck wagon, cabins to rent, a laundromat, and an ice machine, all of these owned and operated by the same family who runs the store.

What our village of Moose lacks in size is certainly made up for in quality. We are speaking now directly of the flourishing Moose Enterprises. The grocery store, though small and unprepossessing in appearance, sells some of the finest products we have seen anywhere. Its line of gourmet foods is impressive as is the quality of its produce, meats, baked goods. We remember a friend of ours who had just returned from a European trip. As a very special gift for us she brought back a jar of Dijon style mustard, our very favorite of all mustards. We were happy to receive the gift but could not suppress a smile as we thought of our little grocery store and its plentiful supply of Dijon mustard. One of us returned recently from a trip to France and Switzerland, and she told us of a delicious cheese she had been served there, a cheese called Suprème. One day she came home from our grocery store in Moose and laughed as she said, "I might have known!" She said that she had seen in the cheese department the very same Supreme cheese she had been served as a treat in Europe. A friend of ours from a large Midwest city visited us and happened to say she had looked everywhere for a Spice Island rack for her spices and herbs but could not find one. We took her to our little grocery store where she found precisely what she wanted. Hearts of palm, artichoke hearts, grape leaves—all can be had at our grocery store, plus a wide variety of fancy pickles, preserves, spices, coffees, and teas. In the summer time a baker comes in, and his bread—French bread, sesame seed bread, raisin bread, cinnamon bread—is famous throughout the Valley. His cookies of all kinds, his Danish pastries, his coffee cakes, his pies— all are delicious and add a great deal to the meals of tourists as well as local people.

The meats which our grocery store offers in the summertime are unsurpassed. Late in August we give the butcher a meat order for our winter supply. By Labor Day we have it, all neatly wrapped and marked, ready to go into the freezer. The steaks, the roasts, the chops are the finest meats we have ever eaten. Even the ground round meat, lean and tender, makes a feast of a humble hamburger. An exciting day it is when we are told our meat is ready and we drive down to the meat department, open the tail gate of the car, and see the big boxes of packaged meat shoved in.

During the winter months there are not many people living at Moose so the store is kept open only for special hours as a convenience for those of us who live here the year around. We are grateful for this thoughtful service as we can remember the time before the store was here when we had to drive the twenty miles into town every few days for fresh milk, eggs, produce, or gas for the cars or snow machines. Now all we need is practically at our door which makes shopping in the winter months an easy task instead of a burden.

The bar which adjoins the grocery store is entirely unique. It is not large, but its shelves, well stocked with the finest of domestic and imported wines, liquors, cordials, and liqueurs, make it famous throughout the West.

The chuck wagon which is open during the summer months is the only one in this entire area. Both tourists and local people flock to it for the delicious sourdough hot cake breakfasts, the hearty lunches, the dinners. One of the most popular of the summer activities is an early morning float trip down the river with a chuck wagon breakfast at the end. Most of the time meals are eaten out of doors at long tables overlooking the river and the peaks beyond. In cool or rainy weather tables

277

are ready in two enormous and authentic tepees where fires are kept burning to warm the guests. Dinners are served from huge black iron kettles, each set over a log fire. One goes from kettle to kettle, choosing what he likes best, always welcome to return for more if he wishes. In one kettle will be peeled boiled potatoes, in another hot, steaming gravy, in another bubbling beef stew. Then come the baked beans, done to a turn, sliced beef and gravy, and finally cole slaw, fresh bread from the bakery, and Wyoming cherries, better known as stewed prunes. Hot coffee and cocoa are served from large urns. When one has finished a meal at the chuck wagon, he knows he has eaten the same kind of meal which the early cowboys enjoyed from their own chuck wagons as they rode the open range and cared for their cattle.

We remember how the father started the bar, the store, the chuck wagon, the cabins to rent, the laundromat. Then, though still very interested in Moose Enterprises, he passed his share of the business to his sons. Now we see the grandsons working there and beginning to assume many of the responsibilities. It is a friendly store, and always, particularly in the winter when things are not so busy, we stop briefly for a visit with whoever happens to be there. We meet friends there, chat with members of the family who own the store, and find that our shopping expeditions consist of far more than the mere buying of groceries and supplies. Our shopping trips are real social events, and the butter or eggs or milk we buy are usually second in importance to the news and friendly visits which we know will always be waiting for us when we go to the Moose Enterprises.

August, 1976

AT THIS TIME of year, July and August, our coat closet and glove rack always carry an aroma of fly repellent. We think it is a pleasant odor, fresh and clean, and we don't object if it clings to our jackets and especially our work gloves. It is during these hot months that flies and mosquitoes are a nuisance to the burros. Early mornings when we go to see them in their pasture, we take a curry to smooth down their coats and comb out any burrs. We also go well equipped with a big can of bug repellent, and if our front hall smells of it, it is nothing compared to the aroma that surrounds the burros after we have daubed it on their chests, their ears, their noses, their legs, their backs.

Each burro has a decided and distinct personality, and we have long since learned what to expect from the behavior of each. First we curry Fidelity, the mother of the family, and she stands patiently as we run the curry over her back, down her legs, and over her long ears. When we

278

have finished, she turns her head expectantly, knowing it is time for her first carrot. Then we move on to Loli who has made a nuisance of herself as we were busy with Fidelity. She rubs her nose against our back, tries to get between us and Fidelity, and shows her lack of manners by nudging our pocket where she knows her carrot is waiting. She is the baby of the family, and we are more indulgent than we should be. When she has been curried and is noisily munching her carrot, we go to Esso, but Loli insists on following and again tries to push her way forward and shove her sister out of the way. Esso is completely feminine in looks and behavior and would never stoop to the unmannerly ways of Loli. She loves beyond all else to have the back of her ears scratched, and, when we have pleased her in this way, we begin her currying. She, more than the others, has remnants of her winter coat, particularly in her bangs which frequently are matted, hang into her eyes, and need badly to be combed. But Esso dislikes having her bangs fussed with, so she turns her head, but only a little way as she knows her carrot waits for her in our pocket. She never grabs it in the rude fashion of Loli, but waits until it is handed to her, although her lips twitch in happy anticipation. Loli is still at our elbow bothering and teasing as we move on to TNT who, being the only male in the group and a perfect gentleman, knows he must wait until "the girls" have been cared for. He loves his currying and moves his head from side to side in ecstasy, following our every movement with his big brown eyes until we have finished and reward him for his patience and courtesy with his carrot.

Now it is time for the bug repellent. We pour a little of the liquid onto a turkish towel and decide that Fidelity will be the first to have the treatment. She loves every moment of it and thinks it is pure delight to have her chest rubbed, the back of her ears, the inside of her ears, her legs, and her soft nose. There never is any problem in treating our gentle Fidelity. Loli makes demands to come next; she loves all the attention of the treatment and lifts her head in an accommodating fashion when we are ready to give the application to her cheeks and nose. She seems to relish the smell of the medicine and twitches her nostrils in deep enjoyment as the aroma rises around her. In the meantime, however, Esso and TNT are watching the treatment, realize that their turn is next, and move away. They view the whole procedure with suspicion and distaste, TNT objecting to such nonsense, Esso too fastidious to have herself daubed with such unpleasant smelling mediciation. We pour a little more of the liquid on the towel, hold it behind our back, and cautiously approach Esso. We hold out her second carrot, hoping to distract her while we apply some of the medicine, but she is not to be fooled. She knows only too well what we have behind our back, flicks her tail disdainfully, and off she trots. We are lucky if we have managed to get a little of the medicine on her back as she fled. TNT, too, is poised, ready to take off as we approach him, but the temptation of the carrot is too great. He pauses a second to snatch it swiftly from the palm of our hand, and then he, too, hastily departs. We can only hope that since the burro family is never more than ten or fifteen feet apart that some of the odor of the medicine we have been able to apply so generously to Fidelity and Loli will permeate the air around all of them and do some good to the stubborn and squeamish Esso and TNT. It must work that way as the two objectors seem to be as free of flies and mosquitoes as the more willing and cooperative members of the family.

October, 1976

ONE OF US has not left this Valley since she came to live here permanently. That is longer than she cares to tell. All invitations from the outside world to visit friends or to take trips has left her indifferent and only too glad to remain at home. The other two prefer life here, too, but, on occasion, they have been willing to visit families or friends or to take excursions to interesting places. Not so our Alice-sit-by-the-fire who, however alluring a trip may have sounded, always said, "I'd rather stay here." But, wonder of wonders, a miracle occurred, and this is the strange tale.

One of us had taken to the nearest city two antique chairs which she wanted to have refinished. This happened early in June and, since then, the chairs had nearly been forgotten. But a phone call from the man who had done the work said the chairs were finished. This was in late August and made us realize that another trip to the city must be arranged to pick them up. "And who will go with me?" asked the one who had had the work done. After a moment's silence—could the others believe their ears?—the stay-at-home spoke up in a strong, determined voice and said, "*I* will go." The other two gasped in disbelief and could only wonder what had happened that she would be willing to leave the Valley even for one day. But it was arranged. The following Tuesday was the day set and plans were made.

Tuesday was bright and sunny, bad weather could not be offered as an excuse not to go. Immediately after breakfast the two were ready to leave, warm jackets ready for the chilly trip over the high pass. The one unaccustomed to travel glanced back longingly at the cabin, but she squared her shoulders and got into the car, determined to carry the project through and even find some fun in it if possible.

280

The trip down the back road was unusually beautiful. The bright sun shone through the trees making patterns of light on the road. The blue of the last lupin mingled with the scarlet of the Indian paint brush. Lively chipmunks and pine squirrels scampered here and there in the underbrush. The brilliant yellow of the arnica blossoms added to the gaiety and feeling of festivity as on they drove around curves, up hills, through the little village at the foot of the pass, and then up the pass itself. The mountain ash berries were crimson and shining in the sun as up, up the car climbed. The passengers looked back frequently to see the Valley lying below, quiet and peaceful, the river winding sinuously on its way. Up, still up they drove until they reached the top of the pass and began the winding, precipitous road down. They crossed the state line and reached the flat lands with rolling hills in the distance. Enormous fields of potatoes, oats, wheat, alfalfa stretched ahead, acres of dark green, then tawny brown, then pale yellow. Huge irrigation sprinklers were twirling this way, then that, leaving the fields clean and glistening. Occasionally a sprinkler, sending its spray far into the air, would create a rainbow, then there would be another farther back, still another to one side. The great potato storage barns with their sod roofs had doors open at both ends to let in the fresh breezes. In many fields mighty combines were at work, sending up twirls of dust which could be seen far in the distance in the form of dust devils. Bronze-faced farmers waved as the car passed, and herds of cows, quietly resting or grazing in green meadows, glanced up. Big skies, big country, big crops, incredible fertility of soil which produced abundance to help feed the people of this nation and other nations, too. Well, thought the unaccustomed traveler, this was worth coming to see. Different from our Valley, but spectacular in its own way, too. The prosperous looking farm houses became more frequent, there were big signs advertising the stores, motels, and restaurants in the city, and soon they passed outlying stores and shopping districts. The traffic became heavier and the honking of car horns, the smell of exhausts filled the air. The unaccustomed traveler shrank back at the sight of so many people, so many cars, so many buildings. Occasionally they got into the wrong lane of traffic and were accosted by shrieking horns and angry voices, but on they went, unperturbed, and righted their mistakes as quickly as possible. On they drove, carefully weaving their way through the traffic, avoiding a bus here, a semi there, a pedestrian a little farther on. Traffic lights blinked red and orange and yellow and green, arrows pointed in this direction and then that, flashing signs, "Don't Walk." "Do Walk," "Get Ready to Walk" blinked on and off and bells rang to direct traffic. Finally the furniture renewal shop was seen in the distance, the passengers drew up to the curb, and got out. The chairs were ready, beautifully finished, and were soon loaded into the back of the car. The travelers were hungry by this time and headed straight down town to the city's most popular restaurant. The unaccustomed traveler had often been told of this restaurant and expected a large, cool dining room, exquisite table appointments, silent, accommodating waitresses, delectable food. But instead, oh dear, it was just another restaurant, the usual hub-bub, the chattering of silver and dishes, no fine linen on the tables, no flowers. The food, too, was most ordinary and served in a hurried fashion by. rushed, harrassed waitresses. There was none of the anticipated delicacy and grace. Lunch over, the two from the country again braved the traffic, going the wrong way on one-way streets, again besieged everywhere by flashing, multi-colored lights, blinking arrows, more horns honking, more impatient voices shouting, "Learn to drive, lady!"

Back finally and gratefully to the outskirts, and soon the city was left behind. Ahead lay the country highway winding again through lush fields of crops, rolling hills. Friendly farmers again waved as the car passed. And mountains, there were mountains in the distance. They crossed tumbling mountain brooks, saw and admired the colors all around. Through two little towns they drove, stopping at one for a chocolate soda to compensate in part for the mediocre lunch, and then on they drove toward the pass. Up, up the car began to climb, around broad curves, down steep inclines, but then up and up again. At the top of the pass the passengers looked around, particularly down to our Valley lying just ahead and below. And then, before they knew it, they were there, bumping down the rough road, the cabin just ahead. The one left behind and the dogs were at the gate to greet them. The minute they stepped into the cabin, just as they had expected, the aroma of baked chicken greeted the tired travelers. The chairs were carried in. The unaccustomed traveler took off her jacket, stretched, and looked around at all the dear, familiar things around her. Fine, she thought, to get away for a day once in a while, but it will be a long time before it will happen again. Great for a few hours perhaps, but how wonderful, how simply wonderful to get back, to settle in again, and to know that no one of us has to leave for a long, long time. This homecoming and comforting thought of not having to leave soon again was the very nicest part of the entire trip to our stubborn old stay-at-home.

IT WAS ONE of those strange and mystifying experiences that we call wilderness surprises. One of us kept saying over and over, "It's about the size of a robin." When the other two asked her *what* was about the size of a robin, she answered, "An unusual bird or small animal which I saw in the big cottonwood this morning." Then during the next day or two she would not once see the creature which had baffled her. But, nevertheless, she would continue to say as she was filling the suet cage or scattering crumbs and seeds on the feeder, "About the size of a robin." One morning she called excitedly, "Come see. Here it is again!" The other two rushed to the window, but all that could be seen was an uninteresting and motionless lump on one of the cottonwood branches. One day soon after, however, we were greeted by cries of "Come here and look quick. Whatever it is has moved its head." Again we hurried to see and this time managed to catch a glimpse of the movements of the strange object, but bird or animal, none of us could say.

Last Sunday morning the mystery was solved. Our watchful one again called for the other two to come quickly. The little creature was moving about. We grabbed our binoculars and rushed to the kitchen windows. There perched on a branch was what looked like a miniature owl. Its saucy little tail was held upright, almost like the tail of a wren, but there were no tufts over its ears as is common with most owls. There was a striped chest and two black patches at the back of the neck. "A pygmy owl!" one of us cried. "As sure as can be, it's a pygmy owl." Someone ran to get our bird book from the shelf, quickly turned the pages until she came to a picture of a pygmy owl, and beyond the question of a doubt there sat the exact same thing in the old cottonwood. It turned its head this way and that, seeming to turn it completely around as it watched the other birds in the tree. One of us went to the phone to call a friend of ours who is deeply interested in birds. We told him our

283

news. He could hardly believe what he heard and asked for a description of it. In a few minutes he called back and asked if the little fellow was still there. "I'm coming over right away to see it; I've never seen one before, and I'm on my way." He was coming fifty miles round trip to catch a glimpse of the rare sight. We could only hope that the owl would still be there when he arrived. We watched the road and in about forty-five minutes saw his car pull into our parking lot. One of us hurried out on a snowmobile to bring him in. The owl had moved about but was still in full sight and seemed settled in the tree for the rest of the morning.

Our friend arrived, carrying his camera, equipped with a telephoto lens. He tossed off his cap and parka and rushed to the window. "A pygmy owl!" he exclaimed. "I've heard of a rare one or two being here, and now I actually see one!" We all moved from window to window as the owl moved. The Steller's jays flew about to investigate the strange creature. The woodpeckers darted at him, but the wise owl remained undisturbed. He only fluffed out his feathers and crouched lower when several chickadees flew toward him.

Our friend said, "He should be getting hungry, and I think he is. See how he is looking around for something to eat." Wisely, the owl remained quiet and motionless, waiting until his dinner approached him. He swooped down and in a flash flew back to his perch with a mouse which he proceeded to devour greedily. After he had finished his meal, our friend said, "Now he'll be sleepy and want to rest a while." Sure enough, he soon settled down. Cameras had been clicking during the entire watch, but now was the time to go out of doors to try to get a close up of him as he was sleeping. Cautiously, quietly, step after careful step, our friend and one of us waded through the snowy garden and out the back gate. Closer and closer they got to the branch where the owl was. Cameras were raised, lenses were adjusted, and the pictures were taken. At the moment, we are eagerly waiting to have them developed. We think we will call him Solomon.

May, 1977

We're eagerly awaiting
    The arrival of a friend.
She's sent us messages for days.
    Each one we comprehend.
The chickadees are leaving,
    We'll miss their songs and grace,
But juncos and the purple finch
    Are taking now their place.
Our weasel's coat of snowy white
    Is mottled with dark brown.
He's putting on his summer suit
    And looks a funny clown.
The blue birds perch on wires
    Inspecting where they'll nest.
This house or that one will you choose
    As suiting you the best?
The ponds below the cabin
    Are filled with melting snow.
Each day we watch and wonder
    As black water starts to show.
The ducks and geese are talking
    By the river shores below.
Their quacks and honks are noisy
    As hunting homes they go.

The redwings' cheery trillings
    From opening ponds arise.
Each thinks that his spot is the best
    And claims it as his prize.
Is that an early robin?
    It *is,* we do declare—
Not one, but two we plainly see,
    The first courageous pair.
The ground on sunny slopes is bare,
    But edged with snow and chilly.
But what is that? Can it be true?
    Green shoots of daffy dilly!
The twigs of willow bushes
    Show tiny flecks of white,
The promise of gray pussies
    Who'll grow there overnight.
Oh, yes, we've had forewarning
    That our friend is on her way.
She'll be here any moment now,
    Dancing in gay ballet.
She'll come, we know quite surely,
    So bright and debonair,
With bird songs, budding leaves, and grass.
    A daisy in her hair!
Oh, then we'll fling wide open
    Our doors and windows, too.
We want so much to share with her
    A happy rendezvous.